THE
NEW
VEGETARIAN

THE
NEW
VEGETARIAN

BUILDING YOUR HEALTH THROUGH NATURAL EATING

by
GARY NULL
with STEVE NULL

WILLIAM MORROW AND COMPANY, INC.
NEW YORK   1978

Library of Congress Cataloging in Publication Data

Null, Gary.
 The new vegetarian.

 Bibliography: p.
 Includes index.
 1. Vegetarianism.   I. Title.
TX392.N84   613.2′6   78-2776
ISBN 0-688-03292-3

BOOK DESIGN   CARL WEISS

Printed in the United States of America.

First Edition

1   2   3   4   5   6   7   8   9   10

FOREWORD

OUR PURPOSE IN WRITING THIS BOOK IS TO PRESENT RAtional alternatives to the average American diet. We have included information on such diversified topics as the difference between organic and synthetic foods, the quality of meat, fish, chicken, milk, and eggs; we have tried to unravel the controversy surrounding cholesterol to give you a better understanding of cholesterol-rich foods and their possible link to heart disease.

The first part of this book is largely devoted to the subject of protein. Anyone contemplating a switch from a meat-centered diet to a primarily vegetable-plant diet needs to understand the importance of meeting protein requirements.

The greatest nutritional problem associated with most vegetarian diets is, in fact, how to obtain complete, high-quality protein through incomplete protein sources.

The potential health hazards associated with commercial food processing, along with the nutritional benefits, are also discussed in these chapters. We feel there is no glossing over the manipulation and adulteration of our nation's food supply. While some people would prefer to ignore the potential hazards of eating many apparently healthful foods, we feel a responsibility to present balanced, unbiased information so that you, the consumer, will know what to look for and avoid when buying food.

If you are a vegetarian, or if you are considering making a serious change in your diet, this book will help you decide which foods are most beneficial to you, which offer superior nutrition.

Vegetarians normally eat foods—grains, seeds, nuts, legumes, and fruit—that offer an abundance of the essential vitamins, minerals, unrefined carbohydrates, and unsaturated fats. For them, our second section, on nutritional requirements, will be a helpful refresher course. For those who are undecided, our chapters on vitamins, minerals, carbohydrates, and fats will provide a more complete understanding of the importance of a nutritionally sound diet, and direct them to the right foods for them.

We've written this book as a reference companion. Keep it with you in the kitchen to find out the best way to pan-fry rice. Take it to the supermarket to find out whether the ingredients listed on the back of that box of breakfast cereal mean good nutrition or a health hazard.

In short, *The New Vegetarian* represents as broad a spectrum of alternatives as we can offer in one book. We have intentionally placed more facts in this book than you would normally find in a nutrition book. We believe it is better to have too much information than too little. Those readers who, having initially glanced through certain chapters, have questions in need of detailed answers can then go back and refer to additional chapters.

We hope you carry this book with you for a long, long time.

GARY AND STEVE NULL

CONTENTS

ACKNOWLEDGMENTS

We would like to thank Pat Whitcomb and Nancy Lyons for their assistance in the collection and assimilation of research findings.

We wish to express special appreciation to Ron Gilbert for contributing information on food selection and preparation.

INTRODUCTION

WHEN SEARCHING THROUGH THE AVAILABLE LITERATURE ON vegetarianism, you'll find enough cookbooks to start your own library, featuring every imaginable way to prepare vegetarian meals. You'll find material on the esoteric philosophies of meatless diets. There's plenty of natural hygiene literature on the impurities of flesh and its pollution of your body ecology. But if you simply want to know what vegetarianism is and what you can do to sensibly modify and improve your diet—and why you should do it in the first place—this book is *the* compendium of information for you. All the more so if you can't afford to pay the high prices of meat products, or if you're tired of polluting yourself and your family with chemical additives and adulterations.

What is a vegetarian?

The common belief is that a vegetarian is strictly herbivorous, eating only vegetables, fruits, nuts, etc. But the name vegetarian originally doesn't come from *vegetable*; it is a derivative of the Latin *vegetare,* "to enliven." However, we realize that most people think of a vegetarian as someone who abstains from all flesh eating. Even most dictionaries concur.

However, we wish to show vegetarianism in its broadest possible definition. For instance: there are lactovegetarians who eat milk products, ovovegetarians who eat eggs, ovo-lactovegetarians, even fish-eating vegetarians. Their common bond is that they don't eat the flesh of warm-blooded animals.

How many vegetarians are there?

In the world, hundreds of millions. Of the more than 4 billion people on earth, only a small minority eat meat daily. There are 621 million people in India who, by and large, don't eat meat. Eight hundred and forty million Chinese, 113 million Japanese, 135 million Indonesians, and 200 million other Asians live largely on fish-and-rice diets. Only in Western, industrialized countries has meat become the dietary center.

Why should I become a vegetarian?

Because meat can be less healthful than other foods, and more expensive. Vegetarians tend to live longer, often have more stamina and endurance, and in some countries even suffer fewer maladies. Meat has become highly adulterated over the past few years, loaded down with too much moisture, fat, and potentially dangerous chemicals.

Is it easy to become a vegetarian?

Easier than you think. Once you see what the alternatives are—once you *taste* them—you shouldn't yearn much for meat. Your wallet certainly won't resent the change. And today, fewer people will think you're a weirdo, because more and more people are turning to various forms of vegetarianism.

Are there any dangers to being a vegetarian?

Frankly, yes—if you don't know what you're doing. Meat provides many nutrients, especially protein, in your diet. When you give it up you must replace those nutrients and proteins. Vitamin B_{12}, for instance, is not found in vegetables, and some essential minerals are found only in small amounts in vegetables. This poses no problem if you include fish and dairy and eggs in your diet, but if you limit yourself to vegetables you must know which ones to eat and in what combinations if you're to get proper nutrition.

Can I get what I want and need in my supermarket?

Yes. Supermarkets are slowly turning into wholesome-food stores because Americans are beginning to demand certain quality foods. Most supermarkets now carry brown rice and whole-wheat products in addition to their white, refined grain products. And nearly every town has some sort of fruit or vegetable market. There is nothing exotic about a vegetarian diet. You just have to know what to look for.

Is vegetarianism more than eating (ugh) spinach?

Sure. Vegetables come in every imaginable color, shape, and taste. Fruits do too. Nuts and seeds comprise a part of the diverse vegetarian diet. And if you want to include eggs and dairy products and fish, your diet really isn't going to change that much. A vegetarian diet usually becomes more varied than meat diets, because vegetarians need a greater variety of food

Can I be a part-time vegetarian?

Why not? Simply cutting down your meat consumption will save you money, give your digestive system—particularly your kidneys—a break, and possibly improve your health.

How will this book help me?

If nothing else, it will alert you to the world of good eating and nutrition. That alone may improve your health and give you a few extra years of active living. It will tell you what you need to know about our pollutant-soaked environment and our contaminated food and our fast-food diet. This book will give you an understanding of different types of food and their makeup, the nature of nutrition, and how vitamins and minerals work in your system to affect you. *The Healthy Vegetarian* is not a book on vegetarianism; it's a book on good eating.

How can I use this book?

Let it be a guide. You may want to sit down and go through it first, then refer back to it when you please. Or you may use it strictly as reference, like an encyclopedia. The chapters are laid out so that you can consult them individually.

The Healthy Vegetarian is a book on proteins and carbohydrates and fats and minerals, a book on agribusiness and world pollution, a reference work on the way your body needs and uses the many foods you put into it. In short, this book is whatever you make of it. Unlike other books written for special audiences, the market for this one includes people who aren't vegetarians, who don't belong to hygiene societies, who don't have a background in nutrition, who haven't shopped in health-food stores. It is simply a guide to show you the pros and cons of meat eating, and how to balance a new diet and integrate it into your family's life without hassle.

PART I

PROTEIN

CHAPTER

1

BECOMING
NUTRITIONALLY
AWARE

NUTRITIONAL AWARENESS IS THE FIRST STEP TO GOOD HEALTH.
"I know there is a definite relationship between my diet and
my health, but I don't have the time, money, or knowledge
to make any rational change in my diet." This is what the
average American might say if asked to generalize about his
or her diet awareness.

In this chapter, we will attempt to provide some basic information for people accepting such an attitude. We aren't
going to propose that a vegetarian diet is the *only* dietary
regimen that will contribute to your good health, or that a
meat-centered diet will lead to a life plagued with disease
and/or your premature demise. We do intend to expose the
subtle mass-media manipulations that change public opinions
and attitudes about food.

Nutrition is a relatively new and highly complex science.
Sound nutritionists are the first to admit that few nutritional
concepts are definitely black or white. We are only now beginning to understand the biochemical interactions in the
human body.

For instance, although all normal human bodies function

in basically the same way, no two persons' metabolism or chemical makeup are the same. Digestion, energy levels, body odors, etc., vary just as much from one person to the other as does our physical appearance. This complexity of differences explains why some people will respond well to a certain diet while others won't. Nutritional studies are filled with contradictions: one scientist comes up with a positive result while another, using the same procedure, finds quite the opposite effect.

However, enough research has been conducted in the last twenty-five years to enable scientists to set nutritional requirements for the general population.

It is our aim to inform you of these latest nutritional findings so that you can apply this information and formulate the diet most suitable to your individual needs. At this point we assume you have already questioned your present diet habits and are seeking guidance and direction. Keep in mind that sound nutritional practices can be applied to any diet regimen.

The vegetarian who restricts his diet to vegetables, grains, beans, nuts, fruits, and seeds exclusively has to compensate for those nutrients found primarily in the meat, fish, dairy, and poultry which he has eliminated from his diet. Otherwise, health problems are certain to result, as they often do when a diet is limited. An obvious example is scurvy, developed by strong, healthy British sailors when their diets at sea lacked sufficient vitamin C. People in the East Indies developed beriberi as a result of a newly discovered food-processing technique: removing the outer layer of rice. Not only was the outer layer removed, but the thiamine content as well.

The poor and the elderly who rely on inexpensive, starchy foods for nourishment usually suffer from an assortment of ailments, diseases, and other disorders linked to their limited diets. It may be hard to comprehend that the lack of a single nutrient—of which the needed amount might fit on the tip of your little finger—could result in so many serious problems. Anyone, vegetarian or meat eater, who undertakes a diet limiting the variety of foods eaten runs the risk of poor health. The degree of risk will depend on the type of diet, its duration, and the amount of compensation made for the deficiencies (as in vitamins and other nutritional supplements).

Meat eaters' diets are likely to be much more restricted than vegetarians' diets. The most nutritious meats (such as organ meats) are rarely eaten. When meat is the center of the meal, contributions from the other food groups (grains, legumes, fruits, and vegetables) are often kept to minimum servings. Meat eaters enjoy the luxury of abundant high-quality protein and some B vitamins. But they also ingest large amounts of saturated fat, synthetic hormones, antibiotics, pesticide residues, nitrates, and other potentially harmful substances. Meat eaters generally rely on highly refined carbohydrates to complement their meals, excluding valuable sources of vegetable roughage and whole-grain breads.

Vegetarians, on the other hand, eat a wide selection of foods which supply them with an abundance of vitamins, minerals, unsaturated fats, and unrefined carbohydrates, all necessary for optimum health. Foods low on the food chain (unprocessed), low in saturated fat, and eaten in a raw, semicooked, unprocessed, or natural state contribute significantly to good health: they are usually less contaminated and contain more nutrients than their commercially processed counterparts.

In this age of self-awareness, it's quite surprising that it has taken so long for people to realize the connection between good eating and good health. After all, it is *food* that nourishes the body and furnishes the essential building materials necessary for life. Through advanced plant-breeding techniques and modern agricultural technology, we are blessed with countless varieties of food. Yet many suffer, nonetheless, from nutritional disorders.

Food processing and insect control have resulted in outstanding harvest percentages, but despite all advances in food technology the nutritional content of food is lower today than ever before. Our natural foods have undergone radical changes. Refining and commercial processing techniques have increasingly altered the natural state of our foods. For thousands of years, the world's food supply remained constant and nutritionally sound—until very recently, when people began tampering and changing the natural compounds with the technology of food processing.

Most natural vitamins and minerals are unstable once the plant containing them has been harvested. Extreme care is needed to protect the food from loss of nutrients. Light, temperature, and oxygen are only a few of the factors relating to nutrient loss. The washing of vegetables and grains after harvesting to remove dirt and pesticide residues can cause leaching of nutrients. Application of heat (sterilization, pasteurization) and other food-processing techniques can drastically alter nutritional content. Food manufacturers frequently fortify foods to make up for such losses.

Vitamins are more easily destroyed than most people realize. Some vitamins are destroyed through cooking, prolonged exposure to heat, or the presence of alkali (baking soda). Vitamin B_2 (riboflavin) is sensitive to light. As much as three fourths of the B_2 in a bottle of milk may be lost if it is exposed to direct sunlight for three and a half hours. The potency of vitamin A is greatly reduced during the dehydration of foods.

Orange juice is a rich source of vitamin C, but today's pasteurization process destroys much of its value. Take a nutritional statement like "You should drink orange juice to obtain vitamin C." Is it referring to freshly squeezed or pasteurized juice? If freshly squeezed: oranges picked ripe from the tree or oranges picked unripe, stored, and then gassed later to induce ripening? If fresh-picked: orange trees grown in soil enriched with natural manure or compost, or trees grown in chemically fertilized soil?

Strawberries are also a good source of vitamin C, but will frozen strawberries contain the same quantity of vitamin

C? Will adding sugar to the strawberries have any effect on the absorption of the vitamin C contained in them?

Tomatoes are a good source of the water-soluble B vitamin niacin, but will cooking and canning them in water lower the niacin content?

People are now becoming aware that the nutritional benefits offered by a particular food will vary from the maximum nutritional level reached before the food is harvested until the moment it is on the plate. The total nutritional value of food will depend upon: 1) the methods used by the farm to raise the crop (such as care of soil, manure, etc.), 2) the degree to which the manufacturer processes the food, 3) the type of food storage and handling by the grocery owner, and 4) how the food is stored, prepared, and consumed.

America has always had a small but vocal consumer movement. When America began massive industrialization with large urban growth, small food firms gave up direct control over their food-supply production and processing to large agribusiness. From the very beginning, consumer groups exposed the filth and abusive practices of the food industry. However, very few Americans were health-conscious and therefore allowed the insidious food pollution to continue unabated. Today, most people have some awareness of food additives and are beginning to question their safety and efficacy.

Today, the consumer movement actively informs the American public of abuses of the food industry: insecticides, more processing, and more chemicals. Until recently, these consumerists were labeled health nuts and fanatics and were the butt of jokes by comedians and politicians. It is difficult for us to understand why a person who is concerned about his health would be called a nut. It seems to be a reasonably sane attitude if not an instinctual drive for self-preservation. With all of the jokes and with its credibility challenged by both government and medical communities, the consumer movement has had its share of criticisms and failings. In fact, from the 1930s to the 1970s, it made little impact.

Why has the public, after over forty years, suddenly become interested in what these "health nuts" have to say? There are several reasons, the primary one being that research is now proving much of what they argued to be true. Too little fiber in a diet *can* cause digestive problems, perhaps cancer. Many ingested chemicals *are* harmful over a long period of time. A diet high in saturated fats *can be* unhealthy. Processing *does* destroy most nutrients. Insecticides *are* toxic. Some artificial food colors *can* cause cancer. Artificial female hormones *can* be dangerous. Excessive sugar and white flour *do* rob the body of some nutrients. And so on.

For the past few years, newspapers and magazines have run countless stories on the dangers of food pollution. It seems that every other week we are warned of new environmental pollutants or dangerous food additives—with ever more substances being banned because they're thought to cause cancer or some other disease.

Thanks to the current lack of trust in governmental agencies, food conglomerates, and business institutions in general, the media are finally giving those opposed to government and industry abuses the time and space to voice their opinions on behalf of the consumer.

Perhaps the strongest motivation for people's sudden interest in nutrition is fear—fear of developing diseases. The rise in the rate of cancer, arthritis, diabetes, and kidney disease has been steady over the last decade, with no letup in sight. Virtually every family in America is affected at one time or another by one of these disabling or killer diseases.

It seems that sooner or later every substance the scientists test proves to have some effect on one's likelihood of contracting a serious disease. For years we had blind faith in science's ability to produce miracle drugs to cure everything. For many of us, this faith has been replaced by the realization that we are often better off with an awareness of the relationship between our diet and our health. Self-reliance seems to be the theme for now.

Is it so surprising that people who are doing something for themselves are seeking nutritional guidance? This is, after all, one factor over which we have some control. Arguments for and against vegetarianism are too often battles using boring statistics and laboratory studies for weapons, and skirting questions about the real concerns of people who are rethinking their eating habits, like "Won't I be hungry between meals if I don't eat a solid meat meal?" "Aren't vegetarian diets boring?" "How can I get my kids to give up hot dogs?" "But macrobiotic diets are dangerous." "Doesn't it take a lot more time to prepare nonmeat meals? I'd lose the cost savings in the time spent in food preparation."

Historically, vegetarians have based their arguments against meat eating on emotion rather than facts, insisting that vegetarianism is more "moral" than meat eating, or that they feel better after going off meat. These arguments just aren't good enough any longer. They aren't necessary, either. *We know more about vegetarianism today than ever before.* Nutritional science provides us today with a far more sophisticated understanding of our bodies' nutrient needs and the chemical makeup of the foods we eat. With research focusing on nutrients—specific vitamins, minerals, and amino acids—rather than foods and food groups, nutritionists now know that we need calcium, not milk; amino acids, not proteins. And they can advise us on the various sources and amounts of these nutrients.

The word *vegetarian* covers a wide range of eating habits. The most common vegetarians are *ovolactovegetarians* who do not eat meat but do consume milk and milk products (*lacto*) and eggs (*ovo*) along with their grains, legumes, vegetables, fruits, nuts and seeds. Occasionally, their diets may include some fish and poultry. *Lactovegetarians* consume milk and milk products along with their vegetables, fruits, and grains, but do not eat eggs.

Vegans, the strictest vegetarians, do not eat any animal by-products. They obtain all their proteins from vegetables, grains, nuts, and seeds. Some vegans won't even eat foods that involve animal-related substances (such as gelatin) in their processing, and other vegans abstain from certain kinds of vegetables—potatoes, turnips, onions—which grow underground. Vegans are often motivated by religious beliefs or strong moral feelings about the use of animals as food producers, even if the animals aren't killed. To avoid nutritional deficiencies, a strict vegan must devise a carefully planned diet based on a thorough understanding of the body's nutrient needs.

Seventh-stage macrobiotic diets are classed as vegan diets because they exclude animal by-products. Considered the highest level of diet by the purists who follow them, seventh-stage macrobiotics are all-cereal diets relying heavily on brown rice. Extreme macrobiotic diets have been sharply criticized. In 1965, it was widely reported that a young New Jersey woman actually starved to death while subsisting on nothing but cereals. She weighed seventy pounds when she died. Extreme macrobiotic diets have also led to anemia, scurvy, emaciation, and loss of kidney function due to low fluid intake. But this doesn't mean that all macrobiotic diets are unhealthful. Some of them are lactovegetarian regimens that include vegetables and fruits, soybean meat analogs (substitutes), even cheese and seafood.

Just as dangerous as extreme, seventh-stage macrobiotic diets are the fad "monodiets" that encourage reliance on one particular "wonder" foodstuff. Living on lettuce, grapefruit, or bran is just as senseless as basing a diet on brown rice.

Many people worry about becoming vegetarians because they're confused about "complementing" incomplete protein foods. The idea of protein complements and amino acid patterns can seem hopelessly complicated and not worth the bother—which is exactly what meat-industry interests want you to think. Take, for example, a pamphlet published in 1976 by the National Livestock and Meat Board entitled "Meat and the Vegetarian Concept." [1] In it, we read: "There's no denying that a nonmeat diet could provide adequate nutrition if one has enough knowledge about nutrition to be able to carefully select and substitute the proper combination of foods to get all of the daily essential nutrients. But from the health standpoint, there is no reason to go to that much trouble when meat represents such a convenient nutrition package."

The January, 1977, edition of *Meat Board Reports*,[2] which devotes twelve pages to refuting claims about the impurity of meat, its wastefulness, and the cholesterol-heart disease question, etc., explains that corn contains one fourth the utilizable protein of meat and concludes that "a person would have to eat four pounds of corn to get the same amount of protein one pound of meat would provide." This is true, but ridiculous. No one is suggesting that you sit down to a plate of four pounds of corn, or sixteen cups of rice or a pile of soybeans to meet your daily protein needs.

If you can follow a simple recipe for pancakes you can learn to combine complementary proteins. It's as simple as that.

Throughout the ages vegetarians have boasted greater longevity, endurance, and mental well-being—and slimmer, trimmer bodies; yet underdeveloped nations with rampant malnutrition and nutritional diseases are invariably ones that depend entirely on nonflesh foods. But nonflesh diets vary widely in their nutritional values, and this must be taken into account in any criticism of vegetarianism.

In a 1964 survey of adequate and inadequate nonflesh diets,[3] Mervyn G. Hardinge, M.D., and Hulda Crooks describe four kinds of diet which can lead to malnutrition: "Vegan diets which have been reported to produce vitamin B_{12} deficiency in some individuals; grossly unbalanced near-vegetarian diets in which as much as 95 percent of the calories were provided by starchy foods extremely low in protein, such as cassava root; diets dependent too largely on refined cereals, such as cornmeal or white rice, even though small amounts of animal foods were included; and diets with an intake of total calories insufficient for maintenance requirements."

Vitamin B_{12} deficiency can be a problem among true vegans and even among lactovegetarians who eat very few dairy products. So far no practical source of vitamin B_{12} outside of animal foods has been found, which means that if a strict vegetarian doesn't take a B_{12} supplement, he or she is likely to develop megaloblastic (pernicious) anemia, which results in the degeneration of the spinal cord and death if untreated.

The tricky thing about a B_{12} deficiency is that it can easily go unnoticed until it has greatly progressed. Green leafy vegetables contain large amounts of folic acid, which masks the symptoms of a B_{12} deficiency. These symptoms include soreness of the tongue, menstrual irregularity, and extreme nervousness. If you intend to drastically alter your diet tomorrow (not that we recommend it) to exclude all animal protein sources, we advise that you start taking a B_{12} supplement. The minimal daily requirement of this vitamin is quite small— 5 micrograms—but it is essential for the proper metabolism of proteins, fats, and carbohydrates.

Zinc deficiency is one of the least known yet most common dangers of some vegetarian diets. Zinc is depleted from the body rapidly under stress, and a zinc deficiency will make you feel light-headed and lose your sense of taste. Why are vegetarians vulnerable to zinc loss? Vegetarian diets rely heavily on grains and legumes which are rich in phytates, compounds which bind zinc, calcium, and other minerals so that they cannot be absorbed through the digestive tract.

Phytates are formed when phytic acid, found in the outer husks of grains such as wheat (and rye, oats, barley, rice, peas, peanuts, cottonseed, flaxseed, soybeans), combines with phosphorus. Unleavened breads, like pita and other Middle Eastern flat breads, contain many phytates, and have been linked with zinc deficiencies among Iranians. If you avoid unleavened bread, sprout your beans and grains, or cook them thoroughly, you will reduce your risk of zinc deficiency. Adding yeast to bread destroys the phytates through the process of fermentation, and the sprouting of grains and beans neutralizes the phytates. If you are on a meatless diet and under stress, you might consider eating more foods containing zinc, such as seafood, whole-wheat bread, peas, corn, egg yolk, brewer's yeast, and carrots.

Plants have fewer commercial contaminants—and smaller concentrations of them—than do animal foods. But natural toxins do occur in certain plants we commonly eat. Fortunately most of these toxins can be neutralized by proper heating. But if you want to prepare your baby's food at home using natural ingredients, it's important to be aware of the potential dangers of certain plant foods to which infants are extremely sensitive. These plant toxins are those found primarily in the legume family.

In addition to phytates, the legume family contains a variety of dangerous toxins, which for the most part become harmless when the legumes are cooked or sprouted. They are *trypsin inhibitors*, which stop the action of the digestive enzyme and interfere with growth; *hemagglutinins*, which also interfere with growth by blocking the absorption of nutrients through the intestines; toxins which cause goiter by blocking the thyroid gland's use of iodine; and a *glycoside factor* (in lima beans) that produces hydrocyanic acid, a deadly poison.

Legumes should never be eaten raw. Raw fava beans can cause hemolytic anemia, leading to headache, fever, abdominal pain, and coma, and raw lima beans have even been known to cause death. Some legume toxins are not neutralized by heat: chick-peas (garbanzos) and green peas contain a heat-resistant trypsin inhibitor, and the hemagglutinin contained in green peas is also unaffected by heat. But these toxins in chick-peas and green peas are present in very small amounts and many adults eat the peas raw without ill effects. And if tofu (soybean curd) is a staple in your diet, you needn't worry about these enzyme inhibitors.[4] The heat generated in the processing of tofu is believed to neutralize them.

Nitrite poisoning is usually associated with eating bacon and luncheon meats, because these foods are routinely treated with nitrite to preserve them and give them a "healthy" red color. But nitrates do occur naturally in some vegetables. Spinach, carrots, and beets contain occasionally high levels of nitrates which, in themselves, are harmless. But under certain conditions these nitrates can be converted to nitrites, which are particularly toxic to infants.

The commercial processing of these vegetables, which includes heating and blanching, inactivates the harmful enzymes and eliminates most of the nitrates and the bacteria. But the medical literature has reported some cases of nitrite poisoning among infants consuming *home-prepared* spinach purée, carrot soup, and carrot juice.[5]

Nitrates are converted to nitrites in the body. The infant is more vulnerable because its stomach contains less acid than the adult's, thereby providing an ideal breeding ground for nitrite-forming bacteria. The nitrites link up with hemoglobin (the pigment in red blood cells that transports oxygen through the body) to form methemoglobin, another pigment which is *unable* to carry oxygen to the tissues. When the level of methemoglobin in the baby's blood becomes too high, its skin will turn bluish. When too much hemoglobin is inactivated by nitrites, acute poisoning and even death can result.

Beets and carrots contain toxins which may affect you cosmetically: if you drink too much carrot juice or too much borsch (beet soup), your skin can turn yellow with deposits of carotene, a yellow pigment used by your body to synthesize vitamin A.

If you've ever gotten hives from eating strawberries, broken into a facial sweat over a dish containing tomato sauce, or felt sick after eating bread covered with caraway seeds, your body was reacting to one of many allergens contained in these and numerous other plant foods. Allergens are widespread in different plant families, but sensitivity to them varies greatly among individuals and usually goes undetected unless the reaction is violent.

Allergens are believed to be contained in the protein parts of plants. Since all plants have protein, allergens can exist even in fruits, which have a protein content generally considered negligible. A few nuts, seeds, and beans contain allergens so strong that small quantities of them injected into animals have caused death in minutes. Cottonseeds contain a particularly potent allergen, as do the seeds of mustard and flax. Heating these seeds substantially reduces the potency of the allergens. Some people have allergic reactions to sesame, poppy, caraway, and anise seeds and to coconut, macadamia, and cashew nuts. This becomes noticeable only when these foods are eaten in large quantities or by themselves on an empty stomach.

Some people have strong allergic reactions to fruits—particularly bananas, pineapples, and mangoes. Fresh fruits eaten in the pollen season can be especially allergenic. These fruit allergens are believed to be concentrated in the skin and the seed. It's impossible to eat strawberries without eating the seeds, but washing them with scalding-hot water and then chilling them will destroy the allergen without destroying their taste or texture.

Allergens within vegetables are contained in different parts of the plants. Some people may experience a reaction after eating the leaf, others the root, and still others the bloom or seed. Carrots, potatoes, squash, and celery can be highly allergenic to a small percentage of people. Among legumes, the peanut is the most allergenic, and the riper it gets the more heat-resistant its allergens become. Green peas and soybeans also contain allergens which are heat-stable even at 120 degrees centigrade. Soybean milk-substitutes sometimes cause allergic reactions in older children and adults even when the milk is heated.

Commonly allergenic grain foods include barley, corn, oats,

rice, rye, and wheat. Even inhaling or touching the dusts of these grains can cause irritation in some sensitive people, producing syndromes known as baker's eczema and baker's asthma. The commercial processing of grains removes most of their allergens, and heating reduces the allergenic potency of whole unprocessed grains.

Antivitamin factors, found in certain plants, destroy or block the absorption of vitamins. *Raw* soybeans contain the enzyme lipoxidase, which destroys the carotene used to make vitamin A. Soybeans also contain a substance that interferes with the absorption of calcium and phosphorus. Tests have shown that diets containing raw kidney beans can possibly increase the incidence of muscular dystrophy by depressing vitamin E levels. (Of course, who eats raw kidney beans?— ugh!) Rhubarb leaves are loaded with oxalic acid, which blocks the absorption of calcium and could possibly lead to kidney damage.

While it's true that a natural plant toxin can make you just as sick as a big dose of chicken-liver arsenic, plant foods still have the edge over meat. Most plant toxins are neutralized or greatly weakened by heating, but hormones, arsenic, and high concentrations of pesticides could present problems of toxicity even after the animal foods containing them have been cooked—no matter what the food industry would have you believe.

Seventeenth-century Japanese Buddhists believed that eating the flesh of any animal caused pollution for a hundred days. Eighteenth-century European vegetarians believed that meat eating excited "animal passion" and that a nonflesh diet led to tranquillity, virtue, and health. Modern vegetarians, aware of how many foods these days can contribute to body pollution, would probably call a vegetarian diet the lesser of two evils.

Eating low on the food chain (unprocessed nonmeat), and eating a wide variety of foods that may contain small traces of different pesticides and natural toxins, is preferable to eating meat soaked with hormones, arsenic, and accumulations of pesticides—or fish loaded with varying concentrations of mercury and other industrial waste. It will take many years of examining the health of meat eaters and vegetarians to determine the comparative effect of food contamination on the two groups; to know whether a vegetarian diet is in fact safer —we think it is—and if so, just how much safer. Comparative studies of vegetarians and meat eaters today haven't focused on food contaminants in different diets, but have set out to determine whether or not meat eaters are biologically different from vegetarians, and, if so, in what ways.

In a 1965 study [6] of meat eaters, ovolactovegetarians, and vegans including adolescents, pregnant women, and adults over forty-five, only slight differences in physical measurements, blood pressures and protein, albumin and globulin levels were observed. The laboratory and physical findings were similar in all groups, except that the vegans weighed an average of twenty pounds less than the others, who averaged twelve to fifteen pounds above their ideal weight. Weight gains and losses among all the pregnant women were about the same, as were the average birth weights of the infants, and adolescents in all the groups grew at the same rate.

The idea that people who do hard physical labor need a hearty meat-and-potatoes diet is a cultural illusion. Even if you are a six-foot, two-hundred-pound lumberjack, you can get just as much stamina from eating a meal of complementary grains as you can from steak and fries. In fact, studies have shown that a vegetarian diet can provide you with even more stamina. Dr. Irving Fisher of Yale University [7] put meat eaters and vegetarians through a series of endurance tests and found that the vegetarians could perform better than the meat eaters. It may not be just a coincidence that animals noted for their great strength and endurance—such as the gorilla, the elephant, the horse, and the ox—are all vegetarians.

We can't talk about stamina among vegetarians without mentioning the Hunza people of northwest Pakistan. They live on the simplest diet of wheat, corn, potatoes, onions, goat products, and fruits. For thousands of years they have spent their lives trudging up and down the rough mountain paths for up to thirty miles a day, and they are remarkable for their physical fitness, healthy teeth, and longevity.

In the period between the world wars, vegetarianism lost much of its stigma of culturism—brought about by the association of vegetarianism with asceticism and religious fervor—and began to be taken seriously by scientists. Wartime food shortages, particularly of meat, meant that national diets had to be reevaluated and alternate sources of protein found among available nonanimal foods.

When the Allied Blockade of 1917 substantially cut off imports to Denmark, the Danish government sought help from the vegetarian society in restructuring the national diet. Following the society's advice, grain-consuming animals were slaughtered for food, and the grain formerly fed to these animals was fed to the Danes in its whole unprocessed form. On a diet based on whole-grain and bran bread, barley porridge, potatoes, greens, and dairy products, the Danish people survived the war with improved health and lowered mortality rates.[8] This is often cited as evidence of the association between diet and heart disease, for when the Danes went back on their meat-centered diet after the war, mortality rates from circulatory disease returned to prewar levels. Similar substantiation of the benefits of the vegetarian diet is offered by the experience of the Norwegians, who also gave up meat from 1940 to 1945 and experienced lower mortality rates. They too returned to a meat diet after the war, only to suffer an increase in mortality rates.[9]

We are bombarded with books preaching high-protein diets, high-protein food snacks, protein supplements, and protein lotions for hair, skin and nails that promise renewed beauty and vitality. Faced with this concentrated hype, you have probably asked yourself how much protein you *really* need— not to develop pumping-iron muscles or enter the Olympics, but to maintain good health. And how much food do you have to eat to get *enough* protein? And what will happen if you *don't* get enough protein?

Today, the answers to these questions are more important than ever before.

What is protein?

The word itself comes from the Greek *protos*, first. Protein is "unquestionably the most important of all known substances in the organic kingdom," according to the Dutch chemist Gerard J. Mulder. He is credited with first isolating proteins in 1838 and naming them according to the importance he believed they had for all living matter.

Subsequent research has substantiated Mulder's theory. We now have evidence to show that protein is a part of every living cell. Only water is more plentiful in the human body. If you're an adult, half the dry matter in your body is protein. The only bodily substances that normally contain no protein are sweat, bile, and urine. One third of your body's protein is concentrated in muscle tissue, one fifth in bones and cartilage, one tenth in skin, and the remaining third in other tissues and fluids.

Proteins are various combinations of different amino acids. Every one of these combinations contains the chemical elements carbon, hydrogen, oxygen, and nitrogen. Some protein molecules also contain sulfur, phosphorus, iron, cobalt, iodine, copper, calcium, and sodium. Proteins—highly complex and numerous as they are—may be grouped nonetheless into three classes: simple protein, compound or conjugated protein, and derived protein.

Simple proteins are substances which, when dissolved in water, break down only into amino acids. Albumen in eggs and milk, keratin in hair, and globin in hemoglobin are simple proteins.

Compound proteins are combinations of simple proteins with some other nonprotein substance. Compound proteins perform functions which neither component of the compound could perform by itself. Casein (protein + phosphoric acid) in milk, lipoprotein (protein + lipid) in blood plasma, and mucin (protein + carbohydrate) in saliva are compound proteins.

Derived proteins are formed at various stages of the breakdown of simple and compound proteins by the action of hydrolysis (water dissolution), heat, and other physical forces.

More important than protein structure is its classification as *complete, incomplete,* or *partially complete.* Most food proteins are composed of 12 to 23 amino acids linked together in a large molecule. Of these 23 amino acids, your body can synthesize 15, which you therefore don't need in your diet. The remaining 8 amino acids are called *essential* because you have to get them from food sources. Whether a protein is complete, incomplete, or partially complete depends on the amounts and proportions of these essential amino acids within it. You'll want to understand this classification before basing your diet on nonanimal sources of protein.

Proteins that contain all eight essential amino acids in sufficient quantities and in the right proportion to maintain life and promote growth are called *complete proteins.* Foods from animal sources, such as meat, fish, fowl, eggs, and milk, generally have complete proteins.

Proteins which you can't depend on to keep you alive or healthy without a supplement are called *incomplete proteins.* Most vegetable proteins are incomplete, but they do contain in differing amounts and proportions the essential amino acids. You can combine them together in a meal to provide all the essential amino acids in the right amounts and ratio to create a source of complete protein.

Partially complete proteins will keep you alive but they will not support cell growth. Some dried beans, peas, nuts, and grains contain only partially complete proteins, meaning the percentages of some available amino acids are very small. In the chapters ahead we will discuss the nutritive value of different food sources, based on the completeness or incompleteness of their protein, and explain how to combine incomplete proteins to make them complete.

Though nutritionists often cite your body's need for protein, it is really the eight essential amino acids—the building blocks of protein—that they're talking about. Amino acids form an extraordinary variety of proteins which perform an equally extraordinary variety of functions. The human body contains hundreds of different proteins, some of which contain as many as two hundred amino acids. Protein, commonly known as a body-building substance, also performs structural functions, regulates body processes, and provides a source of heat and energy.

Protein repairs worn-out tissue proteins in the body and builds new tissue. Only protein can do that, which explains why it is especially important during periods of rapid growth, like infancy, childhood, puberty, and pregnancy. Proteins in body tissue are not stable compounds. Since they are constantly being broken down, they must be replaced by new protein synthesized from the amino acids obtained through your diet and produced in your body. For these proteins to remain in a state of dynamic equilibrium—a perfect balance of breaking down and building up—your system must have a constant supply of essential amino acids from foods or food combinations that give you complete proteins. Without an adequate supply of complete protein, the process of catabolism (breaking down) exceeds anabolism (building up) and results in protein deterioration.

But an adequate supply of complete protein cannot, by itself, prevent the destruction of your body proteins. Though fats and carbohydrates are supposed to be your body's energy store, sometimes amino acids have to take up the slack when these two substances are in short supply. Your body can't use its amino acids for both growth and maintenance, and burn them for energy at the same time. Unless 50 to 60 percent of your caloric intake comes from fats and carbohydrates, your amino acids will oxidize for energy production.

If you had to live on a survival ration of 900 calories or less per day, you wouldn't want to include proteins in your ration. It is actually much more taxing for your body to convert protein into energy than to utilize fats and carbohydrates for energy. Proteins, like carbohydrates, provide 4 calories per gram, but they are a more expensive source of energy for your body as well as your pocketbook. Not only does it take more body energy to convert proteins into fuel, but one of the end products of protein metabolism is nitrogen, which has to be excreted—which in turn costs your body more work. Carbohydrates, a less expensive source of energy, burn completely into carbon dioxide and water, which are easily handled in your system. A survival ration exclusively of protein, therefore, would only produce more work for an already weakened body.

There are a few exceptions: sometimes the body's need for specific tissue development will override its need for energy, and proteins will continue to be used for tissue building in the absence of fat and carbohydrate energy sources. When a pregnant woman isn't getting an adequate supply of complete protein, fats, and carbohydrates, the fetus may deplete her protein supply for its own tissue building. Likewise, a rapidly growing malignant tumor will use up the body's amino acid supply for its own growth.

Protein also functions as a structural substance. One third of your body's amino acids is contained in *collagen*, the structural protein glue that holds all the cells of the various tissues together. Structural proteins organize and support subcellular structures and membranes. They aid the mechanical action of the muscles, and contribute to the elasticity of the blood vessels. They compose the hard and insoluble epithelial tissue of skin, hair, and nails, and the framework containing the mineral matter of bones and teeth. If a beautician sets "permanent waves" into your hair, he is making use of a chemical reaction involving these structural proteins and the amino acid cystine. The permanent-wave solution temporarily breaks some of the chemical bonds which hold the hair proteins in their original form. As your hair is then set into new form, the broken bonds are chemically remade.

Without protein, your body fluids would flow through you like a river without a current. Proteins control the movement of these body fluids in and out of the cells, and to and from the bloodstream, through the process of *osmosis*. In osmosis, fluids move through a semipermeable membrane from a medium of lesser concentration to one of greater concentration.

Proteins are also responsible for maintaining your body's neutrality, which is essential to normal cellular metabolism. Your body fluids—gastric juices, saliva, blood, and urine— must all remain at the constant degrees of acidity and alkalinity appropriate to their functions. For example, if the acidity of gastric juices varied widely from day to day, your digestion would be constantly interrupted. Proteins maintain these fluids by acting as a base when the fluid is too acid, and as an acid when the fluid is too alkaline.

Enzymes are biological catalysts which promote thousands of chemical reactions, and all enzymes so far identified are proteins. Every cell of your body contains many different types of enzymes. The liver itself contains a thousand different enzymes.

Other protein substances which regulate your internal processes are the hormones insulin, adrenalin, and thyroxine, and the constituent of blood called hemoglobin that transports the oxygen and carbon dioxide vital for breathing. Mucus and milk are largely protein, as is sperm and the fluid which contains it. Sweat, bile, and urine are the only fluids that have no protein.

One of the first effects of protein deficiency is a lowered

resistance to disease. Protein is essential for the production of antibodies needed to fight infection. A low-protein diet can also leave you more vulnerable to the harmful effects of drugs, poisons, and food toxins. Your body's ability to detoxify these substances is controlled by enzymes, which, as we said, are protein substances.

Before protein substances can be absorbed through the intestinal walls into the bloodstream, they must be broken down into amino acids through digestion. Protein digestion has two phases, mechanical and chemical. The mechanical phase involves the breakdown of the food by chewing and by muscular activity within the walls of the digestive tract, where one group of muscle fibers will break up the food while another set of fibers pushes it along. This coordinated movement is called *peristalsis.*

The chemical phase of digestion, responsible for "dissolving" food, is brought about by enzymes. They break down protein substances by splitting the links in their molecules. But every enzyme is capable of splitting only certain specific linkages: many different ones have to take their turn at the food as it's pushed through your stomach, until it's finally broken down into its ultimate constituents.

The end products of protein digestion—amino acids—are chemically simple enough to pass through capillaries from the intestinal walls into the bloodstream. The portal vein carries the amino acids to the liver. From there, they are released into the general circulation and then carried to various tissues and cells. There is a steady flow of amino acids from the bloodstream to the cells and back. This creates an "amino acid pool" whereby at any given location and at any given moment, a tissue has a ready supply of amino acids.

When amino acids are absorbed, your body may use them in many ways. It may synthesize new protein and build new cells. It may replace worn-out cells. The amino acids may be used to form such body regulators as hormones, enzymes, and antibodies. Or they might contribute to the formation of non-protein compounds. When an adequate supply of fats and carbohydrates is lacking, amino acids may undergo oxidation for energy production.

Every day the average adult can synthesize new body protein at the rate of about 1.3 grams per kilogram of body weight (about 91 grams for a person weighing 154 pounds); but certain conditions are necessary before this can happen. In addition to the need for an adequate fat and carbohydrate intake, an "all or none" law prevails as a requirement for protein synthesis: all the essential amino acids needed for the synthesis of a new protein must be present in the proper amounts *at the same time*. If one essential amino acid is missing, no new protein will be created—not even incomplete protein. This is analogous to building a house with wood and nails: when the nails run out, work comes to a halt, no matter how much wood you've got left, until you go out and buy more nails. If there's a limited supply of even one amino acid, protein synthesis will go on only as long as that supply lasts. After that, synthesis ceases and your body uses the rest of the amino acids for energy. That is why the *balance* of amino acids contained within the protein—not the *quantity* of protein—is so important to a vegetarian diet.

Amino acids may one day replace many of our unsafe drugs. Tested on insomniacs at the Maryland Psychiatric Institute in Catonsville, Maryland, the amino acid tryptophan—abundant in milk—was found to be an effective sleep-inducing agent. The insomniacs fell asleep twice as fast with the tryptophan as they did without it, and slept forty-five minutes longer. More important, the amino acid did not disturb their normal stages of sleep as would barbiturates. The F.D.A. has already given L-tryptophan clearance to be sold as an antidepressant; it may soon be marketed as a sleeping pill.

If enough protein is good, is more better? High-protein diets are creating as much excitement as vitamin therapy these days, but the same question might be asked about both:

once you've met your minimal nutritional needs, do supplementary vitamins and diets rich in protein contribute anything to your health or resistance to disease? Some people maintain that since protein is stored like fat for periods of stress and deprivation, someone on a high-protein diet will have the advantage of a protein supply for resisting an illness or dealing with trauma. The Food and Nutrition Board of the National Academy of Sciences—National Research Council made the point that its recommendations for higher protein requirements were planned to provide a buffer against the added needs caused by various stresses. On the other side are those who believe that a high-protein diet offers no advantage over minimum adequate nutrition. They point out that your body adapts to its intake of protein: that on a high-protein diet it maintains its metabolic equilibrium by excreting the same amount of protein as it synthesizes.

The arguments for and against high-protein diets really center around the question of whether or not there are protein stores in your body. The concept of protein stores was first proposed by Eduard F. W. Pflueger in 1903; since that time it has received support from many studies examining increased nitrogen excretion in states of stress. It has been observed that a poorly nourished person who undergoes physical stress has no significant nitrogen loss. However, a well-nourished person who undergoes the shock of a surgical operation, physical injury, or infection has a striking but temporary loss of nitrogen in the urine, indicating a loss of protein. The big question is, where does the protein go?

Some researchers have interpreted this protein loss as a valuable defense mechanism, a mobilization of cellular protein to limit the injury or aid in the process of repair. Others see nothing beneficial about this striking loss of nitrogen in the urine. It is accompanied by a loss of vitamins and minerals, indicating a loss not just of protein but of tissue as well.

Study of the relationship between a generous protein diet and the body's resistance to stress—and its ability to withstand subsequent protein deprivation—sheds light on the question of protein stores. In 1962, the *Journal of the American Medical Association* reviewed a study by Dr. Elias Halac of New York City. He put two groups of rats on either moderate- or high-protein diets; then he subjected them, together and separately, to the various stresses of swimming in a cold bath, X irradiation, drug-induced shock, and deprivation of food and water. Dr. Halac reported no difference between the two groups of rats in response to shock and X irradiation stress, but in the cold-water-swimming and the food-and-water deprivation tests, the high-protein group did not perform as well as those on the moderate-protein diet.

In another experiment, Dr. Halac placed 29 rats on a high-protein diet and 19 rats on a normal-protein diet for a period of 80 days. After the 80 days, he performed autopsies on 6 rats, then put the remaining ones on a protein-free diet to study the rate of weight loss and survival. Dr. Halac found that after 169 days on the protein-free diet, 10 of the 13 rats formerly on the normal-protein diet were alive, but only 9 of the 23 high-protein rats survived. Dr. Halac concluded that his tests did not support the concept of protein stores.

Research on the question of protein stores is not yet conclusive. Experiments with human subjects are difficult to control, and at this point it would be premature to extrapolate the results of animal tests to human beings. Still, we can safely say that when it comes to protein, *more is not necessarily better*. It seems reasonable to be more concerned with the quality of protein in your diet than with quantities that exceed the generally established minimum requirements.

FACTS TO PONDER

— No food is indispensable in human nutrition.
— Soybeans and their derived products are the most complete of the plant foods.
— Physicians practicing in the United States are rarely con-

fronted with cases of protein deficiency. In fact, the diet of most American adults provides two to five times their minimum protein requirements.

— Milk and eggs are the only foods designed by nature for the nourishment of the young. Experiments show that they are well suited for this purpose and are equally valuable for adults.

— An acre of land planted in soybeans can produce ten times as much protein as animals grazing on an acre of land.

— North Americans make up only 7 percent of the world's population, but they consume 30 percent of world supplies of animal protein. We eat 30 times as much meat as the Japanese and 66 times as much as the average Asian.

— The average American has been estimated to consume from 10 to 12 percent more protein than his or her body can use.

— Milk contains nutritionally superior proteins. It contains all the essential amino acids plus extra amounts of certain amino acids that are often low in plant proteins.

— In the ten countries where life expectancy is highest (Sweden, the Netherlands, Norway, Denmark, Canada, France, Britain, Switzerland, New Zealand, Australia), the per capita consumption of milk averages 955 pounds; per capita consumption in the United States is only 254 pounds.

— National health surveys estimate that 5 to 10 million cases of acute intestinal illnesses, many of them meat-related, occur annually in the United States.

— More antibiotics are now used by farmers than by doctors. Over half of the nation's annual antibiotic production goes to livestock and poultry.

— The poultry industry estimates the annual loss from cancerous chickens (which must be destroyed) at $150 million.

CHAPTER

2

DETERMINING
PROTEIN NEEDS

IF YOU SIT DOWN TO A PLATE OF FETTUCCINE ALFREDO, YOU probably aren't enticed by its amino acid composition. Knowing all about protein functions, chemical composition, and protein metabolism is fine, but it has little meaning unless you can apply it to the everyday world of having to decide what kind of food to buy, where to buy it, how to prepare it to best get its nutritional benefits and enjoy it. So we are concerned here with giving you nutritional theory and formulas and explaining metabolic processes only as they can help you to create a healthful and enjoyable diet. Discussions of protein function and metabolism are important in an overview of vegetarian nutrition, but they are peripheral to the question, How much protein do I need?

This is a tough question. Even a computer fed a pile of figures on nitrogen-balance formulas, your age, weight, and amino acid composition, would have a hard time calculating a protein prescription for you.

The amount of protein in a given food isn't hard to measure, but it is your body's *utilization* of the protein that really counts, and this is influenced by many variables. There are variables among different samples of the same protein food: nutritionally, no one cup of milk is exactly like another. There are variables in your diet—breakfast cheese is metabolized differently than supper cheese—variables between you and other consumers, even variables in your own body from day to day. Any recommended dietary allowance drawn up for an entire population would be about as useful to you as a newspaper horoscope.

Two different protein foods may have the same amino acid composition and yet differ widely in their nutritional values. These values are influenced by the conditions that produced the food, its processing and preparation (whether the food is canned, frozen, fresh, boiled, fried, baked), and seasonal variations (winter wheat is different from spring wheat).

The figures commonly relied upon in the United States for protein requirements are in the recommended dietary allowance established by the Food and Nutrition Board of the National Research Council. The board's recommended allowance for average adults is .4 gram of protein daily per pound of body weight if your diet is based on animal protein.

If your diet is based primarily on plant proteins, they suggest 1.5 grams of protein per pound of body weight daily. These requirements are increased for infants by 250 percent, for young children by 175 percent, for lactating women by 70 percent, and for pregnant women by 35 percent. A stress situation (physical or emotional) automatically doubles your requirements.

These figures take into account the variations in protein quality and personal variations which might influence the amount of protein you can utilize. They are approximately double what the safe minimum protein intake is thought to be. The following table includes the recommended daily dietary protein allowances for infants, children, male and female adults of different ages, and pregnant and lactating women:

RECOMMENDED DAILY DIETARY ALLOWANCES FOR PROTEIN
REVISED 1968

Designed for the maintenance of good nutrition of practically all people in the U.S.A. (Allowances are intended for persons normally active in a temperate climate.)

	AGE (years)	WEIGHT (kg.) (lbs.)		HEIGHT (cm.) (in.)		KILOCALORIES	PROTEIN (g.)
INFANTS	0–1/6	4	9	55	22	kg. × 120	kg. × 2.2
	1/6–½	7	15	63	25	kg. × 110	kg. × 2.0
	½–1	9	20	72	28	kg. × 100	kg. × 1.8
CHILDREN	1–2	12	26	81	32	1100	25
	2–3	14	31	91	36	1250	25
	3–4	16	35	100	39	1400	30
	4–6	19	42	110	43	1600	30
	6–8	23	51	121	48	2000	35
	8–10	28	62	131	52	2200	40
MALES	10–12	35	77	140	55	2500	45
	12–14	43	95	151	59	2700	50
	14–18	59	130	170	67	3000	60
	18–22	67	147	175	69	2800	60
	22–35	70	154	175	69	2800	65
	35–55	70	154	173	68	2600	65
	55–75+	70	154	171	67	2400	65
FEMALES	10–12	35	77	142	56	2250	50
	12–14	44	97	154	61	2300	50
	14–16	52	114	157	62	2400	55
	16–18	54	119	160	63	2300	55
	18–22	58	128	163	64	2000	55
	22–35	58	128	163	64	2000	55
	35–55	58	128	160	63	1850	55
	55–75+	58	128	157	62	1700	75
PREGNANCY						+200	65
LACTATION						+1000	75

SOURCE: *Recommended Dietary Allowances,* 7th ed., Food and Nutrition Board, National Academy of Sciences—National Research Council, Washington, D.C., 1968.

These protein allowances are not as rigid as they may appear; they are intended only to serve as recommendations. As such, they are simply rough guidelines to be adapted to each person's individual needs.

Out of necessity, people in many countries exist on a daily protein intake well below .9 gram per kilogram of body weight. Depending on the quality of the protein ingested, it is possible for an adult to get along on as little as 30 to 40 grams of protein per day. At that level, the urinary nitrogen output drops drastically, indicating an adaptative compensation for the low protein intake. An equilibrium can be reestablished at the lower level, unless the protein intake has fallen below the critical point.

What foods provide the best sources of protein? Animal sources like milk, eggs, cheese, meat, poultry, and fish are all valuable. Three of these foods alone can provide 51 grams of protein: 1 pint of milk, 1 egg, or 4 ounces of meat, fish, poultry, or cheese. Grains such as wheat, corn, and rice, as well as soybeans, nuts, peas, lentils, and beans provide a good second source of protein.

Since the value of different protein sources varies widely, the best way to ensure the most efficient use of protein is to eat a combination of protein foods at each meal. Actually, many popular eating habits reflect this principle. Some examples: macaroni and cheese; casseroles containing legumes and small amounts of meat; sandwiches that combine the grain in bread with meat, cheese, or vegetables; and cereal with milk.

In general, if two types of high-quality plant protein are eaten together the mixture is almost as effective as a moderate amount of animal protein. When certain plant foods, such as corn and dried beans, are eaten together, the value of their proteins is improved. This is because different plant foods lack different amino acids, and one may provide what is missing from another. This means that you *can* get a satisfactory combination of amino acids from a diet consisting of whole grains, nuts, legumes, and vegetables—in other words, a purely vegetarian diet.

Some people whose protein intake is adequate neglect the spacing of their protein sources. For optimum protein utilization, high-quality protein must be available in the body at all times. A good rule of thumb is to eat at least one complete protein (dairy, eggs, fish, fowl, meat) at each meal. It is especially important to eat a complete protein food at breakfast, the first meal after the night's fast.

Researchers have designed a formula that simply expresses the factors involved in evaluating the utilization of a protein food. It is called *net protein utilization*, or NPU.

The NPU is a chemical rating that tells you exactly how much protein a given food makes available to your body—assuming it's eaten with enough fats and carbohydrates. The NPU takes into account two important factors: the digestibility of the protein food, and its amino acid composition.

Digestibility influences a food's NPU in a very simple way. If a food can't be thoroughly digested, all its protein can't be made available for your body's use. Digestibility in turn is influenced by the fiber content (roughage) in your diet. All parts of plants—seeds, fruits, stems, leaves, bulbs, and tubers—are sources of fiber. Unrefined grains, particularly bran and brown rice, are good fiber foods, as are raw fruits and vegetables.

Fiber itself contributes virtually no nourishment to your diet, but it is extremely important nonetheless. The contents of a low-fiber meal pass sluggishly through your digestive tract, allowing more time for harmful bacteria to form and stay in your intestines. High-fiber meals travel more quickly through the intestinal tract, allowing a shorter time for bacteria to act on them. Fiber also partially insulates a protein food from contact with the digestive enzymes. The digestibility of protein foods ranges from 78 percent for dried legumes to 97 percent for animal foods (meat, milk, and eggs). Cereal grains and fruits have about 85 percent digestibility, and vegetables 83 percent.

The NPU of a given food is also influenced by its "biological value," which is based on its amino acid composition and its ability to be used by the cells. As we have already explained, the amino acid pattern of a food determines how your body will use it.

Of all known edible protein sources the egg most nearly matches the amino acid pattern ideal for synthesis in your body. (Scientists use egg protein as a model for evaluating the amino acid composition in other foods.) Egg protein has been assigned an NPU value of 94 on a scale of 100. Theoretically, a protein with a biological value of 100 would produce 1 gram of protein tissue for each gram of food consumed. Milk's NPU is about 82, fish 80, cheese 70, and meat and poultry 67. Just below meat is tofu—soybean curd—with a rating of 65; nuts, seeds, legumes, and grains are in the range of 60 to 40 on the scale.

The biological value of a protein food also expresses the proportion of protein you retain to the protein you lose. This gain and loss is measured by your nitrogen balance. A negative nitrogen balance indicates that your body is breaking down more protein than it is building up, a positive balance means it's building more protein than it's breaking down (as in pregnancy), and a perfect balance of nitrogen retention and excretion means that your protein synthesis and breakdown process are in equilibrium—the state appropriate to the well-nourished average adult. Foods which contribute at least as much protein for synthesis as is being broken down have a high biological value.

It is important to consider the NPUs of protein foods when considering your daily protein requirement. The amount of protein you need to eat depends on its quality: 55 grams of protein from eggs might be adequate, 55 grams from meat or seeds may not. A diet based largely on plant protein calls for a higher protein allowance than one based on protein from animal sources.

There is a simple formula for figuring an appropriate protein allowance for a particular population, based on the NPU of its primary protein source. We use the figure .28 gram of protein per pound of body weight to represent minimum protein needs plus an additional safety factor of 30 percent. We divide 100 by the NPU of the main protein food and multiply the result by .28. For most Americans, whose protein staple is still meat (which has an NPU of 67), the equation would be as follows:

$$.28 \times \frac{100,}{67} \quad \textit{which equals} \quad \frac{28}{67} \quad \textit{grams,}$$

$$\textit{which equals about .4 gram.}$$

If your main protein staple is meat you need .4 gram of meat protein per pound of body weight per day. If you base your diet on protein from plant sources (which have an average NPU of about 55), you'll need to consume .51 gram of protein per pound of body weight every day.

Apart from obvious differences in age, weight, and sex, there are many subtle factors which influence individual protein needs. If you sleep irregular hours or lose sleep, your protein need may be as much as a third higher than someone the same age, sex, and weight who gets a solid eight hours every night. People undergoing physical or emotional stress will probably have higher protein needs. States of physical and emotional health can account for wide variances in protein needs.

If your daily intake of protein is evenly distributed throughout the day—not contained in any one meal—there is a steady supply of amino acids for your body's ongoing process of protein synthesis. If you take too much protein at any one meal, the chances are that some of the amino acids will be used for synthesizing protein, but the rest will be excreted since they can't be stored for later use. How you chew protein foods can also be important since some protein foods, like whole grains, have coverings which must be broken before the proteins within can be reached by the enzymes in your stomach. We stress that unless the protein you eat is accompanied by an adequate intake of fats and carbohydrates—about 50 to 60 percent of total diet calories—the amino acids will be used to fill your body's energy needs instead of building new protein.

Cooking techniques can have a significant, and frequently detrimental, effect on the nutritional value of a food. Overheating, especially with dry heat, may destroy some of the essential amino acids (such as lysine) or tie them up in new chemical linkages. These new linkages make the protein resistant to digestive enzymes or retard the release of individual amino acids in the intestinal tract. High dry heat has a negative effect on the nutritional value of wheat and oat protein, as in the toasting of bread.

Some protein foods have a *higher* biological value when cooked, especially in the presence of water or steam. The cooking process increases the digestibility of some proteins, and may also liberate certain amino acids. The nutritional value and digestibility of navy beans, for example, are improved by their cooking in water.

The cooking temperature may be the determining factor. Extreme heat will lower the protein availability of soybeans, whereas mild heat will raise it. It is interesting to note that although heat apparently lowers the nutritional value of fresh milk used in cooking, the heat used to prepare evaporated or dried milk increases protein digestibility and utilization.

NATURAL TOXINS

Natural toxins pose a problem in that they cannot be banned by legislation. Most of them are rendered harmless by cooking. As we've said, soybeans are a good example of a food that contains dangerous toxins when eaten raw. One of the primary effects of eating raw soybeans can be an increase in size of the pancreas, which leads to a decrease in the protein it secretes. The result is a loss of sulfur-containing amino acids; for this reason, people eating raw soybeans often have an acute need for the amino acid methionine.

Another natural toxin in beans is PHA, a protein which has the unique ability to make red blood cells come together in clumps or clusters. Studies have shown that purified PHA retards growth in rats. Fortunately, the PHA in legumes is destroyed by cooking. All beans should be soaked before cooking. Cases of human poisoning have been reported from the eating of partially cooked beans. Be wary of recipes calling for the use of bean flour in baking, which uses dry heat.

Certain species of pea can cause a paralyzing disease called lathyrism. The chickling vetch, the type of pea that causes the paralysis in humans, is a potentially useful source of protein for the world's population. Soaking the dehusked seeds overnight detoxifies them.

Although most of us have heard of cyanide, we may be unaware of its presence in a number of common foods, including lima beans. In the early twentieth century, lima beans imported into Europe from Java, Puerto Rico, and Burma sometimes caused minor outbreaks of cyanide poisoning. Even today, cases of poisoning from certain varieties of lima beans occur in some tropical countries. The toxic level of lima beans sold in the United States, however, is well below a health-threatening level, especially if they are cooked properly.

Seafood infrequently contains substances which can be dangerous when consumed by humans. Sometimes shellfish will eat a poisonous alga from which they themselves are protected by a special gland called the "dark gland" which binds the toxin. When a human consumes the shellfish, the bound poison is released; it can cause paralysis or even death. A mussel weighing only 50 grams can contain enough poison to kill ten people. Unfortunately, the poison of this alga is unaffected by heat, and an antidote has not yet been found.

The puff-fish contains a substance in its testes and ovaries so poisonous that it is the cause of almost half the fatal cases of food poisoning in Japan.

Some foods that are normally nontoxic may be toxic under certain circumstances. An example is cheese, which contains large amounts of certain amines derived through the fermenting action of bacteria. Although these amines are toxic in nature, they are generally harmless because they are detoxified in the body by monoamone oxidase. But some antidepressant drugs can inhibit this detoxification process. Cases have been reported of people on antidepressant drugs who became very ill after eating only a small amount of cheese. To be on the safe side, avoid cheese if you are taking antidepressants.

The first three weeks of life coincide with the most critical protein needs. If the infant does not get an adequate protein supply during this period, the cell population of its brain will be permanently reduced. Babies and young children also need an amino acid called histidine which is not required by adults. The recommended protein allowances for children based upon a diet with human milk as the source of protein are as follows: birth to six months, 2.2 grams per kilogram of body weight per day; one year, 1.8 grams per kilogram; up to adolescence, 1.2 grams; during adolescence, 1 gram per kilogram.

Since protein is believed to be stored early on in pregnancy and utilized later, the high-protein requirement of a pregnant woman should be distributed over the *entire period* of pregnancy. Since as much as 12 to 15 grams of protein may be secreted daily in breast milk, a lactating woman is advised to increase her daily intake by 20 grams while breast-feeding.

For social, economic, and physical reasons, elderly people tend to decrease their caloric intake. The protein they do consume goes largely to satisfy their body's energy needs, which is why they should increase their daily protein intake by a safety margin. In a diet providing 2000 calories a day, the older person weighing 60 kilograms (132 pounds) should maintain a protein intake of 60 to 90 grams of protein per day.

Evidence indicates that exercise alone does not increase your protein need, provided your caloric requirements are being met. But a number of claims have been made for the beneficial effects of supplementary protein during exercise. Some researchers have observed that strenuous work and exercise in a warm environment can lead to nitrogen loss in sweat and a greater protein requirement. If you are doing exercises specifically to build up your muscles, you will need extra protein during the period of accelerated muscle growth. During the training period, when an athlete is increasing his total muscle mass, he needs extra protein. But beyond the muscle-building period, the athlete's daily protein needs are not really different from those of the average person.

Stress includes emotional upsets and crises, sleep loss, anxiety, illness, injury, and surgery. Fear, anxiety, and anger increase the secretion of adrenaline, which creates a biochemical chain reaction resulting in loss of protein. Jet lag and other changes of sleep patterns can also cause protein losses. Any physical illness—even a cold—increases protein breakdown in your body. Staying in bed and cutting down on food for several days will put you in a negative nitrogen balance; even a healthy person confined to bed loses up to two pounds of body protein during each week of bed rest. The solution to this negative nitrogen balance is not necessarily to consume more protein. The amount of protein in your diet should be no more than 15 to 20 percent of the total calories consumed. If your protein intake is increased out of proportion to the intake of carbohydrates and fats, your body will convert protein to glucose to provide energy. This is more taxing than burning fats and carbohydrates for energy.

While a high-protein diet before illness or surgery may not

help you, what about protein intake during convalescence? Nutritionists generally agree that the protein requirements of the convalescent are very different from those of the healthy person. The convalescent can gain weight and retain nitrogen at a rate otherwise impossible, and during his recovery he should increase his protein and caloric intake accordingly or till he regains his previous normal weight.

Chronic kidney disease may call for protein consumption well below or above normal requirements. In chronic kidney disease with nitrogen retention, too much protein can be harmful because the malfunctioning kidney can't dispose of nitrogenous wastes. The protein merely adds to the kidney's burden. But in chronic kidney disease during which blood proteins are lost through the kidney and there is no excessive nitrogen retention, the patient needs a high-protein diet to compensate for urinary losses. Hyperthyroidism—the condition in which the thyroid gland is overactive—also creates a need for more protein.

Depending on the quality of the protein you eat and what makes up the balance of your diet, you can get by on as little as 30 to 40 grams of protein daily. On such a diet your body maintains nitrogen equilibrium at a lower level by reducing its loss of nitrogen. But if your protein intake is below the critical point—and that point varies among individuals— you'll develop signs of protein malnutrition such as loss of vigor, muscle weakness, retardation of growth, weight loss, irritability, decreased resistance to disease, retarded wound healing, and anemia. A pregnant woman's protein shortage may lead to anemia, miscarriage, premature delivery, or the birth of a child with a chronic degenerative disease which will show itself later in life. Because of their slower metabolism, elderly people are more susceptible more quickly to the effects of mild protein deficiencies than younger people.

Serious prolonged protein deficiency may lead to one of four protein-calorie-malnutrition syndromes: nutritional liver disease, kwashiorkor, marasmus, and abnormal water balance.

In the United States nutritional liver disease is more prevalent than the other three. The usual victims are people on junk food or overly restricted diets. Fortunately, an adequate diet can improve simple forms of nutritional liver disease, except for alcoholics, who tend to get liver damage regardless of their diet.

Kwashiorkor, the major nutritional problem in the world today, usually develops in children between the ages of one and four who are seriously deprived of good-quality protein. It is prevalent in populations whose protein supply comes mainly from vegetables and whose diet does not provide a complementary balance to these incomplete proteins. Kwashiorkor is characterized by growth failure, skin lesions, abnormal water retention, underdeveloped muscles, dental caries, anemia, and changes in hair color. Both this disease and marasmus, which usually develops during infancy, are caused by a deficiency of both protein and calories. If not treated, they can lead to mental retardation. Another syndrome associated with protein deficiency is edema, a disturbance in the body's water balance in which an excess accumulation of fluids makes the tissues soft and spongy.

Excess protein can also cause problems. Though normal adults seem to tolerate a protein intake far above actual requirements, infants and children do not adapt well to it. The actual needs of the body (adult's or child's) for protein building and maintenance limit the utilization of amino acids for protein synthesis; any excess protein will only be converted to glucose and burned as energy, hardly an efficient use of such an expensive foodstuff.

Too much protein may lead to other subtle consequences perhaps not even noticeable to someone on a high-protein diet. Fluid imbalances may be created by what researchers have described recently as the "protein-overload effect": whereas 350 grams of water are required for the metabolism of 100 calories of protein, only about 50 grams of water are needed to metabolize 100 calories of either carbohydrates or fats, which means that consuming protein over and above 15 percent of the total caloric intake *can* lead to increased water requirements and increased levels of metabolic end products in the bloodstream. And though results are still not conclusive, some animal feeding experiments seem to indicate that too much protein over a prolonged period can reduce longevity.

FACTS TO PONDER

— Each protein has an upper limit for utilization. Eating more than that amount is inefficient and may put an excessive burden on your body as it forms and excretes organic compounds containing waste nitrogen.
— Protein allowances should be based upon ideal body weight: what you *should* weigh, not what you *do* weigh.
— When you eat a large amount of vegetable protein with a small amount of animal protein, the quality of the mixture is as effective as that of animal protein alone.
— The presence of free protein (containing all eight essential amino acids) in nature is very rare; an outstanding exception is egg white.
— The protein content of one lot of wheat can be almost double that of another.
— With the exception of sulfur amino acids, the estimated average recommended daily allowance of essential amino acids for adult humans can be provided by one pint of milk.
— Goat's milk, more easily digested than cow's milk, is frequently recommended for infants and invalids.
— The protein content of eggs is relatively constant. The diet of the hen, however, has a large influence on the vitamin content of the egg.
— An increase in urinary calcium excretion accompanies a high-protein diet.
— Most of the nutrients found in meat are contained in the lean portions. The composition of lean meat—77 percent

water, 22 percent protein, 1 percent minerals—doesn't vary much.

— The nutrients in meat become more concentrated during cooking. Cooked rare, a piece of meat contains 3 percent fat, 21 percent protein, 75 percent water; cooked medium it has 5 percent fat, 29 percent protein, 65 percent water.

— Wheat germ and bran, the only truly nutritious parts of wheat, are considered impurities in the American milling process and are duly disposed of. You get the chaff.

— Department of Agriculture figures indicate that almost twice as much protein is available to the American public than is needed for adequate nutrition.

CHAPTER

3

DIETARY PROTEIN:
COMPLETE AND
INCOMPLETE SOURCES

A SAMPLING OF THE PROTEIN SOURCES HUMAN BEINGS HAVE
relied upon through the ages would read like the contents of
a witch's caldron: newts, moths, flamingo tongues, white
worms, water flies, lizards, locusts, dormice, ants, termites,
tadpoles, camel's hair, blood and bone marrow, peacock
brains, and sharks' fins. At the very least, these foods provide
protein to sustain life and promote growth.

The number of edible protein sources on this planet is mind-
boggling, yet most Americans can name only a few: beef,
fish, chicken, eggs, milk, cheese, wheat, and soybeans.

The food industry and the government regulatory agencies
it controls, like the F.D.A. and the Food and Nutrition Board,
are not likely to educate us about the qualities of the least
expensive and most abundant sources of protein available. Nor
are they likely to tell us the whole truth about problems that
abound in both our animal and our plant protein sources—
problems that affect our health, the ecology of our planet, and
the future of the human race as we know it.

Some protein sources are more efficient, more nutritious,
more economical, and more pure than others, but it is not a

black-or-white picture. There are benefits and drawbacks to nearly all protein foods. It's important for you to know what they are so you can create a diet from the best of both protein worlds, plant and animal. What follows is a breakdown of the benefits and drawbacks of both complete and incomplete protein food groups. In later chapters the status of each of these staple protein foods in the American diet today is described in detail.

Complete protein foods are those which have an amino acid pattern closely matching the one you need for maintaining life and promoting growth. Foods that come from animal sources are complete protein, "complete" because they have just the right amount and proportion of amino acids to promote protein synthesis in the human body.

Complete protein foods are desirable because they have high net protein utilization (NPU) values. A relatively small amount of any one of them can satisfy a large percentage of your daily protein needs. Only 5 ounces of meat, a quart of milk, 5 ounces of fish, 4 ounces of cheese, or 5 large eggs are sufficient for the daily protein requirements of the average adult American male.

Complete protein foods usually have a high "nutrient density": large proportions of nutrients, protein, vitamins, and minerals contained within a relatively small number of calories. An obvious example: the nutrient density of milk is far greater than that of whole-wheat bread. Although both contain B vitamins and protein, you would have to eat sixteen slices of whole-wheat bread to obtain the same amount of protein contained in one quart of milk—which also will supply one quarter of your daily requirement of calories; *all* the fat, calcium, phosphorus, and riboflavin you need; one third the vitamin A, vitamin C, and thiamine; and, with the exception of iron, copper, manganese, and magnesium, all the minerals you need daily.

Foods from animal sources generally have high nutrient densities but limited quantities of vitamin C. Some fruits and vegetables have high nutrient densities, simply because they provide so few calories. This is an important consideration when you are planning a diet; you must not only fulfill your body's nutrient requirements but also take in enough calories for the nutrients to do their work. Nutrients and calories, in fact, go hand in hand to keep all your body's systems and protective mechanisms in good working order. If you know about the nutrient densities of different foods you can see clearly why different foods provide different nutritional advantages and why a varied diet is so important.

Complete protein foods present drawbacks as well as benefits. Protein foods are consistently more expensive than carbohydrates and fatty foods. And animal protein foods are many times more expensive than complementary combinations of plant proteins. For example, the combination of ¾ of a cup of beans and 2 cups of rice, which costs approximately 50 cents, has the same amount of *usable* protein as a 9½-ounce steak that costs four times as much. The price of cheese (except for cottage cheese) is as high as beef now; fish and poultry are no longer the cheaper alternatives they used to be. Egg and milk prices continue to escalate.

The reason for these higher prices is not (as meat-industry representatives maintain) a protein shortage. Frances Moore Lappé calls this idea about as logical as blaming the sinking of the *Titanic* on an overabundance of water. Animal protein foods are so expensive because the food industry knows the demand for them is equal to the price. And somehow it's not surprising that the price of beans has doubled in the last few years as more and more people turn to them as an alternative to cheese, which used to be an alternative to meat, which . . .

Environmentalists and nutritionists generally agree that raising cattle is a very inefficient way of producing protein for human consumption. The average steer, fed twenty-one pounds of high-quality grain, produces one to two pounds of beef. Seventy-eight percent of the grain in this country is fed to animals. An acre of land devoted to meat production can produce only one fifth the amount of protein produced by an acre of grain crop. There are exceptions to this argument which justify the use of land for cattle raising: much of the land in this country is unsuitable for plowing but good for grazing; and there are many agricultural by-products not fit for human consumption which can readily be converted by cattle into protein suitable for humans. But as long as cattle are fed high-quality grains, the argument against cattle raising as a waste of world food resources remains valid.

Animal foods are the most adulterated of protein foods. They contain the greatest concentration of pesticides and herbicides as well as industrial and sewage-pollution residues. Contrary to what you might think, animals and fish do not excrete all the chemical residues they ingest; they steadily accumulate them in their tissues and vital organs. Most of these residues are still there waiting for you even after you wash your food and cook it thoroughly. They are also present in eggs and dairy by-products.

The fatty storage depots in the bodies of animals act as biological magnifiers. An animal ingesting as little as .1 part per million of a chemical may end up storing about 10 to 15 parts per million—which means a hundredfold increase for the final consumer, you. This magnification occurs because pesticides and similar compounds are biologically stable, not broken down by digestion and then excreted.

Far worse than these "accidental" contaminations of animal protein foods is the deliberate adulteration of these foods for profit. Chickens are fed arsenic to make them grow faster. Cows are fed antibiotics to protect them against the unsanitary conditions they are raised in. Livestock grain companies add antibiotics to cattle feed so routinely that a farmer wishing to feed his cattle undoctored grain must have it custom blended. And pay *more* for it. Fish are often coated with an antibiotic dip to keep them from rotting on their way to the super-market. Some butchers and packers paint luncheon meats with potentially dangerous sodium nitrate to make them appear red and fresh. To make matters worse, neither the F.D.A. nor current meat-inspection practices consistently protect you from the constant and widespread use of these additives. When chickens are found to have cancerous tumors (a recent U.S. government report states that over 90 percent of the chickens sold in this country have leukosis—chicken cancer), the tumors are cut out and the rest of the bird is sold in your supermarket as chicken parts.

The high saturated-fat content of animal protein foods may or may not contribute to the incidence of atherosclerosis, hardening of the arteries by fatty cholesterol deposits. The cholesterol theory of heart disease is still a controversy. Though it may pose a hazard, cholesterol is important to many vital functions of the body. It comprises most of the dry weight of the brain and conducts the transmission of nerve impulses throughout the body. Cholesterol is also necessary for the synthesis of sex hormones; it is synthesized in your body by the liver, muscles, skin, and intestinal walls. Apart from dietary cholesterol—milk, eggs, butter, etc.—your own body produces nearly 70 percent of the cholesterol in your system (serum cholesterol).

There is widespread evidence that your body maintains its own balance between the amount of cholesterol it produces and the amount it absorbs through your diet. Which means that if you reduce your cholesterol intake, your body will produce more to compensate—and that if your diet is high in cholesterol your body will compensate by producing less. Again, it must be stressed, production and buildup of cholesterol vary from one person to another.

Anticholesterol propaganda and massive advertising campaigns dominate the media. The food industry is jumping on the bandwagon by producing new synthetic low-cholesterol fat-free foods. Doctors stress the potential health hazards for normal healthy people of drastically changing the fat content of their diet without medical consultation. Still, many questions about cholesterol remain unanswered. But in the meantime, the big fuss over the cholesterol content of meat and dairy products has distracted us from the real menace of these foods—their *adulteration*. At least we know that DES and DDT are dangerous.

In deciding whether or not to include meat as a protein source in your diet, you should keep in mind the fact that a meat-centered diet creates more waste products for the kidneys to dispose of. Dr. John Harvey Kellogg, writing in *The New Dietetic*, said that "even moderate meat eaters require of their kidneys three times the amount of work in the elimination of nitrogenous wastes than is demanded of the kidney of flesh abstainers. While the kidneys are young they are usually able to bear this extra burden so that no evidence of injury appears; but as they become worn with advancing age, they become unable to do their work efficiently." In this regard, the decision to eat some meat, no meat, or less meat may have greater significance for the elderly. Meat—provided it is not loaded with adulterants—is an excellent source of protein for the elderly who can't tolerate a lot of bulk in their diet.

Most people would agree that a plant-centered diet is dull, unappetizing, and time-consuming to prepare. Food manufacturers have provided a vast array of attractively packaged, precooked, preseasoned, and ready-to-serve convenience foods. Enticing combinations of frozen vegetables sealed in plastic bags need only be dropped into a pan of boiling water. Meat, fish, and poultry products come precooked, breaded, and seasoned. Microwave ovens can heat or cook meals in minutes at the push of a button. Beef sliced into steaks can quickly be pan-fried or broiled to perfection. With such conveniences at hand, it is easy to understand why so many people are reluctant to adopt a diet that seems to require so much time in preparation.

Eating convenience foods, of course, has its drawbacks, and these are reflected in the general health of our population. Obesity, diabetes, hypertension, gout, indigestion, ulcers, constipation, and gum and tooth disease are only a few of the health problems that are directly linked to our eating habits. Millions of dollars are spent yearly on antacids, laxatives, and other self-prescribed aids for gastrointestinal ailments, on multivitamins and health-food supplements intended to make up for what's lacking in our foods, on sugar substitutes and diet foods and drinks.

The irony of all this is that while it is the food you eat that causes many health problems, food can also correct them. For years now, health advocates and nutritionists have said, "You are what you eat." Nothing could be truer. A well-balanced diet that offers a wide variety of vegetables, fruits, whole-grain cereals, and quality protein foods is most important in obtaining and maintaining optimum health.

Television bombards us with commercials hawking yogurt, high-fiber bread and "back to nature" cereal. Many consumers buy these products thinking "health foods" will make them healthy. While it's true that yogurt, whole-grain cereals, and high-fiber breads are good foods—certainly better than the synthetic chemical concoctions that line most supermarket shelves—they won't of themselves make you healthy.

For centuries Orientals have known how to sprout, grind, and roast soybeans, how to make them into curds and milk, as a remarkably cheap and valuable source of high-quality protein. By comparison, we Westerners are in the Dark Ages when it comes to knowing what to do with our bounty of nonflesh protein sources. Which brings us back to the advantages of plant-centered diets.

Most of the people in the world get the protein in their diets from grains, vegetables, legumes, fruits, nuts, and seeds. Grains (including rice, corn, wheat, rye, oats, buckwheat, barley, and millet) provide almost half the protein consumed in the world. Their net protein values range from the low 50s to the low 60s, except for rice, which has an NPU of 70, greater than that of beef.

Among the vegetables, corn, mushrooms, potatoes, and soybean sprouts have the highest NPUs, but this food group does not contribute significantly to the daily protein requirement. Vegetables contain such high proportions of moisture that we can't eat enough of them to fulfill our protein needs. And those 73 vegetables which contain less than 2 percent protein (such as cabbage, eggplant, onions, green peppers, tomatoes, and lettuce) cannot be considered protein sources at all. But vegetables are a valuable low-calorie source of vitamins A and C, and excellent sources of many minerals and trace elements.

The legume family of soybean sprouts, peas, and all varieties of beans, limas, and lentils have NPUs nearly equal to that of meat. Soybeans and mung beans have NPUs of 61 and 57 respectively. These NPUs represent only the amount of protein available to the consumer *if the legumes are not complemented by another source of protein at the same meal.* When they are complemented by other incomplete protein sources, such as wheat or rice, their NPU can go up as much as 50 percent.

Although the plant foods commonly eaten for their protein content contain the eight essential amino acids, they do have certain deficiencies in their amino acid patterns that render them less useful to the body than other complete protein sources. If only one of the eight amino acids is available in limited amounts it reduces the effectiveness of the other seven proportionately. Remember, not only do the eight amino acids need to be present simultaneously but *all need to be present in the right proportions.* The deficiencies in incomplete plant sources can, however, be offset in combination with other foods containing the limited amino acid. They can produce protein quality equivalent, and sometimes superior, to animal protein.

Once you know the technique of combining different sources of proteins, you'll see why food combinations like rice and beans or bread and cheese have sustained populations for centuries. These people did not understand the biochemistry of these food combinations, but over the generations they saw that these combinations provided enough of *something* to maintain life and promote growth. This "something" is the complementary mixture of amino acids necessary for protein synthesis.

The claim that plant-centered diets are dull and unappetizing couldn't be further from the truth. Agricultural technology has produced forty to fifty different varieties of vegetables, twenty-four different types of nuts, and nine forms of grain. Just imagine eating a lunch with a mixed salad of dark greens, shredded red cabbage, diced carrots, sliced onions, cucumbers, radishes, red pepper, and celery, garnished with black olives and a sprig of parsley. The main course could consist of a hearty mushroom, eggplant, and cheese casserole, accompanied by freshly steamed pieces of crisp broccoli, cauliflower, and zucchini, with rich dark whole-grain bread on the side, a cup of lightly spiced herb coffee or tea, and for dessert a baked apple or fresh fruit covered with yogurt.

Plant foods are generally considered to be high in carbohydrates, and therefore high in calories and more fattening than meat. Plant foods do contain carbohydrates, but they usually don't contain the fat found in animal and animal by-products. Ounce for ounce, most plant foods have either the same or considerably fewer calories than meat and dairy products. For example, many fruits have one third the calories of meat, cooked beans one half, and most varieties of green vegetables one eighth.

Carbohydrate foods, of course, supply energy along with their calories. As far as your body is concerned, carbohydrate energy requirements come *before* protein requirements. Vegetables, fruits, whole grains, and cereals also offer an abundance of fiber. Fiber—cellulose, or the indigestible part of the plant —speeds up the process of eliminating bodily waste, allowing less time for it to accumulate in the body. Adequate amounts of fiber in the diet are also known to prevent constipation and other gastrointestinal disorders. The best sources of fiber are dried fruits, whole-grain cereals, nuts, fresh fruits, and vegetables. Milk, meat, eggs, cheese, and highly refined foods (such as white flour) are poor sources of fiber. Because the fiber in meat is protein, it is digestible and provides the intestinal tract with little if any bulk. The daily need for fiber—estimated to be 4 to 7 milligrams—may easily be obtained if the diet includes a serving of whole-grain cereal or bread, two servings of vegetables, and two servings of fruit.

In short, if you plan your daily eating habits around the basic four food groups, you'll have enough high-protein and vitamin- and mineral-rich foods, as well as enough fiber, carbohydrates, and fats, to ensure a healthful diet.

COMPLETE
PROTEIN
FOODS

4

MEAT

IN THE UNITED STATES, MEAT HAS A LONG AND SOLID REPUTA-
tion as a highly important food. How did it get this reputation?
As protein food meat is not at the top of the scale; eggs are,
remember, first. Meat is, in fact, generally no more than 22
percent protein. But meat does contain several nutrients in a
concentrated form, some of which are not so readily available
from plant sources. These nutrients, found in the lean portions
of meat, include iron and several B vitamins—notably B_{12},
which is not practically available from plant sources. Meat
is also valuable as a source of lipids (fats), which are not available from plant sources.

Your body needs fat, and you should not exclude it from
your diet. Concentrated sources of energy, fats supply 9
calories per gram compared to the 4 calories per gram supplied by proteins and carbohydrates. You need an adequate
intake of fats to spare your body's proteins from being used
as fuel. Fat is also important as an insulator. Stored under the
skin, it protects your body from heat loss in cold weather, and
the fat around your internal organs, filling about 45 percent
of your abdominal cavity, cushions these organs from physi-

cal injury. Your intermuscular fat stores are important as suppliers of immediate energy when it is needed, and you need fat for the digestion, absorption, and transport of the fat-soluble vitamins A, D, E, and K. And, most important, you need fats for the development and growth of your brain and nervous system.

The fats in your body are of two types—saturated and unsaturated. Saturated fats, which make up your body's visible storage fat, are composed of largely nonessential fatty acids. Among these are the triglycerides, which many doctors believe contribute to heart disease if retained in the body in large quantities. The unsaturated fats, composed of essential fatty acids, are involved in vital cell construction and maintenance functions, and are necessary for the development of your brain and nervous system.

All plants and animals depend on both saturated storage fats and unsaturated structural fats. Plants generally contain a predominant amount of unsaturated fatty acids, while animals usually have greater concentrations of saturated than unsaturated fat.

The accelerating incidence of heart disease in America has been linked with increased beef consumption. The saturated fat in beef is believed to be a "risk factor" in the development of arteriosclerosis. But the increased *consumption* of beef—from 60 pounds per person annually in 1950 to 122 pounds today—is only part of the story. Perhaps more important is the fact that the composition of the beef we eat today is somewhat different from what it was twenty years ago.

In the fifties, beef fat was largely unsaturated. Beef provided us with more lipids for cellular construction than it does today, and more nutrients as well. Today's cattle, intensively raised on high-energy feeds, deprived of exercise, and treated with drugs and hormones, carry approximately 30 percent of their total weight in carcass fat. Grass-fed, naturally raised cattle are only 5 to 10 percent carcass fat.

Before the days of the animal drug culture, cattle grazed on open pastures, roaming from acre to acre. They ate when they felt hungry; slept, exercised, and mated when the urge took them; grew lean, strong, relaxed, and, for the most part, healthy. They matured slowly over two or three years, and when time came for their slaughter they were taken directly from the pasture to the slaughterhouse. The meat from these animals was tasty, requiring no doctoring with tenderizers and spicy sauces. Today it's not so easy to buy a steak that tastes delicious with only a sprinkling of salt. The history of this transformation is a long story summarized in one word: *profit*.

The life expectancy of a steer, once two to four years, is now eighteen months. A steer is born. The moment he is dry from the womb, he is taken from his mother. The cattleman places him on a "calf starter ration" consisting of milk powder, synthetic vitamins, minerals, and antibiotics—because suckling temporarily reduces the amount of salable milk produced by the mother. Just 25 pounds of calf food replaces the 225 pounds of milk he would normally drink. The drug-spiked food also reduces the calf's natural desire for activity, thus reducing his need for more energy-sustaining food.

After the calf has outgrown this food, he may be fed a combination of pasture grass and processed feed, which comes to the cattle farmer premixed with antibiotics and other drugs to promote faster growth. By the end of a year the steer will have reached "middle age," with only six months to live before slaughter. He now weights 500 pounds—less than half of his final weight.

When the steer arrives at the commercical feedlot, he is forced off the boxcar and through a tank filled with pesticides that cleanses him of worms and flies. He is then confined in a pen continuously lit to encourage him to feed around the clock. Several times a day his trough is refilled with a feed mixture computer-blended that morning. In addition to starchy, high-protein grains, these ingredients may include urea carbohydrate mixtures and artificial roughage such as ground-up newspaper mixed with molasses, tasteless plastic pellets, feathers, or treated wood mixtures. In fairness, we must state that this is not a common practice, though it does exist.

Sometimes the force-feeding of a steer will create a painful liver abscess, which can slow his rate of weight gain. But this is no longer a problem for feedlot owners: cattle with abscessed livers are simply treated with 75 milligrams daily of the antibiotic oxytetracycline. During his marathon feeding our steer gains upwards of three pounds of muscle and fat a day from approximately thirty pounds of feed. Not enough. Pellets are shot into his ear containing the female hormone diethylstilbestrol (DES), which relaxes his muscles and pads the body with moisture and fat. And why not? Drug companies claim that DES makes cattle 10 to 15 percent fatter on 10 to 15 percent less feed.

Meanwhile, the steer's female counterpart, the heifer, is getting the hormone melengestrol acetate (MGA) in her feed every day to kill her sex drive. After all, the feedlot manager can't have her jumping around mounting other animals. With MGA she'll stay glued to the feed trough.

Scientists know that hormones encourage overeating by somehow manipulating the behavior of the animals, which also affects their metabolism. Some scientists believe antibiotics make the intestinal walls thinner so that food is absorbed more rapidly; others believe that the antibiotics stupefy the cattle so they just stand and stare at the food and eat it.

As for antibiotics, they may increase profits by reducing the incidence of some disease among cattle, but sooner or later disease-producing organisms can develop immunity to the antibiotics, and these drugs become less effective against infection.

Another set of drugs in the feedlot manager's medicine chest is tranquilizers. They induce animals to eat more food in a given period of time and convert it faster into body tissue. When tranquilizers are used along with antibiotics and DES, the results are really dramatic. In steers the combination hastens weight gain by slowing down metabolism; in cows it increases milk production by stimulating the hypothalamus.

By now our steer more resembles a test tube than an animal, but his chemical diet isn't quite complete. He is sprayed and dusted with pesticides from time to time, and he eats the insecticide with his feed. It passes through his digestive system and is eliminated in his manure, where it serves the purpose of keeping flies from breeding. Charcoal may be added to dairy feeds to absorb the pesticide, preventing their excretion into the milk.

This modern development of systemic pesticides liberates feedlot owners from the need to remove manure from the cattle stalls. In some feedlots manure is cleaned up only four times a year. You can see the cattle standing numbly in a soup of it, eating away.

After four months of ingesting the equivalent of three huge Christmas dinners a day, the steer weighs about 1200 pounds, almost enough for slaughter. During the last three to five days, he is fed a booster of 1000 milligrams of oxytetracycline or chlortetracycline a day, and given one last shot of streptomycin for the road to the slaughterhouse.

Meat packers used to hang beef in a refrigerated room for fourteen to twenty-one days to tenderize it. But this lengthy process took up warehouse space, and caused both meat and profits to shrink. Now meat is tenderized on the hoof or dipped in a solution of enzymes prior to freezing.

Given a political system reluctant to regulate business aggressively, meat inspection is often less effective than it should be. Twenty percent of the meat sold in this country has not been federally inspected. Meats processed and sold in the same state are subject only to state inspections, which range from thorough to practically nonexistent. From time to time there are scandals which expose the laxity of the inspection regulations or the corruption of the inspectors. In 1971, forty U.S.D.A. inspectors were indicted for soliciting bribes from the meat-packing companies whose products they "inspected." And three years earlier a large plant in California was caught doctoring and repackaging spoiled meat returned by retail stores. This plant then resold it, without the reinspection required by law, in the predominantly black Watts area of Los Angeles.

Meat sold in interstate commerce is examined by U.S.D.A. inspectors who take a four-week training course covering anatomy, sanitation, the composition requirements for different grades of ground meat, safety regulations, and labeling laws. This course is followed by one week of on-the-job training, in which they learn to inspect slaughtered livestock for gross defects like diseased internal organs, bruises, cancerous tumors, abscessed livers, and fecal contamination—all in only a few minutes. If cancer is found, inspectors don't condemn the whole carcass; cutters are directed to remove cancerous organs and send the rest of the carcass on for processing. In 1954 alone, we ate the meat from 2.4 million cattle whose livers had been cancerous or tubercular. Inspectors do not examine meat for microbial contaminants such as salmonella, trichina, staphylococcus, and pesticide residues, since no cheap and easy way of doing so has been found.

The labels for federally inspected canned, packaged, or frozen meats must list all the ingredients, the name of the product, the name and address of the processor or distributor, a mark of approval, and accurate weight. But you will rarely see the purple approval stamp on the meat you buy, because the carcass has been cut up into serving sizes and placed in coolers along with meat from many different animals. If you should find that a piece of meat is not fresh when you get it home—or, even worse, if you get food poisoning from eating it—the only person you can complain to is your store owner, who may not even know by this time where the piece of meat came from.

Passing federal or state inspection does not mean that a piece of meat is disease-free. Dr. Oscar Sussman, chief of New Jersey's veterinary public health program, warns, "No present method of U.S. meat or poultry inspection can assure disease-free, noncontaminated raw meat or poultry products. Reliance by the housewife on the U.S.-inspected legend alone has, can and will cause countless cases of food infection such as salmonellosis [food poisoning] and trichinosis. . . . Elimination of such hazards lies in proper food processing, food handling, and cooking techniques." [1]

Proper cooking will destroy disease-carrying bacteria in meat, but your hands can carry these organisms to other foods that won't be cooked. Always be sure to wash your hands after handling raw meat and wash the cooking utensils you have used in preparing the meat.

What goes on in the cutting room behind the meat counter of your local supermarket? You may shop at a store whose owners are conscientious about the quality of meat they sell and would themselves eat anything in their own meat coolers. But you might be shopping at a store like the one described by former meatcutter Jon A. McClure in his book *The Meat Eaters Are Threatened.*[2] McClure exposed the practices and conditions he encountered during his ten years in sixty different stores in the East and Midwest, where city and state health inspections were infrequent and superficial. He describes the routine doctoring of rotten meat for sale to poor and old people, the use of rotten meat in spicy deli foods, the filthy conditions that could contaminate all products.

Many of the incidents he describes are downright lurid: "Adulteration of hams has taken place in every store I've worked in during the past ten years. In one store there were three grocery cans full of hams left over from a ham sale a month ago. They had been wrapped and rewrapped a dozen times, but we couldn't sell them. By this time the hams were slick with bacteria and green and white mold. Many of the hams had dark spots on them from where the mold had eaten into the tissues. I was ordered to fill a large sink with water and scrub the hams with a scrub brush until I removed all the mold. Some of the mold came off but the black spots remained. The hams were putrid, and the pleasant smoke flavor had dissipated by decomposition and adulteration. The hams were full of contaminated water, and when you squeezed them on the face side they resembled a sponge full of water. The 'boss' brought back three bottles of 'liquid smoke' from the grocery shelf and ordered me to 'doctor them up' and rub the smoke all over the surface of the ham. The hams were rotten and there was no way anyone could argue the fact. However, for weeks after that we sold the hams. Finally, when we couldn't sell any more we sliced some of them and diced some others for ham seasoning. And then he called a local restaurant to take the balance off his hands. There were twenty hams left, all were sold to a restaurant."

McClure also describes how meat managers use sodium sulfite, a powerful chemical illegally used to hold the color in meats, to change the color of rotten meat from green to red. Treated ground meats like chuck, round, sirloin, and sausage are especially dangerous because the chemical is mixed throughout to completely disguise the rotten odor and color.

The increase of environmental contaminants and the rise of cancer has made scientists more concerned with the investigation of long-range toxins—substances which are toxic over a long period of time. The damage from some of these toxins may not show up for twenty or thirty years, while others may wreak havoc after a year or two. The F.D.A., more concerned about substances that can cause immediate damage in humans or in laboratory animals, is shortsighted about the restriction of chemicals that may be long-term toxins.

And so today we have some 2700 drug compounds available for use in our meats, a few of which may be necessary, many of which involve risks, either known or unknown. Most of these drugs have been used for only the past twenty years. We may just now be ready to discover which of them are twenty-year carcinogens.

It is currently estimated that upwards of 80 percent of all

beef cattle are still being fattened on DES. This female hormone has been identified as the cause of a rare vaginal cancer. It has also been known to produce breast cancer, fibroid tumors, and excessive menstrual bleeding in women, sterility and impotence in men, and arrested growth in children. After DES was exposed as a powerful carcinogen, public pressure forced the F.D.A. to ban it as an additive to animal feed as of January, 1973. So now steers are being fattened with DES pellets—"growth-promoting pellets"—injected into their ears. DES increases the weight gain to cattle, but it produces watery fat rather than protein and results in meat that is marbled with fat throughout. No one knows how much DES and other growth hormones end up in our meat, since U.S.D.A. inspectors rarely test for them. Residues are hard to detect by scientific means, and may remain in the meat even after thorough cooking.

If DES is eventually banned from feedlots, cattle growers won't be without a replacement arsenal of other growth hormones. One of them being used now is called Synovex S, a combination of estrogens contained in a pellet ready for injection into the steer's ear.

The F.D.A. is aware of the potential risks growth hormones pose for the consumer. An internal F.D.A. memorandum has reported that "all estrogens are considered to be carcinogenic, since all estrogens that have been adequately tested have been shown to be carcinogenic in animals." The F.D.A. hasn't yet determined what levels of estrogens can be dangerous to humans, and it may take years to find out.

We know that bacteria exposed to antibiotics over periods of time develop resistance to them, making the diseases the bacteria produce untreatable by these drugs. An F.D.A. task force warns that there has been a "marked increase" in resistant bacteria in animals; that means an increase in diseases carried by animals that can no longer be wiped out by antibiotics. These diseases can be passed on to humans. Dr. Henry

Isenberg, a microbiologist at the Long Island Jewish Medical Center, says so many strains of the food-poisoning virus salmonella have developed resistance to antibiotics that we face food-poisoning epidemics "of staggering proportions." Government inspectors, in a random sampling of supermarkets, have found salmonella contamination in over 50 percent of the poultry sold. The National Communicable Disease Center estimates that each year 38 million Americans suffer salmonella poisoning in varying degrees, from headache and nausea to violent illness.

Heralded as miracle drugs when they were discovered after World War II, antibiotics have saved many lives. But they also can be hazardous, as the 17 to 20 million Americans who are allergic to them are aware. Severe reactions to these drugs have caused shock, irritating rashes, nausea, and, in some cases, death. Since antibiotics kill all bacteria that aren't resistant to them—even the healthy, disease-fighting bacteria —they can disrupt the intestinal system by eliminating those bacteria necessary for proper digestion.

Antibiotics are used in feedlots only incidentally to fight specific animal diseases. They are added to feed to make cattle grow faster and to prevent diseases likely to occur because of unsanitary, stressful conditions in feedlots. Since cooking doesn't destroy antibiotic residues, the meat you eat today may make you more vulnerable to infection tomorrow. Ingesting small amounts of antibiotics over a period of time can lower your resistance to many types of disease, and increase the danger that the diseases you do contract will be resistant to treatment.

If you feel slightly sluggish after eating a big steak, one possible explanation is that you've just had a small amount of tranquilizers. They have been used in animal feed since the late 1950s, when experiments showed that tranquilized animals ate more food in a shorter time and converted it faster to body tissue. Animals fatten on tranquilizers because their metabolic rate is slowed down. At present, nobody knows how much of these drugs accumulate in the animals' bodies or what effect they have on our health.

The argument usually given for the use of all these drugs is that without them we would face a severe protein shortage in this country. Secretary of Agriculture Earl Butz once said that America could revert to the organic method of cattle raising if it wanted to, but someone would first have to pick the 30 million people who would starve. The implication was clear: we'd starve without meat.

To test the true importance of antibiotics in animal feed, Dr. H. Dwight Mercer, a former deputy director of the F.D.A.'s veterinary research farm in Beltsville, Maryland, raised groups of livestock for eighteen months with and without these drugs. When Mercer raised the animals on high-protein feed in clean conditions he found no growth response from antibiotics. When he let the conditions in the feedlot become filthy, he could maintain the health of the animals only if they were given antibiotics. The worse the living conditions, the better the cattle responded to antibiotics. Mercer and other veterinarians have concluded that the factors that make antibiotics most efficient are manure pile-ups, mediocre food, extreme temperatures, crowding, and stress.

Twenty years ago you'd buy a hot dog at the beach and you'd get a little mustard, a little sand, and a fair amount of protein for your money. Today, though the flavor may seem the same and the color looks healthy and inviting, what you are paying for is very often a neat package of spice-flavored fat, a little protein and water, and certain ingredients added to give it the old hot dog "mouth feel," as they say in the industry. Recent research conducted at the Nutrition Institute of America showed that the average hot dog contains 60 percent moisture, 30 to 40 percent fat, and only 7 percent protein.

Depending on whether the hot dog is labeled "all beef," "all meat," "frankfurters," "wieners," or "imitation frankfurters," you'll possibly be getting artificial flavor, MSG (monosodium glutamate), nitrites, sugar, dextrose, water, and a wide variety of "animal products." The animal products in all-beef and kosher franks must be all beef, but the "all meat" label does not mean that the hot dog must really be all beef.

Under the law, it may contain up to 15 percent nonmeat ingredients, including artificial coloring, flavorings, and preservatives. "All meat" hot dogs can contain beef, pork, veal, lamb, or goat in any proportion, and up to 15 percent chicken. Hot dogs with general labels such as "frankfurters" could contain animal products like beef lips, pork lips, snout, tail gristle, blood, lung, spleen, tripe, and stomach. And if chicken is added, it may be chicken skin, chicken fat, giblets, even pulverized chicken bone. Labels that say "cereal added" mean that the hot dog may contain up to 3.5 percent of such "extenders."

Imitation frankfurters contain, in addition to quantities of cereal fillers and artificial flavors, animal parts that you might not have even heard of. As a source of protein, even the best hot dogs provide only 10 grams—compared to an equal weight of chicken, which provides 26 grams, or fresh fish, which provides 25. And as a source of protein, hot dogs are not cheap. *Consumer Reports* [3] has calculated that the average cost of one pound of protein from hot dogs is from $6.98 to $7.94, while a pound of protein from ground beef only costs $3.91.

Hot dogs and other ground and processed meats—such as hamburger, bologna and sliced luncheon meats—are particularly susceptible to bacterial growth: the grinding process breaks down tissues and cell fluids, creating a perfect environment for bacteria to breed. Food analysts generally agree that when the bacterial count of a piece of meat is about 10 million per gram, putrefaction has set in. *Consumer Reports* analyzed thirty-two brands of widely available U.S.D.A.-inspected hot dogs and found that 40 percent of the samples tested had begun to spoil.[4] The "vacuum packs" that contain hot dogs and other luncheon meats don't fully protect you from buying spoiled products. Some bacteria can grow in airtight containers, and some airtight containers aren't airtight. They are easily accidentally punctured. A package bloated with the gas produced by bacterial action can look "salable" with the prick of a pin. *Consumer Reports* says that bacteria counts as high as 5 million per gram are likely to cause nothing more serious than a mild gastric upset—but it cautions against eating franks that haven't been properly cooked. Never, but never, eat them from the package without cooking them.

A staple food for many Americans, bacon is loaded with higher concentrations of nitrites than other preserved meats, but hot dogs, bologna, corned beef, ham, and luncheon meats are also treated with nitrites. In fact, about a third of the federally inspected meat you eat contains nitrites.

The way in which nitrites turn meat from unappetizing gray to robust red makes them potentially unhealthy for human beings. Once added to meat, the nitrite is broken down into nitrous acid, which combines with the hemoglobin of the meat to form a permanent red color. Unfortunately, just as the nitrites react with the blood of a carcass, so will they react with the blood of living humans: inactivating the red blood cells which carry oxygen through the body. The disease which nitrites can produce is called methemoglobinemia, or "inactivated hemoglobin." If too many red blood cells are temporarily inactivated by the nitrites, severe poisoning and sometimes death can result. Reported cases of nitrite poisoning involve food containing more nitrites than the legally allowed 200 parts per million. The victims are, as a rule, susceptible to small quantities of nitrites—particularly infants, small children, and anemic people with heart disease or low blood pressure. In Buffalo, New York, six persons were hospitalized with "cardiovascular collapse" after they ate blood sausage containing excessive amounts of nitrite. In New Jersey, two persons died and many others were critically poisoned after eating fish illegally loaded with nitrite. In Florida, a three-year-old boy died after eating hot dogs with only three times greater nitrite concentration than the government allows.

Physicians used to prescribe sodium nitrite—a salt nitrite compound—for high blood pressure. The therapeutic dose was usually 30 milligrams, the amount legally allowed in one third of a pound of cured meat or fish. Even if you don't have high blood pressure, your blood pressure can be lowered for up to two hours after eating meat and fish treated with *legal* levels of nitrites.

Another cause for concern is the fact that nitrites are one of three ingredients which can combine in the stomach to form nitrosamines. These compounds are so potent that a dose of only 2 parts per million has induced cancer in rats. An F.D.A. report notes, "Nitrosamines have been described as one of the most formidable and versatile groups of carcinogens yet discovered." [5] Nitrosamines are considered versatile for their ability to attack any organ of the body, and potent because they have produced cancer in animals after a single dose. Unlike many other carcinogens, they have produced cancers in every species of animal tested—mice, guinea pigs, dogs, monkeys, rats, and hamsters—and in the offspring of pregnant animals.

Nitrosamines are formed by the combination of a mildly acid solution, nitrites, and amines, found naturally in many foods and synthetically in certain drugs. Beer, wine, tea, cigarette smoke (which can be dissolved in saliva and swallowed), fish, cereals, and many other foods contain amines. They are also found in prescription drugs and over-the-counter preparations, including oral contraceptives, muscle relaxants, antidepressants, tranquilizers, analgesics, nasal decongestants, diuretics, and antihistamines.

Nitrites and amines come together in the stomach, which is like a test tube already containing the first necessary ingredient, the mildly acid solution. For nitrosamines to form in the stomach, you must ingest nitrites and amines at the same time. The possibility for this chemical reaction is hardly remote: what about ham or salami (nitrites) and beer (amines)? Or smoking a cigarette after eating a corned beef sandwich? (Some investigators have speculated that since the carcinogen in cigarette smoke has not been identified, perhaps cancer from smoking results not from the smoke alone, but from the interaction of the amines in smoke with the nitrites in foods.)

Sometimes nitrites can react chemically with the amines in meat and fish even before we eat them. In February, 1972, the F.D.A. found nitrosamines in eight samples of processed meat from packing plants and retail stores.[6] The F.D.A. found nitrosamine levels of 11 to 48 parts per billion in dried beef and cured pork, 26 parts per billion in smoked salmon, 5 parts per billion in hams, 80 parts per billion in hot dogs, and 106 per billion in bacon. The nitrosamines in bacon were found only in *cooked* bacon, suggesting that heat had accelerated the formation of nitrosamines. The drippings were discovered to contain *twice* the nitrosamine amount of the bacon itself—over 200 parts per billion, which easily makes bacon a potentially unsafe food.

With all this evidence on the dangers of nitrites, why are they still allowed in our meat and fish? Other countries have banned their use as color fixatives and replaced them with vitamin C and citric acid. The F.D.A. and the U.S.D.A. are not making any moves until a joint industry and government task force has "evaluated the problem."

By now we hope you've concluded that the only person who can protect you from unsafe, unhealthful foods is *you*. By shopping and preparing foods knowledgeably, you can avoid or minimize the dangers of eating meat. Here are some guidelines for getting the best and safest protein and nutrients from meat:

Use caution when buying ham, hot dogs, luncheon meat, smoked fish, and bacon unless the label states clearly that the product is pure—like kosher hot dogs. If the list of ingredients includes nitrites, complain to the storekeeper and your neighbors.

The ground beef you buy should be ground in your presence. Better yet, grind your own beef and pork. *You* can be sure that the meat grinder is clean every time you use it, with no pork residues possibly bearing trichina organisms, or particles or spoiled meat which could contain salmonella bacteria.

Minimize precut packaged meat. Ask to have your meats cut and trimmed of fat in your presence, and ask to see the inspection and grading mark on the carcass. Initially your store manager may balk at this request, but the more often consumers show an awareness of meat-inspection procedures, the harder it will be for packers and retail stores to pass off low-quality meat. The best guarantee of good meat is to find producers who raise their animals in sanitary conditions free of drugs. Your local health food store or consumer union may be able to supply you with sources.

Never buy beef liver unless you are sure that the beef has been raised without drugs. The liver, the organ of detoxification, is a repository for all kinds of chemical residues.

Avoid fatty meat as much as possible, since pesticide residues generally accumulate in the fatty portions. Choose cuts of meat that aren't marbled, but instead have the fat contained in strips that can be cut away.

FACTS TO PONDER

— Organ meats have a higher biological value than muscle meats.
— Senator Maurine Neuberger has charged that since ham may be pumped with water up to 10 percent of its total weight, and since ham sales totaled $875 million in 1960, the public paid for $87.5 million worth of federally inspected water.
— Although the federal government limits the fat content of

meat to 30 percent, most states lack proper enforcement of this regulation. Some states that have a fat regulation allow as much as 50 percent fat in a piece of meat or meat product.

— We have at least three times as many cases of trichinosis in the United States as does the rest of the world.

— There are 485 food chemicals which, according to federal law, do not have to be listed on food labels.

— A Department of Agriculture scientist has estimated that of the 700 chemicals now used for flavoring, about 30 could accomplish the same thing. In France, only seven chemical flavorings are widely used.

— About one third of all hot dogs are not federally inspected.

— The world population increased beyond the point at which it could be supported by a meat-centered diet over a century ago.

CHAPTER

5

MILK AND
DAIRY PRODUCTS

MILK HAS BEEN CALLED THE PERFECT FOOD. ITS AMINO
acid composition makes it a complete protein, and it contains
extra amounts of the amino acids that are often hard to get
in plant proteins, so milk is an ideal complement to any vegetarian dish. Milk is also an important food because it contains
calcium, phosphorus, and most of the essential vitamins.

Milk is the best nutritional source of calcium. High in both
calcium and fat, which aids the absorption of calcium, it also
offers an ideal calcium-phosphorus ratio. Americans obtain
more than three fourths of their dietary calcium and half of
their dietary phosphorus from milk and milk products. Milk
products provide a rich and well-balanced supply of fat-
soluble vitamins A, D, E, and K and the water-soluble B
vitamins, particularly riboflavin. A quart of cow's milk per
day will furnish you with approximately all the fat, calcium,
phosphorus, and riboflavin you need, one half your daily protein need, one third your vitamin A, and one fourth the calories you need daily. And, except for people suffering from a
lactose (milk sugar) intolerance, milk is nearly 100 percent
digestible.

Of course, there is no genuinely perfect food. Like any food, milk is strong in some nutrients and weak in others, such as vitamin C, iron, and copper. The milk products of different species vary in content. Cow's milk, the most widely consumed in the Western world, is 87 percent water, 4 percent fat, 3.5 percent protein, 4.8 percent milk sugar (lactose) and .7 percent mineral salts. Different breeds of cow produce milk with varying fat content. Cow's milk lacks certain nutrients contained in human milk, which is why infant formulas based on cow's milk must be enriched. Cow's milk contains only one sixth the amount of vitamin C in human milk, and only one third the iron.

Milk is imperfect for other reasons as well. Today milk production and transport is more sanitary and efficient than ever before, but this doesn't mean that the milk and milk products we get are any more pure than they were in the old days when milk came "warm from the cow." Like the beef steer, the dairy cow lives a life manipulated by stressful conditions, forced feeding, and drug ingestion, and the proof is in her milk. This milk, which once caused concern only as to the diseases it might carry, now contains antibiotics, hormones, pesticides, radioactive isotopes, and other toxic materials—as well as, on occasion, disease-producing bacteria. These hazards are compounded by the fact that the standards and laws regulating the dairy industry vary greatly from state to state. Dairy products, most of which are produced and sold within the same state, are not subject to federal regulations.

Before 1945, when antibiotics were introduced, about 35 percent of all dairy cows suffered from a common inflammation called mastitis. Today an estimated 50 percent of all dairy cows become infected with this disease, and there are more different strains of mastitis-producing bacteria than ever before.[1] Over the years, these bacteria have developed a hearty resistance to penicillin and other antibiotics, and farmers and veterinarians are finding it increasingly difficult to treat.

Penicillin is the least toxic of all the antibiotics, but some people are so allergic to it that even one millionth of the normal medical dose can cause them severe, sometimes fatal, shock. Penicillin can also cause gastrointestinal disorders, asthma, dermatitis, enlarged glands, swellings, and fever. Often these symptoms don't occur until fifteen days after it has been injected, which makes it even more difficult to determine their cause. Despite penicillin's potential hazards for some patients, and the fact that physicians are very cautious in their administration of this antibiotic to humans, tons of it are used in dairy feed each year. Penicillin residues end up in the milk we drink; surveys by the F.D.A. in 1956 showed that penicillin residues in milk were almost universal. These residues cannot, unfortunately, be destroyed by the heat of pasteurization or cooking, and there is every reason to think that these levels are even higher today. The size of antibiotic dosages for the treatment of mastitis has increased over the years, and many of these antibiotic preparations are now contained in an oil rather than a water base. The oil base delays the excretion of penicillin and other antibiotics from the milk, meaning that the treated cow will produce contaminated milk for a longer period of time than before.

Dairy owners are supposed to withhold from sale all milk from treated cows for seventy-two to ninety-six hours after the administration of antibiotics, but they don't always comply.

Even though a relatively small percentage of the population is sensitive to penicillin, prolonged exposure to tiny amounts of it could cause nonsensitive people to develop sensitivities which will not show up until a therapeutic dose is administered later. And people ingesting small doses of antibiotics through milk products could develop a resistance to them, so that a therapeutic dose administered in the crisis of a severe infection may prove less effective.

"No milk available on the market today, in any part of the U.S., is 100 percent free of pesticide residues." This statement comes directly from the United States Dairy Association.[2] Pesticide residues are a more severe problem in dairy products than in meat because the chlorinated hydrocarbons used to kill insects accumulate in the fat of animals and are excreted in milk. You can trim the fat off a piece of meat, but you can't trim the fat off a glass of milk or piece of cheese unless you drink skim milk and eat low-fat cheese. The pesticide concentrations legally allowed in milk fat are twenty-five times those allowed in milk, so dairy products with high concentrations of milk fat—such as butter and cream—will have higher concentrations of these residues than nonfat dairy products.[3]

It is important for you to know that the legal tolerances set for DDT and similar substances in milk do *not* represent quantities which are safe, but only those which the dairy industry can practically achieve.

After the extensive tests of nuclear weapons in the 1950s, radioactive fallout was discovered in milk and milk products. Today milk is still contaminated with strontium 89, strontium 90, iodine 131, cesium 137, and barium 140.[4] A technique for decontaminating milk has been devised, but it is still too expensive for commercial use. Decontamination of milk would cost the dairy industry an estimated 9 cents a quart.[5]

Even so, we don't advise you to give up milk or milk products. Milk is too valuable a food, and the calcium it contains can actually protect us from certain types of radioactive materials. As mentioned above, milk is contaminated with strontium 90. We are, however, relatively safe from the small amounts of this radioactive material found in milk because the body absorbs calcium more readily than strontium 90. The amount of strontium deposited in human bones depends upon the strontium–calcium ratio in the total diet. Cows screen out 90 percent of the strontium 90 before it enters their milk, and most of the remaining 10 percent is kept from entering our bones, where it could cause severe damage. Most importantly, strontium poisoning is combated by the great amount of calcium we receive from milk. We can, by drinking milk, actually *reduce* the amount of strontium in our bones.

Milk contamination can also come from hormones, detergents, and wax particles. Hormones, given to cows to increase their milk production or reduce their sex drive, may end up in milk and milk products. And if milking equipment is not rinsed completely, residues of detergents and disinfectants can pass into the milk. This does not seem to pose any serious health hazards; even so, it is a problem for the cheese industry, since detergent residues lower the bacteria count necessary to produce cheese and cultured milk products. If you can buy milk packaged in glass or plastic containers, do so. A hydrocarbon that may be a carcinogen is sometimes present as an impurity in the wax used to coat some milk cartons, and wax particles from containers do find their way into milk and milk products.[6]

The natural toxins (mycotoxins or aflatoxins) found in mold growing on grains or seeds can contaminate milk. They can be passed through to the milk if cows eat contaminated feed, and they are suspected carcinogens in test animals. But potentially unhealthy feeds can be subjected to an ammoniating process to destroy aflatoxins without altering the nutritional value of the feed.

MILK PROCESSING

The old horse-drawn milk wagons carried milk, butter, and eggs. The milk was just milk. Now milk is either raw, whole, skim, low-fat, homogenized, fortified, evaporated, sweetened, condensed, whole dry, nonfat dry, or filled. What are the differences?

Raw milk comes straight from the cow without being pasteurized or homogenized. Some people adhere to the idea that raw milk is more healthful than pasteurized milk because the heat of pasteurization kills the lactic-acid-producing bacteria. But pasteurization also retards the development of decay-producing bacteria which can make milk unsafe to drink.

All raw milk sold must be certified to specific limits for bacterial count and freshness. Before the advent of pasteurization, illness and death from milk drinking were not uncommon, since raw milk was a carrier of many disease-producing microorganisms. There were milk-produced diarrhea epidemics, as well as milk-derived scarlet fever, tuberculosis, gastroenteritis, septic sore throat, and other diseases.

Milk is graded on the basis of its bacterial count, grade A milk having the lowest standard bacterial count. Pasteurization does cause a loss of 10 percent of the vitamin B_1 and 25 percent of the vitamin C, but it does not alter the other nutrients milk contains. Far more destructive to the nutritional value of milk is the heat of ordinary cooking. When you boil milk you reduce its nutritional value by 10 to 15 percent. The deposit of milk on the saucepan, and the skin that forms on the top, contain valuable protein, fat, and calcium salts. Their waste is a loss of important nutrients, which is why it's best to heat milk to just below the boiling point.

In Europe milk is usually pasteurized but not homogenized, so you can find a layer of sweet rich cream on top of the milk as you pour it from the container. In America milk has an even color and consistency; you'll find no layer of cream to pour off into your coffee. Milk is homogenized not for hygienic purposes, but simply to sell milk. In the 1930s, people in the milk industry, believing that milk might be more attractive if its cream did not separate from the rest of the milk, developed a process to make milk whiter, more opaque and viscous. In homogenization, pasteurized milk is forced under pressure through a sievelike machine which breaks down its fat globules into tiny droplets one tenth their original size. These particles are then distributed evenly enough throughout the liquid to remain suspended.

Skim milk and **nonfat milk** have become popular in recent years. These milks contain only half the calories of whole milk, since most of the fat content of the milk is removed in processing. Removing milk fat also removes much of the fat-soluble vitamins A, D, E, and K, but these vitamins are usually added back to the skim milk after processing to fortify it. Removing the fat of the milk doesn't disturb any of the proteins or water-soluble B vitamins and minerals.

Cream is milk which is extra rich in emulsified milk-fat droplets. The heavier the cream, the higher the proportion of fat droplets to the milk. Half-and-half has a fat content of 10 percent, coffee cream a content of 30 percent, and heavy whipping cream 35 percent.

Evaporated milk has 60 percent of its water content removed through a heat-vacuum evaporation process. The concentrated portion is then homogenized and sterilized, and emulsifiers and stabilizers are usually added. Vitamin D is added and the milk is sealed in a tin. A reaction during processing gives evaporated milk a slightly beige color. Sealed cans of evaporated milk can keep a long time, but the milk should be refrigerated immediately after opening. You can reconstitute evaporated milk by adding equal parts of water to the concentrate.

Sweetened condensed milk is also canned, but only 50 percent of its water is removed and it is *not* sterilized. Instead, sufficient sugar—about 44 percent—is added to preserve it.

Dried milk can be stored unrefrigerated for months, shipped long distances, and used to supplement the protein content of many foods, especially baked goods.

There are two processes for drying milk, one of which—spray drying—leaves the food values intact. The other, drum drying, can destroy some proteins and vitamins. The labels on the dried milk you buy don't tell you which process was used, nor are they required to. (Writing the manufacturer of dried milk is the way to find out.) In spray drying the butterfat of the milk is removed, and the nonfat portion of the milk is pasteurized and some of its water content removed by evaporation. The remaining liquid is blown as a fine spray into a preheated vacuum chamber and turned into a powder with a moisture content of 2 to 3 percent. Spray drying has no effect on the important amino acid lysine.

Drum drying requires excessively high heat. In this process a thin film of milk is poured over the surface of a very hot revolving drum and scraped off the drum as it dries. Certain conditions in drum drying may scorch the milk and destroy its proteins. Obviously, this process isn't very desirable. Manufacturers use it because bakers find that milk dried under high heat improves the "loaf volume" when it is added to bread.

Nonfat dry milk is a convenient food for complementing incomplete protein foods. Just 2 tablespoons of nonfat dried milk added to 1 cup of wheat or rye flour will increase its protein quality by 45 percent. But dried milk is an unbalanced food compared with whole fresh milk and it should be used only occasionally to replace whole milk. It is sometimes used in infant formulas, but many doctors advise against this. Dried milk has a much higher sugar content than fluid milk, a potential danger to the infant's teeth formation, and it is relatively low in essential fatty acids and high in synthetic vitamin D.

Even though dried milk can have a long shelf life, it should always be stored in an airtight container, kept cool, and used before it becomes stale. Once a box of dried milk is opened, even a small amount of moisture can cause the powder's bacteria count to double or triple. Nor is dried milk immune to salmonella contamination, although cases are relatively rare.[7]

The cholesterol scare has created an overnight industry of chemical milks, cheeses and eggs claiming low cholesterol. **Filled and imitation milks** have had their butterfat removed and replaced with vegetable fats, to give the milk a whole-milk consistency. Filled milk is a combination of skim milk and vegetable fat—or of nonfat milk solids, water, and vegetable fats—that sells for slightly less than whole milk. Filled milk is sometimes promoted as a low-cholesterol food, but the vegetable oil used to "fill" it is usually coconut oil, which is high in saturated fatty acids. Filled milk, higher in saturated fat than whole milk with butterfat, is not recommended to anyone cutting down on saturated fats. And the coconut oil in filled milk can cause diarrhea and low growth rates in infants given it in formulas.[8]

Imitation milk is usually a combination of water, corn syrup, hydrogenated coconut oil, sodium caseinate (a protein derived from soybean or milk), potassium phosphate, stabilizer, emulsifier, synthetic vitamins and minerals, and artificial flavoring and coloring. Imitation milk is popular because it's two thirds the price of regular milk, it meets the specifications of the Jewish dietary laws, contains no saturated facts, and has a longer shelf life. Nutritionally, it's no bargain. Whereas cow's milk and filled milk contain about 3.7 percent protein, most imitation milks have only .9 percent, and they are low in essential amino acids and minerals. Recent research shows that filled and imitation milks do not replace milk effectively in terms of nutrition and are unsuitable for infants, children, pregnant and lactating women, and people subsisting on marginal diets.

Since the time of Hippocrates, physicians have recommended **goat's milk** for infants and invalids because it is so easily digested. It's also frequently prescribed for people with stomach ulcers or for those who are allergic to cow's milk. It is easy to digest because of its very small fat globules, which compare in size to those in homogenized cow's milk. It has slightly less protein and slightly more fat than cow's milk, and a little more calcium and vitamin A. Although goat's milk provides less than 3 percent of the world milk supply, more people may well consume goat's than cow's milk since 70 percent of the world's goats are found in the densely populated countries of Asia and Africa.

Milk is an outstanding source of protein, calcium, and riboflavin. Three fourths of the calcium, nearly half the riboflavin, and one fourth of the protein in this country's food supply come from milk. If milk or dairy products are omitted or used sparingly in the diet, it is difficult to meet calcium and riboflavin requirements.

The protein in milk, casein, is of the highest quality and is particularly suitable for building muscle tissue and supporting growth. The minerals found in milk—especially calcium and phosphorus—are essential for the structure of bones and teeth. Although milk contains only small amounts of iron, it is available in a form readily used by the body. Milk and other dairy products are dependable sources of vitamin A, thiamine, niacin, and riboflavin, and milk provides small amounts of B_{12}. Those on a vegan diet should substitute soy products for milk and dairy products. Those who wish to include milk and dairy products in their diet should consume the equivalent of three eight-ounce glasses of milk per day.

BUTTER

Manufactured for at least five thousand years, butter has been used as a food only in the last few hundred years. The ancient Greeks and Romans employed butter as a remedy for skin injuries, and as late as three hundred years ago butter was available only as a medicine in Spain. It was probably the Scandinavians who first used butter in their diet and introduced it as food to the rest of Europe. Today, between a quarter and a third of the world's milk production is used to make butter. Its composition is usually 16 percent water, 80.6 percent fat, .6 percent protein, .4 percent lactose, 2.4 percent ash, 20 mg. of calcium per 100 grams of butter, and 2 percent added salt. Butter is a concentrate of milkfat obtained by "churning" the milk or cream to separate the fat from the water; it takes nearly nine quarts of whole milk to make one pound of butter. Churning breaks down the emulsion of the fat and causes the fat to stick together. You may have accidentally made your own butter while beating heavy whipping cream past the point of fluffiness. The watery part of the cream will start to separate, leaving you with fresh butter.

On the farm, butter was always made from sweet cream, but today factory-made butter can be derived from stale cream. Calcium carbonate, sodium bicarbonate (or calcium, sodium, or magnesium hydroxide) can then be added to neutralize its acid taste. Manufacturers also use bleachers and antioxidants to prolong shelf life. Butter made from sweet cream is labeled as such, so always check the label.

When farmers made their own butter, its color reflected the concentration of carotene (a yellow, fat-soluble pigment used by the body to produce vitamin A) present in the cream from which it was made. The color of the cream would vary with seasonal changes in the carotene content of cow feeds. The cream was deep yellow in summer when the cows ate green forage; paler in winter months when the cows ate dry feeds. To deepen the color of winter butter, early commercial buttermakers added carrot juice to their butter. Today the carrot juice has been replaced by cheap coal-tar dyes, some of which, the American Medical Association suspects, may be carcinogenic. Natural vegetable dyes, such as carotene and annatto, would probably be safer, but they are more expensive than synthetic dyes.

Salt is added to butter to retard the growth of yeast and molds and lengthen its shelf life, so it's hard to know just how long that package of salted butter has been in the dairy cooler. Even if it is slightly rancid—you can't always tell by the taste —fat-soluble vitamins in your digestive tract may be destroyed. You're much better off buying unsalted butter. Its shorter shelf life means that it is usually handled more carefully and sold more promptly. And it has fewer additives. You can always salt your own butter at the table, and you will know exactly how much salt you are getting. Try to purchase well-wrapped butter in small quantities rather than bargain special tubs that may go rancid before you can use them up.

FERMENTED OR CULTURED MILK PRODUCTS

These products result from the action of bacteria cultures that ferment milk sugar, producing lactic acid. Acidified milks are produced by the addition of acid to the fresh milk. Regardless of the type of cultured milk product, the same basic steps are used: a starter culture is prepared; the milk, skim milk, or cream is pasteurized and homogenized; the bacteria culture is added to the mixture, which then incubates while the process of fermentation takes place. After the mixture incubates, it is cooled to stop the fermentation activity.

For thousands of years, Mongolians, Armenians, Persians, and Arabs have been fermenting milk into **yogurt**, calling it *mast* in Iran and the Middle East, *koumiss* and *kefir* in Russia, *laban* in Arabia and *matzoon* in Armenia. As the French pride themselves on their wine, the Bulgarians pride themselves on their yogurt, saying that only the mountains of their country produce the bacteria, *bacillus bulgaricus,* that can curdle milk the right way for good yogurt. They insist too that the yogurt be made from a mixture of goat's milk and water buffalo milk, which is twice as rich in butterfat as cow's milk. Bulgarians devotedly eat on the average of several pounds of yogurt a day.

Yogurt's popularity in this country started with the advent of the health-food store, which sold yogurt as a food having fewer calories than pasteurized whole milk, but the same amount of vitamins and minerals. Yogurt was eaten plain, with no syrupy fruit preserves to neutralize its bold, sharp flavor. Today, with processors making yogurt Swiss style, lowcal, with every sweetened fruit from boysenberries to bing cherries, we eat over 110 million cups of it a year. More than 90 percent of American yogurt eaters live on our East and West coasts. Yogurt is replacing the hot dog as a quick lunch food, and it's the steadfast friend of the diet-conscious. Even so, Europeans still consume ten times as much as we do (per capita).

Today yogurt is made from homogenized, low-fat, or skim milk, with nonfat dry milk added to increase its body firmness. Dry milk is not added to yogurt made in European countries, which is why European yogurt has a more liquid consistency. Either way, yogurt is a highly nutritious food with a nutrient composition similar to that of whole and low-fat milk. It can be eaten plain, mixed with either fruits or vegetables, used as a low-calorie substitute for rich sour cream dressings, or served as a protein-rich dessert. Yogurt has long been associated with longevity, and a standard nutrition textbook, *Newer Knowledge of Nutrition* by McCollum and Simonds, states, "Wherever yogurt is used in liberal amounts as human food the people are of exceptional physical perfection." [9] Khem M. Shahani, of the Department of Food Science and Technology, University of Nebraska, reports on recent research into the nutritional value of yogurt: "Last year we isolated a natural antibiotic produced by *Lactobacillus bulgaricus,* one of the two organisms used in the manufacture of yogurt. The thought here is that through yogurt the consumer may ingest the natural antibiotic type constituents which may provide him with a sort of natural resistance against infections. However, here again more research work needs to be done." Shahani and his group also observed that yogurt synthesizes several B vitamins in its fermentation process, and they noted that in one study with cancer and mice, yogurt seemed to partially inhibit the growth of certain tumor cells. [10]

Nutrient percentages of yogurt may vary from brand to brand, depending on processing and additives, but the differences are not great unless high quantities of sugar (as in preserves) are added to the product. Yogurt is even more digestible than whole milk, and individuals with a mild lactose intolerance can more easily digest yogurt. Persons with a lactose intolerance lack the enzyme necessary to digect lactose, or milk sugar, but in yogurt the lactose has been fermented to lactic acid, which is easily digested. Yogurt is often prescribed by physicians for patients taking antibiotics. These drugs destroy all intestinal bacteria, even the healthful kind; yogurt helps to restore the healthful bacteria necessary for proper digestion. Women who tend to get vaginal yeast infections when they take antibiotics often find that eating a pint or so of yogurt each day with the antibiotics maintains the acid balance in the vagina, preventing yeast infections.

Yogurt is promoted as a diet food, but it may not be saving you as many calories as you think, especially if you eat it with fruit preserves. American yogurt is made from homogenized, pasteurized cow's milk which has had half its butterfat content removed. Because the butterfat is reduced by half, many people think that yogurt has half the calories of whole milk. Well, it may have half the *fat* of whole milk, but its proteins and carbohydrates contain calories too. An amount of *plain* yogurt equivalent to one glass of whole milk (170 calories) contains 125 calories. Yogurt with sweet preserves may contain many more calories than a glass of milk.

Buttermilk is actually the thin, watery fluid—sometimes called whey—left over from the churning of cream into butter. It is consumed as a beverage, but more often dried for use by the baking industry. The buttermilk we drink today—*cultured buttermilk*—is made from skim or low-fat milk by fermentation with bacteria. Buttermilk has only 43 calories per glass and its proteins, like those of yogurt, are easily digested.

Scientists have debated the virtues of **acidophilus milk** since 1907, when Dr. Elie Metchnikoff published a treatise associating the consumption of some fermented-milk products with longevity. He observed that large numbers of centenarians living in southeastern Europe drank milk fermented with *Lactobacilli* bacteria, or acidophilus milk. Today more acidophilus milk is sold in the United States than anywhere else, usually for therapeutic reasons rather than for its taste.

Acidophilus milk is prepared basically the same way as

yogurt, except that it is fermented with different bacteria cultures and heated to higher temperatures. Its flavor is less "buttery" than yogurt, and more astringent. Though refrigerated acidophilus milk can keep for up to six months, it should be consumed as soon as possible to get the greatest benefit from the high *Lactobacilli* bacteria count.

Sour cream is made by adding acid or a culture of acid-producing bacteria to fresh cream. Cultured sour cream contains 18 percent milk fat and is comparable in calories to mayonnaise and salad oils. Sometimes stabilizers (vegetable gums and gelatin, mono- and diglycerides, sodium phosphates) are added to give it a smooth consistency.

CHEESE

Novelist Amanda Covey described cheese as "milk's leap to immortality," for cheese can last hundreds of times longer than the fresh milk it is made from. Unprocessed cheese comes in hundreds of varieties created by differences in the grasses and herbs the cows feed upon; and in climate, season, and aging. Even two cheeses made by the same person in the same place, using the same process, can be vastly different from one another.

The history of cheese dates to the first domestication of animals, which was about 9000 B.C. Stories explaining how it was discovered vary from country to country, but they usually involve a traveler setting out on a journey carrying some milk in a leather pouch. He finds, when he drinks the milk some hours later, that it is now a watery clear liquid (whey) and curds. The traveler tastes the curds and whey and finds it delicious. He shares the good news with his friends, who start curdling their own milk in leather pouches made from a young cow's stomach.

All cheeses are classified according to whether or not they are ripened, and how they are ripened. *Unripened* cheeses are ready to eat as soon as they are made. They are made with very little rennet and have a slightly acid flavor because the lactic acids have not been entirely fermented out of them. Cottage cheese, ricotta, pot cheese, cream cheese, mozzarella, and Neufchâtel are characterized by a high moisture content (from 55 to 80 percent), which makes them highly perishable. But there are some unripened cheeses which are low in moisture content and may be stored for some time. Gjetost and mysost are firm unripened cheeses made from whey.

Ripened cheeses must be aged for various lengths of time before they are ready to eat. They vary in consistency from soft to very hard, depending on their moisture content. Soft ripened cheeses with a moisture content of about 50 percent include Brie, Camembert, and Limburger. Semisoft ripened cheeses have a moisture content ranging from 40 to 45 percent; for example, Muenster, Bel Paese, Roquefort, and Stilton. Firm ripened cheeses, like Cheddar, Edam, Gouda, Gruyère, and Swiss have even less moisture, 35 to 40 percent. The hardest cheeses of all—which are grated before they are eaten—are Parmesan and Romano, with a moisture content of 30 to 35 percent.

Cheese today is made by coagulating milk. Rennin, an enzyme found in the fourth stomach of calves, is most often used, but some processes depend on a bacteria starter that develops acid by fermenting the lactose. The rennet, or acid, makes the milk separate into our traveler's curds and whey. The curds are then cut and pressed to drain off the whey. At that point the curds can be eaten, as in cottage or pot cheese, or else ripened in a variety of ways, depending on the type of cheese to be produced.

Unripened (green) cheese is tough, rubbery, and bland in taste. During ripening, enzymes break down some of the components of the cheese, making it softer and more flavorful. As the cheese ripens, the physical and chemical conditions inside it are always changing, depending on the growth of the microorganisms and the activity of the enzymes inside it. Many factors are used to control the rate of ripening, and

federal regulations require that cheese made from unpas-
teurized milk be ripened for not less than sixty days at a
temperature no lower than 35 degrees F. in order to kill
disease-producing bacteria.

While the price of Cheddar and Swiss has gone up 72
percent since 1967, **cottage cheese** is still a great bargain. It
has long been a staple for dieters, because it is high in protein and low in calories. Its delicate flavor gives it great
versatility. If you are a moderately active woman, only 14
ounces of cottage cheese will supply you with all the protein
you need, two thirds of the riboflavin and phosphorus, and
one third of the calcium—while providing only one fifth of
your daily requirement of calories. Cottage cheese is also
more digestible than hard cheese because the stomach can
easily manage its soft curd.

Although cottage cheese is made with skim milk, it is usually "creamed" to create its characteristic velvety body. In
creaming, cream with 18 percent fat is added to the skim milk
curd, resulting in a fat concentration of 4 percent. Cottage
cheese is generally 74 percent moisture, 15.8 percent protein, 4 percent fat, and 4.2 percent carbohydrate. It contains
464 calories per pound. Considering that whole milk has only
3.2 percent protein, you might regard cottage cheese as a
protein-enriched milk. You would have to drink 500 grams of
milk to get the protein contained in 100 grams of cottage
cheese. At 66 calories per 100 grams of whole milk you
would be consuming 330 calories to get this protein. When
cottage cheese is eaten with grains, nuts, seeds, and other
plant foods in about equal proportions, all the incomplete
proteins become complete, creating high nutritional value.

Cheddar cheese was first made in the sixteenth century, in
the village of Cheddar, England. Since that time it has become so popular in this country that 70 percent of the cheese
we produce is Cheddar of one variety or another. Cheddar is
a hard, white-to-yellow cheese usually made from pasteurized
cow's milk. It has a composition of 35.1 percent water, 33.1

percent fat, 25.8 percent protein, and 826 milligrams calcium (per 100 grams). Most Cheddars are aged from six months to two years and will keep for months if they are wrapped and stored properly.

Those holes in the **Swiss cheese** you buy are formed by bacteria as the cheese is ripening. Swiss cheese is one of the most difficult cheeses to make. Only the perfect combination of milk, three species of active bacteria, and well-controlled ripening conditions can produce true Swiss. Swiss cheese has a composition of 34.9 percent water, 30.5 percent fat, 27.4 percent protein, and 1180 milligrams calcium per 100 grams.

Hard Italian cheeses like **Parmesan** and **Romano** have the highest protein and calcium concentration. Parmesan is 30.0 percent water, 36.0 percent protein, 26.0 percent fat, and has 1140 milligrams calcium per 100 grams. Parmesan is made from low-fat milk and is usually ripened for two years. Lipase enzymes often promote the development of the sharp *piccante* flavors in Italian cheeses by releasing butyric and caproic fatty acids. The popularity of pizza has increased our consumption of Italian cheeses—we now eat seven times more of them than we did in 1957.[11]

Brie and **Camembert** are surface-ripened by the slow action of molds, bacteria, and yeasts. They are characterized by a feltlike rind outside and a creamy, buttery consistency inside. They often taste like fresh mushrooms or rich earth, and are among the most expensive of cheeses. Next to cottage cheese, they have the highest water content. Camembert has a composition of 51.3 percent water, 22.8 percent fat, 18.7 percent protein, and 382 milligrams calcium per 100 grams.

Roquefort, blue, and other "blue-veined" cheeses are ripened by the blue-green mold *Penicillium roqueforti*. The spores are put into the curd just before it is pressed, and the cheese is exposed to the air, allowing the mold to breathe. Roquefort cheese is made from ewe's milk only in the Roquefort region of France. Blue cheeses, which are much less expensive, are made in the United States, Canada, and Denmark from cow's milk. The composition of these cheeses is generally 40 percent water, 30.5 percent fat, 21.5 percent protein, and 315 milligrams calcium per 100 grams.[12]

Processed cheeses are made by grinding, heating, and mixing hard types of cheese, then emulsifying them with inorganic salts into a homogeneous mass that will no longer age. Different consistencies and ages of cheese are blended together into a uniform product that has greater keeping and melting qualities than any of the individual cheeses. The idea of processed cheese is not bad in itself. Cheeses that would otherwise have to be discarded because of minor imperfections—too high or low a fat content for the type of cheese, too high or low a moisture content, imperfect rind, and gas holes—can be blended together to compensate for one another's slight deficiencies. The problem is that processing can be used to disguise the flavors and textures of defective cheeses, or of those aged improperly or not at all. Processing also involves the use of emulsifiers, preservatives, artificial colors and flavors, stabilizers and other chemicals, and high heat, all of which affect the nutritional values. Even though processed cheeses are ultimately more expensive for the consumer, they continue to dominate the market in this country. Almost half of the cheese marketed in 1964 was processed.[13] Cheddar is the cheese most often used in processing, but Colby, Swiss, Gruyère, brick, and Limburger are also commonly used.

Processing presents the cheese manufacturer with an opportunity to sell cheese "products" that contain progressively smaller quantities of real cheese. *Consumer Reports* calls these products "cheesoids" and warns consumers to be wary of the labels by which many of them are sold. Do you know the difference between cheese, processed cheese, processed cheese spread, processed cheese food, and imitation cheese? The differences, measured in water, butterfat, protein, and real cheese, are great.

Real cheddar cheese has a composition of 35.1 percent water, 33.1 percent butterfat, and 25.8 percent protein; some process cheese products have no legal limits set for butterfat and water content, and contain up to 58.4 percent moisture and as little as 9.4 percent butterfat. Some of them are even more expensive than real cheese. The F.D.A. standards of identity for processed American cheese are a maximum of 43 percent moisture and a minimum of 27 percent butterfat, as compared with F.D.A. standards for unprocessed American cheese, a maximum of 39 percent water and minimum of 31 percent butterfat. F.D.A. requirements for processed cheese foods (which need contain no more than 51 percent cheese), are 44 percent maximum moisture, 23 percent minimum butterfat; and for processed cheese spreads, 60 percent maximum moisture, 20 percent minimum butterfat.

The packaging and labeling of various cheese products makes them hard to differentiate. Processed cheese spreads, cheese foods, and imitation cheese spread all come in crocks, jars, and tins, and are sometimes wrapped in individual slices and packages. Typically the label features the brand name and the word "cheese" in large print; the description according to process category in fine print.

Consumer Reports conducted a survey of five different processed cheese foods and found that though their cheese content varied considerably, their prices did not. American cheese (unprocessed) was priced at 6.9 cents per ounce, processed cheese 6.8 cents, cheese food 6.4 cents, cheese spread 6.1 cents and imitation cheese spread 6.5 cents. The biggest difference was observed with the imitation cheese—promoted as a "diet" product—which sold for 7.4 cents per ounce.

Cold-pack cheeses, sold in crocks and often having the word *club* in their names, are also processed cheeses, but their processing, unlike that of other cheese blends, does not involve heating. Cold-pack cheeses are a blend of two or more natural cheeses, usually Cheddars or blues. They contain a number of additives, have a longer shelf life than pure natural cheeses, and are usually soft and easily spreadable.

We expect processed cheeses to contain added chemicals,

but we assume that the wedge of unprocessed cheese we buy from the big wheel will be completely "natural." It may be; then again, it may not. F.D.A. regulations exempt only the dairy industry from stating on the labels of its products that artificial coloring has been added. Blue or green coloring is added to certain white cheeses to offset the natural yellow color of the fermented milk, and some cheese rinds are coated with a bright red wax that can penetrate the cheese. Cheddar, Swiss, and related cheeses may have their colors altered by bleaching; hydrogen peroxide, which destroys vitamins C and A, is often used. Some other natural hard cheeses are bleached with potassium alum, calcium sulfate, and magnesium carbonate; this information *is* stated on the labels of the large wheels of cheese —which are sometimes cut up before you ever see them.[14]

Because they contain animal fat, cheeses can be contaminated with pesticide residues. Pesticide residues in cheese are a problem abroad as well as in the United States: in 1969, 2 million pounds of imported cheeses were confiscated because of contamination from pesticide residues.[15]

Over the years, more and more additives have been put into cottage cheese. The F.D.A. permits stabilizers for smooth texture, flavor, thickness, and uniform color, and mold inhibitors to give it a longer shelf life. Both additives can disguise cottage cheese that is older than it should be when you bring it home from the store. If you can't find a source for good, fresh cottage cheese, it's not difficult to make your own. A government publication offers directions for making this cheese at home: Home Garden Bulletin No. 129, U.S.D.A., "Making Cottage Cheese at Home" (Superintendent of Documents, U.S. Printing Office, Washington, D.C. 20402, approximately 5 cents).

Many cheeses contain artificial coloring; Gruyère, Neufchâtel, Roquefort, and Limburger do not. When you buy processed cheese, always examine the label to see exactly what you are getting. When selecting unpackaged cheeses, keep in mind that the ones that don't look good probably aren't.

Avoid those that are sweating, cracking, or uneven in color and texture; they may have been mishandled.

Cheese should be stored at temperatures from 35 to 38 degrees. Moist cheeses are more difficult to keep and have shorter lives than firm and medium-firm cheeses. Plastic wrap preserves them better than aluminum foil or waxed paper. Always wrap cheeses separately and avoid placing strong ones next to mild ones—for obvious reasons.

ICE CREAM

Like milk and cheese, ice cream is a complete protein food and a good source of calcium, phosphorus, and vitamins A and B_2. A half pint of ice cream contains from 3.5 to 4.5 grams—or about 10 percent of the recommended daily allowance—of protein, as well as 250 calories. Ice cream contains 10 percent fat, whereas ice milk, its low-calorie counterpart, contains between 2 and 7 percent fat and only 140 calories per half pint.

Taster's manuals for judging ice cream describe the ideal product as smooth, easy to dip, melting to a creamy, homogeneous liquid, free of ice crystals, with just the right amount of air whipped into it, pleasantly sweet, and with no off-flavors. How often do you eat ice cream like this? Like the hot dog, most of today's ice cream is a reservoir of additives—at least 1200 different chemical stabilizers, emulsifiers, bactericides, neutralizers, and artificial flavors and colors are legally permitted. And since federal standards apply only to ice cream made in one state and sold in another, most ice cream is exempt from them; most brands, even the important ones, are manufactured and sold locally. Ice cream labels, according to F.D.A. standards, need say only what the product is—ice cream, ice milk, or sherbet—what the flavor is, and whether or not it is natural. Nothing more. Think of this next time you have a bowl of propylene glycol-flavored chocolate ice cream.

Ice cream manufacturers are not required to declare the presence of artificial colorings. Many of these are coal-tar dyes, some of which are suspected carcinogens.

Another practice used by a few ice cream manufacturers is "reworking," a euphemism for the recycling of old ice cream. Chocolate ice cream is made from a lighter-flavored batch that didn't turn out right or was beginning to spoil. Chocolate ice cream can even be made from other flavors of ice cream returned from retail stores as unacceptable. And manufacturers are not required to identify reworked ice cream. While this practice does not necessarily make reworked ice cream unhealthful, it is unfair to the consumer.

Perhaps the most alarming fact about ice cream regulations is that no federal regulations limit the amount of harmful bacteria in ice cream and similar frozen desserts. The individual states are left to set their own limits. Contrary to what many people suppose, freezing does not kill all bacteria, notably fecal streptococci bacteria from fecal contamination. These bacteria, found in hot dogs and other foods, can be destroyed by cooking, but since when do you cook ice cream? *Consumer Reports* conducted a three-state survey of thirty-four brands of ice cream and tested the samples for bacteria counts, using the limits they had used for their survey of hot dogs. They found that a number of ice cream samples contained fecal streptococci counts well above their limits for hot dogs.[16]

When you buy ice cream there are a few things you can do to get the best product for your money. When buying by the half gallon, check the weight on a scale in the produce department; it should weigh at least two and a half pounds. Make ice cream your very last purchase at the market, and always pick a container that is brick-hard. (You might have to dig under other cartons to find one frozen hard enough.) Ask to have the ice cream wrapped in an insulated bag or in several regular bags, and keep it out of the sun on your way home. Keep it in the coldest part of your freezer, wrapped in a plastic bag to minimize evaporation. And eat it within two weeks.

All-natural ice cream is becoming very popular. At least you're getting your money's worth. Sugar (sucrose) is, however, considered a natural product, so be aware that you are getting plenty of sugar, even in all-natural ice cream.

FACTS TO PONDER

— Milk proteins are good supplements for plant protein—especially corn, potatoes, white bread, and navy beans—and actually increase this plant protein when both are consumed at the same meals, because the amino acid lysine in milk complements plant amino acids.
— Milk is an important source of riboflavin. Keep milk out of light, for light destroys riboflavin.
— One pint of milk contains about 7.2 grams of unsaturated fatty acids and 10.5 grams of saturated fat, which aid in the absorption of calcium (of which milk is the best source).
— You never outgrow your need for milk, yet few Americans over twenty-five drink enough milk to maintain their level of dietary calcium.
— The bone weaknesses of old people, especially women, are due to calcium deficiencies. Inadequate calcium intake over long periods of time is a major contributing factor to these problems and is associated with the large incidence of bone fractures among older people.
— Scientific dairy-farming practices have increased the milk production of the cow from less than 1000 pounds per year to more than 2000 pounds.
— Pasteurization and cooking do not destroy antibiotic residues in milk.
— Pesticides can accumulate in the fat of cattle which eat contaminated grass or hay, and the residues could be excreted in their milk. Since pesticides are fat-soluble, a high percentage of their residues may be stored in fat foods such as butter, cream, and rich cheeses.

— Evaporated milk loses half its vitamin B_6 content in processing. Babies fed on an evaporated milk formula can develop convulsive seizures as a result.

— Unsalted butter has fewer additives than salted butter.

— Penicillin residues have caused so much trouble in fermented milk products by inhibiting the starter cultures that some factories have been forced to discontinue their cheese and yogurt production.

— Low-priced ice cream may contain as much air as it does ice cream.

— Strawberry ice cream may be flavored with alcohol, propylene glycol, glacial acetic acid, aldehyde C16, benzyl acetate, methyl cinnamate, methyl anthranilate, methyl heptine carbonate, methyl salicylate, iodine beta, aldehyde C14, biacetyl, anethole—and no strawberries.

— Diethylene glucol, a cheap chemical that is substituted for eggs as an emulsifier in ice cream, is identically the same chemical used in antifreeze and paint remover. Butyraldehyde, often used to give ice cream a nutty flavor, is a common ingredient of rubber cement.

— When milk is stored at 40 degrees F., the temperature usually recommended, its bacteria count doubles every thirty hours.

— More than 25 percent of the U.S. population drinks no fluid milk.

— Cottage cheese is the most perishable of all cheeses. Generally the higher the moisture content of a cheese and the less its acidity, the shorter its shelf life.

CHAPTER

6

THE CHICKEN
AND THE EGG

THE CHINESE FIRST DOMESTICATED CHICKENS AS EARLY AS 1400 B.C.; today the chicken is a familiar barnyard and road-side bird the world over—especially in America, where 6 percent of the world's population produces one third of the chickens and turkeys, and eats more than 12 billion pounds of poultry each year. Chicken has become an American fixture: the 3000 Kentucky Fried Chicken outlets serve enough chickens each year to lay end to end around the world at the equator seventy-four and a half times. The chicken has scratched its way into our language. Hotrodders play chicken with other cars, organizations have pecking orders, witches cackle, and wives henpeck their husbands. Foolish people are clucks, cowards are chickens, gossipy old ladies are biddies, young girls are chicks, women's gatherings are hen parties, and poor handwriting is chickenscratch.

The chicken is at home anywhere: in the shiny copper pots and rich sauces of exclusive French restaurants, in the paper buckets of take-out fried chicken stands, in elaborate aspics and humble soups. In big cities you can eat it curried, sweet-and-soured, barbecued, sautéed, steamed, stuffed, patéed, or poached, à la paprikash, parmigiana, or paella, Szechuan, or tandoori. Perhaps because of its versatility, its moderate price compared to beef, and its value as a complete protein food, we eat more chicken than ever before; our annual per capita consumption of it increased from 18.7 pounds in 1947–49 to 36.8 pounds in 1968, a 97 percent increase. During this same period, our consumption of beef, veal, lamb, and pork increased only 24 percent.

As a complete protein food, poultry (including chicken, turkeys, ducks, geese, and guineas) is comparable to beef, lamb and pork in composition and nutrient value. Chicken is about 20 percent protein. It's also a good source of B vitamins, iron, phosphorus, and fat. Fat content varies with the age of the bird, from under 5 percent in young chicks to nearly 25 percent in mature birds.[1] Dark meat has more fat than white meat.

Your butcher or grocery store meat department sells chickens of various sizes and labels and prices. Those palm-sized chickens called Rock Cornish Game Hens are chickens killed at 5 to 7 weeks old. They usually weigh about a pound. Broilers or fryers are 9 to 12 weeks old, and roasters are 3 to 5 months old. Capons are castrated male birds under 8 months old, and stewing hens are over 10 months old. Younger chickens are more tender than older ones, and their skin is usually a brighter yellow. Younger chickens are best for frying, roasting, and broiling, and older birds are best suited for stews, soups, and salads.

The increased consumer demand for chicken has sparked the growth of huge breeding farms: chicken-production factories in which as many as 300,000 broilers a week are slaughtered, processed, and sent on their way. This assembly-line approach has made the modern chicken almost a species apart from its ancestor that roamed free on a farm, scratched and rooted in the soil for worms and grubs, and mated with the roosters. Today's chickens suffer the henhouse blues in artificially lighted rooms designed to keep them eating and egg-laying around the clock. They are artificially inseminated, and their processed feed contains drugs, hormones, and "growth factors."

Chickens and eggs are Big Business in America. As late as 1964 there were 1.2 million egg farms; today there are only 200,000. Four thousand of these farms—a mere 2 percent—own more than 90 percent of the country's laying hens, according to poultry-industry analysts.[2] Let's look at a typical poultry plant, the Pennfield Corporation in Lancaster, Pennsylvania, where 9 million hens are contained within a fifty-mile radius. The company's largest chicken house is a complex of nine warehouses, each as long as two football fields, each holding 30,000 hens housed in 12 x 18-inch wire cages, three or four to a cage. Feeding, watering, and egg collecting is all done by machine. Moving troughs carry food and water past the hens; conveyor belts take the eggs away. Gerald Astor, in an article in *Esquire Magazine*, wrote that by the time a Pennfield hen lives out her life she has given the chicken factory everything but her cackle. During her half a year of growth and year of laying, the hen has produced 21 dozen eggs, 50 pounds of high-nitrogen fertilizer (eventually sold by Pennfield), 4.5 pounds of meat, and feathers (which are almost pure protein) and other offal that are ground into food fortifiers and fertilizers.[3]

In 1935 it took at least 16 weeks and five pounds of feed to produce a pound of chicken meat. Today it takes only 9 weeks and 2.5 pounds of feed. But poultry breeders, with the goal of producing a pound of chicken with less than 2 pounds of feed, are trying to mature the chickens even faster. They have, unfortunately, been able to speed up the growth process by using chemicals potentially hazardous to humans: arsenic, antibiotics, and hormones.

Since 1950 the arsenic substance arsanilic acid has been mixed into poultry feed to stimulate growth, make utilization of food more efficient, produce more eggs, and improve skin coloring and feathering. Today approximately 90 percent of all commercially raised chickens have been fed with arsanilic or arsonic acid.[4] Arsenic is a known toxin for humans, yet the F.D.A. allows residues of .5 part per million for it in chicken and turkey tissues, and twice as much in chicken by-products such as eggs and broth. Since the liver is the organ of detoxification in these animals, arsenic and other poisonous compound residues tend to concentrate in this organ, making chicken livers a potentially unhealthful food.

Antibiotics are given to chickens for the same reason they are given to cattle—to help keep them disease-free in a stressful environment where disease is a fact of life. Antibiotics help speed up weight gain, particularly in birds kept in unsanitary conditions. Little consideration is given to the consequences of antibiotic treatment: reduced resistance to disease (both for the chickens and the humans who ingest antibiotic residues), the growth of fungus and mold infections in the intestinal tracts of chickens, the growth of salmonella bacteria, and premature senility and shortened life-span of chickens. Chickens routinely fed antibiotics are also injected with them when they contract disease. Chicken carcasses may be dipped in an antibiotic solution to increase their shelf life up to twenty-one days. The F.D.A. permits up to 7 parts per million of antibiotics in uncooked poultry carcasses.[5]

In addition to arsenic and antibiotics, breeders can add other drugs to poultry feed. Tranquilizers can be used to ease tensions resulting from crowding, hot-weather conditions and transportation, and to facilitate handling chickens being vaccinated or debeaked. Aspirin can also be added to poultry feed to fatten chickens suffering from the discomfort of crowding, and hormones are used routinely to put extra fat on the birds and to tenderize their meat. Male birds, formerly castrated, are now chemically caponized with estrogenic female hormones. They're called the "caponettes." When a bird is castrated, either surgically or chemically, it assumes female characteristics, grows faster, develops greater deposits of fat, and becomes more tender.

DES is administered to poultry of both sexes to put weight on the birds quickly. Not only is DES a known carcinogen; it makes chickens develop fat instead of protein. Consumer groups have pressured the F.D.A. to ban DES in chickens; but whereas DES was banned in cattle feed, then allowed to be administered to cattle in the form of pellets injected into their ears, the opposite tactic has been used for poultry breeding. By law DES can't be injected into chickens, but it is still permitted in poultry feed.

In 1965 the U.S.D.A. tested 2000 samples of poultry from every federally inspected plant in the nation and found them all to be contaminated with pesticide residues. No one area of the country produced poultry less contaminated than another, and the residues were traced to contaminated grain and poor husbandry practices. The U.S.D.A. has yet to disclose the levels of pesticides found.

Sometimes chickens are treated with chemicals for purely deceptive reasons. Chicken flesh can be given a golden-yellow appearance when colorings are added to the feed, and chemicals can be injected into the carcass to eliminate the need for the expensive process of aging. The latest technique is to season the bird *while it is still alive*. This treatment is really a deodorizing process which disguises unsavory cooking odors caused by chemicals and by the conditions under which the bird was raised. Just prior to slaughter, chickens are injected with a solution of the enzyme hyaluronidase mixed with sage, garlic, and nutmeg. The solution, injected beneath the neck and skin of the bird, spreads quickly throughout the flesh before the bird dies.

If chickens are artificially colored and flavored, how can you tell whether or not the chicken you buy is good enough to eat? Poultry inspection is no guarantee of meat quality or the absence of chemical residues, but poultry graded A will be of better quality than other grades, and better than poultry that is inspected but not graded. Grade A poultry should be free of bruises, breaks in the skin, and other defects which would indicate that it has been frozen. Frozen poultry may have been frozen and thawed numerous times during shipment, resulting in a high bacteria count. But a fresh-looking chicken in your meat market may also have been frozen, so ask your meat market manager or butcher whether the chicken has been frozen and thawed or is truly fresh. If you do buy a frozen chicken, cook it immediately after you thaw it. When buying poultry, it can be worth the effort to track down poultry raisers who keep the flocks in clean, well-ventilated poultry houses and feed the chickens with drug-free mixtures. You might write to different poultry raisers to ask them about their breeding and feeding practices.

Eggs have been valued as a highly nutritious, delicious, reasonably priced and perfectly "packaged" food for centuries. In the last decade our egg consumption has decreased drastically, thanks to the cholesterol scare. In 1945 our per capita egg consumption was 400 eggs a year; now it is below 275 and steadily decreasing.[6] The fact that the egg is our greatest single dietary source of cholesterol—a whole fresh egg contains 275 milligrams—has created an unprecedented fear of eggs that threatens the $3 billion-a-year egg industry and deprives consumers of a superior source of complete protein. The egg's status as a public enemy is even official: last year a Federal Trade Commission trial judge ruled that it was misleading for egg industry advertising to state, "There is absolutely no scientific evidence that eating eggs increases the risk of heart disease." The ruling was based on the belief that "there exists a substantial body of competent and reliable evidence that eating eggs increases the risk of heart attack or heart disease."[7]

Does egg eating increase the risk of heart disease? More and more researchers are saying "No," or at least "It's doubtful," and they are pointing out that the cholesterol-level scare has been brought about more by commercial than by scientific interests. Research into cholesterol and heart disease is still inconclusive; yet the makers of polyunsaturated egg substitutes and other products would have you think that you can avoid heart disease simply by consuming their products. Advertisers of such products do not want you to know that the cause of hardening of the arteries is still unknown, that there is no direct scientific proof in humans that eating high-cholesterol foods raises serum (blood) cholesterol, or that high cholesterol contributes to heart disease—or that lowering the blood cholesterol reduces the chance of heart disease. Consuming large amounts of polyunsaturates in an attempt to lower cholesterol may, of itself, be dangerous. Recent studies have linked a high intake of polyunsaturates—over 10 percent of the calorie intake—with vitamin deficiencies, premature aging, liver damage, and blood diseases in infants.[8]

In 1960, after an ambitious fourteen-year study of a middle-class suburban population in Framingham, Mass., researchers isolated cigarette smoking, high blood pressure and high serum cholesterol as prominent "risk factors" in the development of heart disease. The study was well publicized and celebrated, and investigators everywhere used its data as if it represented the male population not only in the United States but in the whole Western industrialized part of the world. Then something happened that changed the cholesterol theory to dogma. On the basis of the Framingham study and others that appeared to confirm its data, the American Heart Association recommended that "the public should be encouraged to avoid egg yolk consumption, and the food industry should be persuaded to minimize the egg yolk content of commercially prepared foods."

After this A.H.A. proclamation, the processed-food industry came out with chemical simulations of butter, bacon, cream, and eggs. Naturally it used the Framingham data and the A.H.A. edict as marketing tools to sell the new products. Now many researchers think that this A.H.A. recommendation was premature, that it unjustifiably frightened the American consumer away from a source of high-quality protein, vitamins, and minerals. To determine the actual effect of eggs on human cholesterol levels, laboratories are conducting studies around the country. Though it is premature to judge their results conclusive, a case is being made to show that the body carefully regulates its level of cholesterol, regardless of what the dietary intake may be.

Dr. Roslyn Alfin-Slater, of the School of Public Health at U.C.L.A., headed an investigating team studying 52 men over a period of ten weeks, which showed no significant increase in blood cholesterol in either the young or the old subjects when they ate additional eggs. The study involved two groups: 25 men between the ages of 20 and 28, and 27 men between the ages of 39 and 66. All 52 subjects normally included eggs in their diet. The group of younger men were asked to eat two eggs a day for eight weeks, and then to abstain from them for two weeks. The group of older men ate one egg a day for the first four weeks, two eggs a day for the second four weeks, then no eggs at all for two weeks. Cholesterol levels were checked daily, and the researchers found no significant cholesterol increase in any of the patients throughout the course of the study, regardless of the egg intake. This U.C.L.A. study was the first of its kind to use people eating normal diets. Previous cholesterol studies involved subjects on rigidly controlled protein-, fat-, or cholesterol-elimination diets, and their results do not relate to the diet of the average American. Dr. Alfin-Slater, while admitting that the study is not a conclusive document of eating eggs, says, "In view of the high protein value of eggs, especially in areas of the world where protein is in short supply, we wonder if we have the right to restrict eggs. While there are some people who are hypersensitive to eggs and should not have them, there is little evidence to support any prejudice against the consumption of eggs by the general public."

Perhaps a more dramatic testimony to the body's ability to regulate its production of cholesterol is the study in which eight severely burned patients were fed *thirty-five eggs a day for at least a month* as a highly concentrated source of protein and calories. Before they were placed on the egg diet, their cholesterol levels were below normal (due to their greatly altered metabolism), but during and after the egg diet their cholesterol levels remained within normal limits and no side effects were observed.

All the evidence to incriminate or acquit cholesterol and eggs is not in yet, and not expected in the near future. But as a consumer you should bear in mind that advertising messages encouraging you to give up eggs or use egg substitutes are often based on scientific half-truths or information taken out of its scientific context, and they should not influence your dietary decisions. For example, if you were to feed your infant egg substitutes in hopes of preventing the early development of atherosclerosis, you might possibly be risking its health.

Out of concern that some pediatricians might encourage mothers to feed Egg Beaters to their infants, two researchers at the University of Illinois made a comparison study of the nutritional values of Egg Beaters with farm-fresh eggs, and published their results in *Pediatrics* in 1974. The researchers placed three groups of newborn rats on three different diets of Egg Beaters, whole eggs, and standard laboratory chow. At the end of three months the weights of the rats on chow averaged 70 grams, those on whole eggs 66.5 grams, and those on Egg Beaters 31.6 grams. The rats fed Egg Beaters and those fed farm-fresh eggs were weaned at five weeks, and all of those fed Egg Beaters died within three to four weeks afterward. Apparently, as closely as egg substitutes may attempt to match real eggs nutritionally, some nutrients essential to growth and health are missing.

Eggs are considered the most nearly perfect source of protein, because their amino acid pattern most nearly matches that needed for human growth and health. All other protein foods are measured against them: on a scale of 100, eggs rank 94. Eggs are also an important source of unsaturated fatty acids, iron, phosphorus, trace minerals, vitamins A, E, K, and the B vitamins, including B_{12}. As a source of vitamin D, eggs rank second only to fish liver oils. Only in vitamin C content do eggs come out as a loser. The fat content of an egg equals that of a tablespoon of heavy cream. Like cottage cheese, they have a high nutrient density contained within few calories (one whole large egg has 81.5 calories), and they are easy for most people to digest.

By composition eggs are 73.7 percent water. They contain 6.45 grams of protein, 5.75 grams of fat, and .45 gram of carbohydrate. The yolk is the nutritional heart. It contains three fourths of the calories, nearly all the fat, iron, vitamin A, thiamine, and calcium, and almost half the protein and ribaflavin of the whole egg. The nutrient composition of eggs is determined by the age and breed of the hens, differences among individual hens, the feeding and health of the hens, the environment they're raised in, egg storage conditions and length of storage time, and cooking methods. The size of the eggs affects nutrient composition by influencing the proportion of yolk to white, which tends to be higher in small eggs than in large ones.

The color of the egg shells—dark brown, light brown, or white—depends on the breed of hen and has nothing to do with the nutrient composition of the egg. Nor does a deep-yellow egg yolk necessarily mean that the egg is more nutritious. Granted, organically raised eggs generally contain yolks of a deeper yellow than eggs laid by hens fed hormones and drugs, but the yellow color is due to the presence of xanthophyll, which has no nutritive value.

You might suppose that fertilized eggs are more nutritious than unfertilized, but there's no scientific proof. It's possible that the developing embryo may provide slightly more nutrients than the sterile yolk, but if an embryo has developed to the point to significantly increase the nutrient content of the egg, you'd be unlikely to eat it.

Organic eggs have not been proven to be higher in nutrients than nonorganic eggs; they are simply supposed to be free of the residues found in eggs laid by chemically fed and treated chickens.

Eating eggs raw, as in a tomato juice cocktail whipped up in a blender, makes them harder to digest, not more nutritious: the protein lost in normal cooking does not significantly alter the egg's value.

The 1977 egg looks like the egg laid twenty years ago: brown or white, oval and smooth. But did you ever wonder why so many eggs are cracked and stuck to the bottom of their cartons? This high percentage of cracked or stuck eggs isn't caused by rough handling in shipment, but by overly thin and fragile shells. The shells are thin because of the conditions under which the hens are raised, and the chemicals they're fed to offset the negative effects of their environment.

If thin eggshells indicate poor egg quality, it is not true that thick shells necessarily indicate good egg quality. Now egg producers can manipulate poorly fed, calcium-deficient hens to lay eggs with thick shells by adding terephthalic acid and antibiotics to the feed and sodium bicarbonate to the drinking water. They can harden eggshells by treating their chickens with a toxic substance called "three-niter mash." It has also been reported that carbon dioxide can be pumped into the laying sheds; birds inhaling this gas will lay eggs with thicker shells. We did not, however, discover this practice in our research.

Infectious diseases are a big problem for caged birds in close quarters. Crowding causes a high mortality rate among young chicks, and a mortality rate among hens of 20 to 25 percent a year. This costs the industry some $240 million a year; and the consumer is the one who eventually pays for it. Your eggs could contain the disease bacteria or residues of antibiotics used to treat sick birds.

Since tranquilized birds tend to lay eggs with pale yolks and watery whites, farmers can put additives such as antioxidants into the feed to "improve yolk pigmentation." If the eggs you buy have blotchy, mottled, unevenly colored yolks, they may come from hens fed estrogenic hormones and disease controlling chemicals.

How fresh are the eggs you buy at your grocery store? Though they may not look it, they could be several weeks old, having been stored in the egg factory for weeks before actually being delivered to your store. Commercial eggs undergo a process which makes it impossible for you to tell whether or not the eggs are one day old or several weeks old.

To extend their shelf life, producers can coat their eggs with an oil which clogs their six to eight thousand pores and keeps the air from hastening spoilage. The oil also keeps them from absorbing the odors associated with their storage conditions. Before these eggs are oiled, they are washed with sanitizers and detergents which can easily pass through the pores and contaminate them.

How can you tell if the eggs you're getting are fresh? Though there is no way of distinguishing between fresh and weeks-old eggs—in some states, cold-storage eggs can still be legally marketed as "fresh"—certain characteristics can help you to identify old eggs. Their yolks look flat rather than firm and round, and they may be mottled, while their whites are runny rather than viscous.

Although graded eggs do not always measure up to state and federal grading standards, grading can give you an idea of the relative qualities of different eggs. Eggs are graded according to the condition of the shell and the interior proportions of yolk to white. Grade AA or Fresh Fancy eggs have small, firm, compact yolks and thick whites. Grade A eggs have fairly thick whites and firm yolks; they differ from grade AA eggs only in that their yolks are less perfectly centered and the whites are slightly thinner. Both grades are good for frying and poaching, where appearance is important. Grade B eggs are fine for cooking and baking.

Eggs are not only graded but sized. If you are buying jumbo eggs, they should weigh at least 30 ounces per dozen; extra large, 27 ounces per dozen; large, 24 ounces per dozen; medium, 21 ounces per dozen; and small, 18 ounces per dozen. Before you buy a carton of eggs, always open it and turn each of the eggs around in its depression to see if any are cracked or sticking to the carton. Never use eggs that are cracked, not even in baking recipes. You never know what else, besides yolk and white, they may contain.

FACTS TO PONDER

— Stimulated with artificial light sixteen hours a day, hens lay an average of 250 to 270 eggs a year. A team of poultry scientists at the University of Missouri is close to breeding a hen that, under twenty-four hours of artificial lighting, will produce an egg a day.
— Today's commercial hens never see a barnyard.
— Currently 90 percent of all commercial chickens are raised with a form of arsenic in their feed. Chicken livers may contain high concentrations of this compound.
— At least twenty-six diseases that infect poultry may be transmitted to humans.
— Poultry industry representatives estimate the annual loss from cancerous chickens, which must be destroyed, to be $200 million.
— Many thawed chickens are sold as "fresh."
— Each egg pore is about one hundred times larger than the salmonella organism.
— Some 80 billion eggs are produced in North America each year.
— The egg is our best source of protein.
— A technique involving ultraviolet radiation and vacuum sealing has been developed to prolong the shelf life of eggs at least two years.
— Less than 30 percent of all eggs sold commercially are graded.
— Whether eggs are hard-boiled or scrambled, the protein

loss during cooking is virtually the same, and not significant.

— A 1 percent increase in the weight of the poultry from water added during freezing may cost consumers $32 million a year.

— The stuffing in roasted poultry will absorb any harmful bacteria in the bird, which is why the stuffing must be cooked thoroughly before eating. The temperature of the stuffing should reach at least 165 degrees F. Leftover cooked poultry and stuffing should be refrigerated immediately.

CHAPTER

7

FISH

FISH HAS ALWAYS BEEN AN IMPORTANT PROTEIN SOURCE FOR humans. The short-order fish stand dates back to at least 2000 B.C., when the narrow winding streets of Mesopotamian cities were filled with stalls selling fried fish to passersby. Fish was always the poor person's protein; widely available and reasonably priced.

Today fish is more expensive and less abundant in the United States than ever before, outpricing chicken and sometimes even beef. The Department of the Interior estimates that some 15 million fish were killed by water pollution in 1968.[1] Millions of tons of crude oil spilled into our seas have sickened or killed fish and upset the chain of marine life straight down to the one-celled organism. Industrial wastes, laundry detergents, and raw sewage have dangerously contaminated lakes, and runoffs of chemical pesticides such as DDT into our waters are threatening nearly every form of aquatic life. Pesticide residues have been found in fish caught far out at sea, even in areas as remote as the Antarctic.

The dumping of raw sewage from urban areas has made the fish in many waters unsafe for eating. Waters with edible fish should not have a fecal coliform count greater than 1000 per 100 milliliters, yet counts as high as 24,000 per 100 milliliters have been recorded in the Potomac—up to 27,000 in some parts of Long Island Sound, and up to 36,000 in the James River below Richmond, Virginia.[2] Lake Erie, the garbage dump for several cities, produced 75 million pounds of fish in 1954 but today produces almost none because only the most primitive forms of aquatic life have been able to survive that environment.

In the fall of 1975, *Caveat Emptor* reported that thirty-three states had waterways contaminated with mercury.[3] It was originally thought that when inorganic mercury from industrial sources was dumped into an ocean or lake, it would harmlessly settle to the bottom, remaining inactive. Unfortunately, bacteria in water convert inorganic mercury into highly toxic and highly absorbable methyl mercury, which travels up the food chain fish by fish in increasingly higher concentrations. Unsafe residues have been found in swordfish, red snapper, tuna, striped bass, and lobster.

Mercury accumulates in humans as well as fish. The mercury you ingest from fish or lobster tomorrow will be with you for the rest of your life, and the effects of accumulation might not show up for years. Symptoms of mercury poisoning are tremors, irritability, fatigue and headaches, unnatural timidity, a metallic taste in the mouth, kidney damage, and eventual insanity. The Mad Hatter in *Alice in Wonderland* may have gone "mad" because of mercury poisoning; it was common for hatmakers to lose their sanity after a lifetime of breathing fumes from mercury-treated felt. Mercury poisoning, in its acute form, can also cause brain damage, coma, and death.

Atomic energy pollution may prove to be the most serious threat of all to the world's fish. Underwater atomic energy plants heat the waters around them to infernal temperatures and change the entire ecology of the surrounding areas, since aquatic organisms have a narrower range of temperature tolerance than do most land creatures. The destruction of tiny plankton organisms by unnaturally warm water threatens the survival of a long chain of dependent marine creatures. When Consolidated Edison opened its nuclear power station at Indian Point on the Hudson River, an estimated 2 million striped bass were killed before a mesh screen was erected to keep the spawning bass from the warm, deadly water that attracted them.[4] Some ecologists feel that in addition to the heat danger they present, atomic energy plants may contaminate our fish with radioactive waste materials.

Since World War II the catch of fisheries in the United States has declined by at least half a billion pounds. While our supply of fish dwindles, our national appetite for it is growing. More and more Americans have been turning to highly nutritious, low-calorie fish as an alternative to beef and chicken. Today the average American eats about twelve pounds of fish a year. This is still modest compared to the Danes, who average over fifty pounds per capita and the Japanese, who average over sixty-five.[5]

There are approximately 19,000 species of fish in the world, of which only 200 are commercially important. The fish we eat are generally classified by anatomical structure: some have vertebrae and fins; others have shells instead. The first group are further classified according to their fat content and whether they spend their adult lives in fresh or salt water. Examples of lean fish, with a fat content under 5 percent, are bass, halibut, flounder, perch, and sole. Examples of fat fish, whose fat content ranges from 5 to 20 percent, are albacore, herring, mackerel, salmon, shad, sardines, smelt, and tuna.[6] Shellfish have their skeletons on the outside of their bodies instead of the inside, and they are divided into two groups, *crustaceans* and *mollusks*. Crustaceans have a segmented shell that allows them freedom of movement; examples are crabs, lobsters, crayfish, prawns, and shrimp. Mollusks have a soft body contained in a hard shell that is not segmented; some examples are abalone, mussels, clams, oysters, scallops, and snails.

The nutrient composition of fish varies somewhat among

different species, but only the fat content varies greatly. All fish provide an excellent source of protein and phosphorus, and salt-water varieties are good sources of iodine. A 100-gram portion of albacore tuna will contain 66½ percent water, 25.3 grams of protein, and 7.6 grams of fat; haddock will contain 80.5 percent water, 18.3 grams of protein and .1 gram of fat. Generally shellfish contain less fat than most species of vertebrate fish. That includes lobster, which many people consider too rich to eat on a frequent basis. A 100-gram portion of lobster contains 78.9 percent water, 16.9 grams of protein, and 1.9 grams of fat. The fatty acids in fish are mostly unsaturated, so fish is an attractive food to those who believe saturated fats contribute to atherosclerosis. Vertebrate fish contain two types of muscle that comprise their edible meat. The great lateral muscle contains the white meat, which is lowest in fat, and the small dark reddish-brown muscle contains a high proportion of the fat.

Fresh vertebrate fish can be bought *whole uncleaned* (straight from the water), *drawn* (with their entrails removed), *dressed* (minus entrails, head, tail, fins, and scales), as *steaks* (big fish cut into cross sections from one half to one inch thick), and as *fillets* (slices parallel to the backbone with the bones removed). But how can you tell if the fish is fresh?

The skin of a fresh fish is shining and iridescent, and covered with a thin, transparent layer of slime. Its eyes are full and bright, the pupil is a jet-black and the cornea is transparent. The gills are bright pink. The flesh is firm and elastic. When you press your finger into it, the flesh should bounce back rather than form a pit. The flesh itself is translucent rather than dull and milky, and its odor should be more like that of seaweed than the heavy pungent odor associated with old fish.

Fish is highly perishable because of the powerful digestive enzymes which perforate the fish intestines and attack the entire carcass. Fresh fish that isn't going to be eaten right away should be frozen immediately, but not for more than a week to ten days. The muscle of fish differs from that of warm-blooded animals in terms of its ability to withstand frozen storage. Prolonged freezing makes the flesh of seafood dry, tough, stringy, and tasteless when cooked. This deterioration progresses throughout the entire storage time, which is why you should use caution when buying frozen fish—you never know how long it has been frozen. In a survey of frozen fish products sold in supermarkets, the U.S. Department of the Interior found that some of the frozen samples they analyzed were up to four years old.[7]

Those frozen fish sticks, convenient as they may be for quick lunches, may contain less fish than you think. Up to 50 percent may be bread, not fish, and even though the fish sticks are prefried, the bacteria count may be high. Always cook them thoroughly, even if the label says they need only be "reheated."

If you buy unfrozen fish that looks and smells fresh, you increase your chances of getting a fresh product, but you may be taking home a fish that has been dipped in antibiotics. Since April, 1959, the F.D.A. has permitted the use of an antibiotic dip to preserve fish during transportation and storage; these fish may contain up to 5 parts per million of antibiotic residue. Cooking will destroy much of it, but some fish dipped in antibiotics, such as oysters and clams, are often eaten raw.

That fresh fish shimmering in its bed of crushed ice may have been treated with preservatives like sodium benzoate, sodium nitrite, hydrogen peroxide, ozone or chlorine. Always ask your fish-market manager if such chemicals are being used to preserve the products sold in his market.

Tuna, salmon, and sardines are most often packaged in cans, in their own oil. You may be surprised to learn that a higher level of quality has been maintained for canned fish than for frozen fish, which means that you're probably better off with the former, and among canned fish, sardines are a better bet than tuna. Tuna are big fish, high up on the aquatic food chain, and they have been found to contain dangerous concentrations of mercury.

When you buy fresh fish, choose small fish over large, and ocean fish over fresh. The swordfish steak may look succulent, but swordfish are huge fish high on the food chain and could contain concentrations of chemical contaminants. You're better off with three or four small fish rather than a chunk off a big carcass. Choose ocean fish over inland fish, which are likely to contain higher concentrations of residues.

Fish is a naturally tender food, tough only when over-cooked. Fish may be broiled, sautéed, baked, fried, steamed and poached in milk or water. Fish with higher fat content should be cooked in very little fat, because it loses enough while cooking to baste itself. Poaching and sautéeing are appropriate methods for lean fish that tend to be dry when cooked without additional fats or oils. Regardless of how it's cooked, the fish is done as soon as its flesh can be separated into flakes. Cooking it beyond this point only shrinks and toughens it, destroying some of its protein in the process.

BUYING, STORING, AND COOKING SHELLFISH

You may have heard about Mafiosi being poisoned by plates of shrimp marinara containing shellfish toxin. Paralytic shell-fish poisoning (PSP), as the syndrome is called, is caused by the biotoxin (natural poison) saxitoxin, which is produced by tiny marine organisms known as *dinoflagellates*. Shellfish ingest these tiny organisms and concentrate the toxic sub-stance they contain within their tissues. Saxitoxin is a power-ful poison, 150,000 times more lethal than curare, the plant poison used by South American Indians on the tips of their arrows.[8] It attacks the central and peripheral nervous system from five to thirty minutes after it is ingested, causing tingling and burning of the lips, tongue, and face, which spreads through the body to the arms and legs, fingers and toes. Later the sensation changes to numbness and muscle movements become spastic. If the amount of toxin ingested exceeds .3 gram the victim may die of convulsions, paralysis, and respiratory failure. Saxitoxin is not destroyed by cooking, and there is no specific treatment or antidote for its victim. And because it is water-soluble, the water or broth that such contaminated shellfish are cooked in will contain especially high concentrations of saxitoxin.[9] In addition to saxitoxin, shellfish can concentrate other substances which are poisonous to humans. This does not mean that you must give up eating shellfish, but that you should understand how shellfish can become contaminated and how you can be assured of finding ones safe to eat.

Except for sea clams and sea mussels, the majority of shellfish live in shallow coastal estuaries which are filled with brackish water. These estuaries are contaminated by the discharge of sewage and other pollutants that concentrate in the same place because estuaries have very little current. Shellfish in these estuaries nourish themselves by pumping several gallons of water through their tiny bodies each hour—up to three hundred gallons per day. Thousands of hairlike cilia paddle water containing suspended particles of nourishing microorganisms, sand, dissolved gases, and chemicals through each shellfish's incurrent siphon. The water and its contents are then passed along through the gills to the mouth and stomach, intestines. The waste products are excreted back into the surrounding water. It is important that shellfish be harvested directly after this excretion process; otherwise they may contain up to half a teaspoon of sediment. These bivalve organisms cannot distinguish between good and harmful bacteria, and both build up in the tissues in far greater concentrations than in the surrounding water. Oysters, for example, have been found to concentrate polio virus from twenty to sixty times greater than the level in the surrounding sea water.[10]

How are you protected from shellfish contamination that

can cause polio, infectious hepatitis, meningitis, typhoid, cholera, strep throat, and gastroenteritis? Since poisonous shellfish cannot be detected by their appearance or smell, and ordinary cooking does not lower their toxicity to a safe degree, the Shellfish Sanitation Branch of the U.S. Public Health Service was set up to make bacteriological surveys of shellfish growing conditions and inspect shellfish harvested for sale. The U.S. Public Health Service oversees and evaluates the National Shellfish Sanitation Program, and issues a bimonthly publication of approved interstate shellfish shippers. Toxicological surveys of shellfish beds have greatly reduced the incidence of shellfish poisoning, and research into more refined and sensitive methods of detecting harmful bacteria is ongoing. But current sampling techniques used by the Public Health Service have sometimes failed to detect dangerous concentrations of paralytic shellfish poisoning, which has resulted in the intoxication of persons who eat these shellfish.

There are precautions you can take when you buy and prepare shellfish. Don't buy shellfish from peddlers; you don't know where it came from, how old it is, whether or not it was ever inspected. Don't harvest your own shellfish unless you have information from either state or local health authorities that the harvesting area is approved for shellfish growing. And don't attempt to extend the storage time of fresh-shucked oysters, clams, or mussels by freezing them.

Avoid eating clams, mussels, or oysters that are dead when you find or buy them. If a clam or oyster's shell is not tightly closed, it has died and should not be eaten. How do you tell whether or not a mussel is dead? Run cold water over the shell for a minute or two; if the shell doesn't close, the mussel is dead.

When buying crab and lobster, choose ones that are still alive. They may possibly be safe enough if they smell right and their flesh is still firm, but smell and firmness, measured subjectively, are not the best criteria for freshness. A live crab should be able to move its legs. Live crabs can be refrigerated, but not for more than twenty-four hours.

When you buy a lobster, try to buy it live from a retailer. The lobster should move its legs when you pick it up, and its tail should curl under its body. Keep lobsters in the coldest part of the refrigerator for a few hours, no longer, and don't try to keep them fresh by putting them in salt water, as the salt content and temperature will not be right.

If you feel uncomfortable with the traditional way of cooking lobsters—throwing them live into a deep covered pot containing a small amount of boiling water—you can soak the lobster in a briny mixture of two quarts of water, one pound of salt. This will anesthetize the lobster so that it can be boiled within the next five minutes without "visible signs of discomfort." When a lobster turns bright red, it is dead. You should not cook it much longer than ten to twelve minutes in a covered pot. You can safely eat any part of the lobster except its shell—even the female lobster's ovaries, considered by some to be quite a delicacy. The green liver, which may have a bittersweet taste, could contain concentrated water pollutants.

Uncontaminated fish is an excellent source of high-quality protein, vitamins, essential minerals, and fats. The nutrient content of fish is similar to that of beef. Varieties of salt-water fish and shellfish offer a better source of iodine, fluorine, and cobalt. Fish is also a fair source of magnesium, phosphorus, iron, and copper. The iron content in fish is lower than that of meat; the amount of calcium is about the same. Shellfish usually contain higher percentages of iodine and calcium than fish. Salmon and mackerel (both fatty fish) are excellent sources of the fat-soluble vitamins D and A. An average serving of either fat or lean-fleshed fish will supply significant amounts of thiamine, riboflavin and niacin.

Easily digestible and of high nutritional value, fish should be included in all but the strictest vegetarian diets.

FACTS TO PONDER

— The U.S. Coast Guard reports that the United States alone had 714 major oil spills in 1968.

— Fish is superior to meat in protein usability. Some fish, like cod and haddock, are virtually *pure* protein, having no carbohydrates and only .1 percent fat.

— Four medium canned sardines satisfy about 20 percent of the daily protein requirement of the average woman.

— The catch of American fisheries has declined by at least half a billion pounds since World War II.

— If fish is truly fresh, it has no fishy odor.

— Americans now eat close to 400 million pounds of fresh and frozen shrimp a year, or 1.4 pounds per person per year.

— Large shrimp are often called *prawns* or *scampi*. The famed Dublin Bay prawn is not a shrimp at all, but really a species of lobster.

— While the French prize and even cultivate mussels, the abundant blue mussel found on our Eastern shores goes largely uneaten in this country.

— New Jersey leads all other states in clam production, accounting for some 40 million pounds a year.

— In the mid-nineteenth century oyster eating was a national mania. There were oyster peddlers in the city streets, and oyster houses in every Eastern city, some of them offering all the oysters you could eat for six cents.

— During the fifteen years after World War I, there were 100,000 cases of typhoid fever in France, all attributed to eating shellfish.

— Fish livers may contain dangerous concentrations of water pollutants.

— U.S. grade A breaded shrimp may contain 25 to 50 percent bread.

INCOMPLETE
PROTEIN
FOODS

CHAPTER

VEGETABLES

VEGETABLES OF EVERY SORT—DOMESTICATED AND CULTI-vated or wild—should play an important part in your diet. The preparation of vegetables becomes simple and creative once you consider what part of the plant is edible. In general, the earthy root portions require the most cooking; the amount of cooking diminishes as you proceed up the plant to the stems, leaves, fruit, or bud. Plan your meals so that during the course of a week you eat a variety of naturally fertilized fruit and vegetables, covering the full spectrum of tastes and textures, from earthy tubers to leafy greens full of sunshine.

Watch for seasonally available vegetables and try to obtain locally grown produce whenever possible. Seasonal limitations become rather arbitrary if you live in a large city; today's methods of production and transportation have made practi-cally everything available most of the time. Your body will benefit in the long run, and you will feel much more in tune with yourself and with the cycles of nature if you follow this simple principle: Combine those vegetables which are avail-able during the same season; they will complement each other and also prove to be the cheapest. Some vegetables are available the year round because they either have several harvests or can be stored well. These vegetables include carrots, onions, potatoes, yams, parsnips, burdock root, cabbage, brussels sprouts, celery, parsley, garlic, ginger, and squashes such as butternut, acorn, or Hubbard. They can provide a variety of textures when used in soups or casseroles or presented in their own right—such as baked onions or a steamed-vegetable still life.

Other vegetables are generally available only in the cooler weather of spring and fall. This group includes other tubers such as beets, turnips, Jerusalem artichokes, celeriac, salsify and rutabagas; bulbs such as daikon (Japanese white radish), kohlrabi, radishes, and leeks; plant shoots such as asparagus greens, including the many varieties of lettuce (ruby, leaf, romaine, Boston, Bibb, endive, bok choy, etc.) and greens such as spinach, corn salad, Swiss chard, salad cress, kale, mustard, and chicory; and the buds such as artichokes, cauliflower, and broccoli.

Still other vegetables can be grouped as summer vegetables because they need the warmth of the sun to mature. These include vegetables which form after first flowering and contain seeds or pods: avocadoes (usually considered fruits), cucumbers, eggplants, green beans of all types, okra, peas and snow peas, peppers, sweet corn, all the varieties of summer squash (zucchini, scalloped, crookneck, spaghetti, etc.), and tomatoes. Also included with the summer vegetables are some of nature's finest greens and healing grasses (often considered weeds), such as collards, alfalfa, comfrey, malva, and dandelion. It is an excellent practice to include these and other greens in your diet by making a juice from their leaves. The remedial properties of herbs and grasses have long been recognized. There are several excellent books on this subject, including *Nature's Healing Grasses* by H. E. Kirschner, and *Back to Eden* by Jethro Kloss.

Some cultures seek out wild vegetables at the change of season and include them for a short time in the daily diet to aid in cleansing the body. Many Japanese people in rural areas still follow the spring custom of searching the hills and valleys for shepherd's purse, chickweed, daikon (white radish) leaves, turnip leaves, coltsfoot buds, wild parsley, and bracken with which to prepare tonics. Wild vegetables, generally rich in minerals and rather bitter in taste, aid in removing excess salt, oil, and protein stored in the body during the winter months. Wild plants, of course, are relatively free from contamination by chemical fertilizers and insecticides.

For salads, raw vegetables straight out of the garden or fresh from a farmer's market taste the best and are most nutritious. If you're not going to use them immediately, store the vegetables in a cool place to retard the breaking down of enzymes into nutrients, which happens when they are mature. There is no reason to soak vegetables; many water-soluble vitamins and minerals can be lost in the process. If raw vegetables are to be chilled for use in a salad, it is a good idea to toss them in a little oil (perhaps with some garlic pressed and rubbed on the inside of the salad bowl) before chilling in order to slow down oxidation.

When cutting vegetables, work the knife with as quick a stroke as possible so as not to loose vitamins by oxidation through cut surfaces. And it is important not to waste anything. Use all parts of the vegetables, discarding only rotten parts or skins which have been waxed—as with supermarket cucumbers and peppers—to lengthen shelf life.

The less done to vegetables the better. Don't attempt to disguise them; let them be what they are. Most vegetables and fruit should be enjoyed raw, but it is necessary to cook others in order to break down their carbohydrate structure and render them more digestible. Take care not to overcook: the vegetable should maintain the texture and color it had before cooking, but become somewhat softer. Learn to judge for yourself how much cooking or baking time it takes to satisfy you.

Juicing is another excellent way to get optimum nutrition

from vegetables; but remember not to drink much more juice than you could eat of an equivalent amount of whole vegetables. The juice is concentrated, so either dilute it or drink it in small quantities.

With some exceptions, vegetables are not usually one's primary source of proteins or fats, although almost all vegetables contain these nutrients in tiny amounts. Nor are they the *primary* source of carbohydrates, although vegetables contain natural sugars in abundance. They are, however, among the best sources of vitamins and minerals. You can get vitamin A from green leafy vegetables (carrot and dandelion greens, kale, lettuce, parsley, spinach, watercress); vitamin D from some seaweeds (nori). Vitamins E and K are present in green leafy vegetables (cabbage, parsley, spinach); vitamin F can be found in vegetable oils.

Their low cost and high nutritional value make vegetables one of the best food bargains available. They have every vitamin except D (which you get from the sun) and nearly every essential mineral and trace element.

Nutritionally, the top-ranked vegetable is kale. Next you have collards, lima beans, turnip greens, peas, mustard greens, brussels sprouts, spinach, broccoli, sweet corn, watercress, sweet potatoes, asparagus, cauliflower, and snap beans.

Vegetables have a high water content that prevents concentration of vitamins and minerals, so you should eat fresh vegetables every day, in combination with carbohydrates and proteins. Because each vegetable is high in some nutrients and low in others, it's important to include many servings and varieties in your diet.

All dark-green, deep-yellow and orange vegetables are outstanding sources of carotene, which your body converts to vitamin A. If you exclude the orange root vegetables like carrots and yams and the dark-leafed vegetables like kale and spinach, you're probably not getting enough vitamin A. Green-leafed vegetables, which seem to be generally unpopular, are important sources of not only vitamin A but riboflavin, available iron, calcium, phosphorus, potassium, and several important trace elements.

Raw fresh vegetables, served as garnishes or appetizers or in salads, yield a generous bounty of vitamin C. Unfortunately, most of this vitamin is lost when vegetables are boiled or cooked.

If you're a calorie counter, you can't beat vegetables. Half a cup of most boiled vegetables contains some 50 calories; starchier vegetables like potatoes, lima beans, peas, and corn supply 50 to 100 calories per half-cup serving.

Vegetables add variety and color to a meal and offer an abundance of textures and flavors to be enjoyed. Their high water content balances more concentrated foods, thereby aiding the digestive process.

Fresh vegetables are enormously superior in every way to those that are frozen or canned. When bought in season, locally grown produce is generally highest in quality and lowest in price. They offer the best taste if you eat them immediately. If you've grown a summer vegetable garden, you can testify to the exceptional flavor of vegetables picked straight from the vine or ground: carrots are sweet, peas from the shell are sugary sweet and tender, tomatoes are juicy and have a firm-bodied flavor beyond any comparison to the mealy-pulped mushballs you find in supermarkets all year.

Though frozen produce is reputed to be nutritionally equal to its fresh cousin, this isn't usually the case. Once harvested, the produce is shipped to processing factories and held in temporary storage bins, where it may deteriorate if not given proper light and refrigeration. The vegetables then are processed: rinsed to remove grit, dirt, and clinging insects, during which the water breaks down the plant cells; blanched and boiled to reduce their bulk and destroy destructive enzymes; peeled, diced, and cut—all of which contribute to nutritional loss. From this point on, keeping these vegetables frozen becomes a problem.

It's important that prepacked frozen vegetables be maintained at 0 degrees F. Unfortunately, transportation and handling procedures interfere with this needed care. By the time the produce gets to the market, it's anyone's guess how long it has been sitting in storage. Most freezers are not checked periodically for fluctuations in temperature, and more often than not temperatures do wander up from 0 degrees F. Frozen vegetables that are soft or partially defrosted run the risk of further nutritional loss, bacterial contamination, speedy deterioration, even spoilage.

Canned vegetables are popular because they're convenient and less expensive than frozen or fresh produce. But canned vegetables suffer the same storage and processing abuses as do frozen vegetables. They're sterilized by heat after being canned to kill bacteria—at extreme temperatures which make the vegetables soggy and drab-looking and leach out their vitamins and minerals into the liquid contents. Consider too that the manufacturers can add assorted chemicals before canning to retard color changes and stabilize texture.

A certain amount of acid is required by law, to retard bacteria contamination. If the vegetable is already acidic, the manufacturers add baking soda to mellow the taste; baking soda not only depletes your B vitamins, but when it's used in combination with the salt the canners invariably add (never mind the plant's natural sodium content), the overall sodium content increases. Excessive sodium causes water retention and, over a period of time, possible hypertension. Before the lid of the can is put on and sealed into place, even more additives may be dumped into the brew: artificial colors, starches, flavorings, flavor enhancers and intensifiers, sugar, et al. Needless to say, canned vegetables are not quite on a par with frozen vegetables. Which, generally, are not as tasty as fresh vegetables.

Most people think fresh produce means fresh. But fresh really isn't fresh unless the produce has been grown locally or in your own garden. Most vegetables are shipped in from distant farms and produce centers—after first being waxed to prevent bruising or gassed for ripening if they've been picked too early. The produce shippers have sleevefuls of tricks to keep their vegetables and fruits looking fresh—nearly all of which strip them of nutritional value. Chemical fertilizers douse the seeds. Farmers routinely spray herbicides and pesticides on their growing plants, and these chemicals not only cling to the surface but are absorbed through the roots and distributed into every plant cell.

No soap or amount of scrubbing can completely clean these vegetables of their wax coverings or chemical residues. To avoid them, you have to peel off the vegetable's skin. In many varieties of vegetables, concentrated vitamins and minerals are stored just below the surface; once the skin is peeled, these nutrients are diminished.

Only a few vegetables—avocadoes and peas—have skins tough enough to resist sprays. Vegetables which can be coated with wax include carrots, parsnips, cucumbers, tomatoes, potatoes, green and red peppers, and eggplant. Below is a selective sampling of readily available vegetables:

Artichokes, French or glove. Grown in California the year round, peak season is March through May. A good source of vitamins A, B_1, and riboflavin. Select small to medium with tightly compacted, closed leaves (spreading leaves are a sign of age). Look for firm, fleshy leaf stalks, free of discoloration.

Asparagus. Peak season for asparagus is March through June; rarely available out of season. Excellent source of vitamins B_1, C, and riboflavin. Good source of vitamin A in the green, unblanched stalks; the white variety contains very little. Asparagus contains 92 to 95 percent water, which helps maintain your body's water balance. The stalks are high in roughage. Select firm, well-rounded stalks with compact tips. Avoid flat stalks and tips that are open or show signs of decay. Use within one or two days.

Beans, green snap. Available May through October, particularly in summer months. Good source of vitamins A, C, and B$_1$. Select crisp, brightly colored pods; bulging and shriveling indicate that beans are old and tough. Store unwashed in the refrigerator, in the crisper or in plastic bags. Use within three to five days.

Beans, yellow. Available May through October, particularly in summer months. Excellent source of vitamin B$_1$ and a good source of A, C, and riboflavin. Green snap and yellow beans are rich in potassium. The high water percentage in both makes them an excellent choice in balancing concentrated starch foods in a meal. Good sources of fiber. Selection: same as green snap beans. Refrigerate in plastic bag, three to five days.

Beet greens (tops). Sometimes available June to October. High in vitamins A, thiamine, riboflavin, and C. Good sources of available iron, manganese, phosphorus, and potassium. Selection and storage: same as kale.

Beets. Peak season is June through August, but available year round. Good source of vitamins A, B$_1$, and riboflavin. Relatively high in sodium; good potassium and magnesium source. Select firm beets, with a rich color. Usually sold in bunches; can be judged for freshness by the appearance of the green tops. Avoid bunches with wilted tops and oblong beet shapes. Store in a cool place; use within two weeks.

Broccoli. Peak season October through May. Excellent source of vitamins A, B$_1$, and C. Rich in potassium, calcium, sulfur, and iron. Select firm, bright-green stalks, not too thick or tough. Flower buds should be closed, compact dark green with no yellow flowering. Use within two days.

Brussels sprouts. Available September through February. Excellent source of vitamins C, B$_1$, and A. Rich in calcium, potassium, and sulfur. Select compact heads of good green color with no yellowed or bruised leaves. Store in coldest part of the refrigerator. Use in one or two days.

Cabbage. Available year round. Good source of vitamins

C and B_2. Rich in phosphorus, magnesium, and potassium. High in roughage. Select compact heads, heavy for their size, with outer leaves that are deep green or red and free of discoloration. Avoid heads with wilted, decayed, or yellow outer leaves. Store wrapped up in coldest part of refrigerator. Use as soon as possible, particularly if cut, because vitamin C oxidizes when exposed. Can be stored for one to two weeks.

Carrots. Available fresh year round. Excellent source of vitamins A, B_1, and riboflavin. Rich in potassium and sodium. Select firm, smooth roots. Avoid carrots with large green spots at the top, or with soft spots. Larger varieties contain more vitamin A than smaller varieties. More nutritious when steamed or cooked. Keep in a cool dry place for no longer than two weeks.

Cauliflower. Peak season September through November; low season May through August. Generally available all year round. Excellent source of vitamins C, B_1, and riboflavin; good source of phosphorus, magnesium, potassium, calcium, and sulfur. Select compact heads, heavy for size, with firm flowerets. White with no discoloration. If buds are spread out and spotted, cauliflower is old or exposed too long to sun. Store with outside leaves attached in coldest part of refrigerator.

Celery. Available year round. Good source of A, B_1, riboflavin, calcium, and phosphorus. One of the highest sodium sources. High in roughage. High water content makes it an excellent food for balancing concentrated starch or protein foods. Select thick, crisp stalks, free of rusty discoloration. Leaves should be bright green and unwilted. Wash stalks well before eating. Use within three to five days.

Chard, Swiss. Excellent source of A, B_1, C, riboflavin, iron, and sulfur. Select crisp, tender leaves and stalks. Refrigerate in plastic bags; use in one or two days.

Chicory, endive. Excellent source of A, C, B_1, riboflavin, calcium, phosphorus, and iron. Select crisp, undamaged leaves. Refrigerate and use within two days.

Collard greens. Available year round, frozen; fresh, June to September. Good source of vitamins A, C, riboflavin, thiamine, and niacin. Rich in magnesium, calcium, phosphorus, sodium, potassium and available iron. Selection and storage: same as kale.

Corn, yellow. Peak season May through September. Buy only in season; corn loses its delicate sweet flavor immediately after harvesting, and unless it's really fresh the kernels will be starchy and flavorless. Good source of vitamin A, thiamine, riboflavin, niacin, phosphorus, magnesium, iron, and copper. Select ears with fresh green husks; once the husks are removed, flavor and nutrition deteriorate. Silk ends of the husk should be free of decay and stems shouldn't be discolored. Carefully strip husk and check for worms. Kernels should be plump and exude a milky substance. Avoid ears with shrunken or oversized kernels. Store unhusked and uncovered in the refrigerator. Remove husks just before cooking. Use within one or two days.

Cucumbers. Available all year. Good source of vitamin B₁ and riboflavin. High water content balances out meals with concentrated starch and protein. Cucumbers aid in the digestion of proteins. Unwaxed cucumbers are a rarity. Since the wax surface can't be washed or scrubbed off, peel before eating. Choose medium-size cucumbers that are uniformly dark green; avoid oversize cucumbers and those streaked with yellow. Shriveling or yellowness indicates age and pithiness. Refrigerate and use in three to five days.

Eggplant. Peak season late summer but available year round. Excellent riboflavin and good B₁ source. High water content. Select firm, glossy, heavy plants with a uniform rich purple color, not streaked with dark spots. Avoid cracked and shriveled skins. Store at cool room temperature, about 60 degrees F. If air is dry, wrap in plastic to retain moisture. Use in one to two days.

Escarole. Good source of A, B₁, riboflavin, calcium, phosphorus, and iron. High water content. Select crisp, undamaged leaves. Refrigerate and use within two days.

Kale. Excellent source of vitamins A, B_1, C, and riboflavin. Contains most of the essential minerals and trace minerals, particularly magnesium, calcium, available iron, sulfur, potassium, sodium, and phosphorus. Excellent source of niacin. Fairly high in roughage when leaves and stalks are eaten. Select crisp, dark-green leaves free of discoloration; bronze coloring indicates exposure to frost. Yellow leaves indicates age. Refrigerate in plastic bag, use in two days.

Lettuce, Boston, Bibb, Romaine, Iceberg. Available year round. Nutritional value: darker-leafed varieties contain about six times the vitamin A and three times the vitamin C content of the lighter variety (iceberg). Dark-leafed is a good source of thiamine and riboflavin, potassium, and other essential mineral elements. Select well-shaped heads, heavy in weight, free of discoloration. In loose-leaf varieties look for a deep rich green color. Avoid discolored, wilted, and yellowed leaves, all indicating age. Use within one or two days.

Mushrooms. Available year round. Good source of thiamine and riboflavin, rich in potassium, phosphorus, copper, and iron. Select small to medium mushrooms. Immature caps are joined to the stem (closed), and as mushrooms mature the caps open to expose the gills. Avoid caps that are wide open, pitted, or discolored. Mushrooms should be firm, not spongy, with a creamy white color (slightly brown is acceptable). Refrigerate and eat within two days.

Mustard greens. Available year round, frozen; fresh June to October. Good source of vitamin C, thiamin, and riboflavin. Rich in niacin, magnesium, calcium, phosphorus, iron, sodium, potassium, and available iron. Selection and storage: same as kale.

Okra. Peak season June through September. Adequate amounts of vitamins A and C, calcium, phosphorus, potassium, and magnesium. Select crisp, bright-green pods, no more than four inches long. Avoid tough, light-colored pods. To store, wrap and refrigerate. Use within three to five days.

Onions, green (scallions). Green tops a good source of vitamins A, C, B₁, and riboflavin; bulbs and tops supply calcium, phosphorus, potassium, and sulfur. Select fresh, firm green tops with small bulbs. White part of the stalk should be at least two inches above the root end. Avoid damaged, discolored, or wilted scallions. Store in a cool, dry place.

Onions, mature. Available year round. Small amounts of vitamins A and C, calcium, and phosphorus. Good source of potassium and sulfur. Select rich-brown, firm bulbs. Skin should be paper-thin, dry but not brittle. Avoid bulbs with soft spots and uneven coloring. Sprouting of bulb indicates age. Store in loosely woven or open-mesh containers at room temperature; onions need adequate ventilation. High humidity of plastic bags will make them sprout faster. Can be stored for several months in a cool, dry place.

Parsnips. Peak season October through April. Good source of vitamin C, phosphorus, calcium, and potassium. Look for small or medium bulbs uniform in size, firm and free of surface damage. Large bulbs are usually tough. Refrigerate and use within one or two days.

Peas, green. Available March through June. Small amount of protein; excellent source of vitamin A and good source of vitamin C, thiamine, riboflavin, and niacin, calcium, phosphorus, iron, and potassium. Pea size doesn't necessarily indicate degree of maturity. Refrigerate and use within one week.

Peppers, green and red. Excellent source of vitamins A and C; also supply calcium, phosphorus, sodium, and potassium. Pick peppers that are firm and crisp, whose skin is smooth without wrinkling or shriveling. Look for bright-green or red color. Discolored areas and soft spots indicate spoilage. Refrigerate in plastic bags or vegetable bin, and use within three to five days.

Potatoes. Available year round. Good source of vitamin C and niacin, iron, potassium, and phosphorus when baked or boiled and eaten with the skin. Potatoes are good sources of incomplete protein, high in ascorbic acid, but this vitamin C is quickly lost during storage. Select well-shaped, firm, reasonably smooth potatoes. Large potatoes may have internal rotting. Those with green spots have been exposed to the sun and are usually bitter. Avoid bruised or cut surfaces. Store in a dark, dry place with adequate ventilation and a temperature of 45 to 50 degrees. Under these conditions can be stored for several months.

The immature potato has more vitamin C than the common all-purpose potato. Caution: skins of new potatoes are often dyed red.

Radishes, red. Available year round. Good source of vitamin C, calcium, iron, sodium, phosphorus, sulfur, and potassium. Radish tops have almost ten times the vitamin C as the bulbs, and should be eaten fresh. Select small, uniform-sized roots with firm smooth surfaces; yellowed, wilted leaves show age. Refrigerate in plastic bag and use within two weeks.

Spinach. Available year round frozen; fresh July to November. Excellent source of vitamins A, C, riboflavin, and potassium. Considerable calcium and iron. Selection and storage: same as kale.

Squash, summer. Varieties include green zucchini, yellow crookneck and straightneck. Eaten with skin, squash provides adequate amounts of vitamin A, potassium, phosphorus, and calcium, and small amounts of vitamin C. Select squash that has rich color, heavy for size, with a soft rind. Avoid cut, discolored, or decayed surfaces. Refrigerate and use in three to five days.

Squash, winter. Available year round. Bright-orange flesh is outstanding source of vitamin A; also supplies calcium, phosphorus, and potassium. Select squash heavy for size, uniform color, unblemished tough rind. Store in a cool dry place (about 60 degrees F.); will keep several months.

Sweet potatoes and yams. Peak season March to June. Outstanding source (more than a hundred times regular potatoes) of vitamin A. Also supplies vitamin C, sodium, phosphorus, potassium, and calcium. Must be boiled or baked within the skin to retain these nutrients. Select moist potatoes with a bright orange color (yams) or light orange color (sweet potatoes). Look for firm, well-shaped potatoes, with bright, evenly colored skin. Avoid potatoes that are cut, discolored, or have any evidence of decay or surface injury. Store in a cool (60°), dry place with adequate ventilation. Storing below 50 degrees can cause chilling injury; *do not refrigerate.* Can be stored for several months.

Tomatoes. Peak season July to September. Available year round but summer tomatoes, locally grown and vine-ripened, are vastly superior in nutrition, taste, and texture to prepacked, year-round tomatoes. Tomatoes are an excellent source of vitamins A and C; they also contain calcium, phosphorus, potassium, and sodium. Select firm, plump tomatoes free of blemishes and soft spots, with a rich red color (unless bought green for home ripening). Ripe tomatoes should be uncovered in the refrigerator; unripe tomatoes should be kept at room temperature *away from direct sunlight* until ripe, then refrigerated. Too much sunlight will prevent development of even color.

Turnips. Peak season October to March. Good source of vitamin C, calcium, sodium, phosphorus, and potassium. Select firm, smooth, uniformly shaped roots; avoid wrinkled, blemished surfaces. Oversize turnips with many thin rootlets are old and have a bad flavor. Store in a cool, dry place (60 degrees F.).

NUTRITIONAL SUMMARY

The dark-green leafy vegetables are important sources of vitamins A, C, K, and riboflavin as well as calcium and iron. These vegetables also provide an excellent source of fiber, and help to keep the digestive tract functioning normally. The outside leaves of lettuce and cabbage vegetables are much higher in vitamin A, calcium, and iron than the lighter, inner leaves. Remember: the thinner and greener the vegetables, the higher in nutritional value.

Broccoli and cauliflower are commonly referred to as flowering vegetables. Broccoli, because of its dark-green color, is an excellent source of iron, phosphorus, vitamins A, C, and riboflavin and is nutritionally superior to cauliflower. The outer leaves of both cauliflower and broccoli are much higher in nutrient value than the flower buds and should be eaten rather than discarded (which is usually the case).

Peas, beans, and lentils, commonly called legumes, provide an excellent source of protein when properly combined with other complementary proteins. (See Chapter 11, "Combining Complementary Proteins.") Besides valuable protein, legumes offer a valuable source of phosphorus, iron, thiamine, and necessary bulk to your diet.

Root vegetables such as carrots, beets, sweet potatoes, and turnips are generally good sources of thiamine. The yellow and deep-orange varieties are rich in vitamin A, and the deeper the color the greater the content. Generally speaking of all vegetables, the deeper the color the higher the nutrient content.

Vegetables are bulky fibrous foods and are essential in the diet for proper digestion and elimination. They are also important sources of minerals and vitamins. Dark-green, leafy vegetables, yellow and orange vegetables, and those rich in vitamin C should be served at least four times a day (raw, in salads, or cooked as a vegetable dish). Most vegetables when lightly steamed will not only retain their crisp texture and color but fewer nutrients are lost in the process.

FACTS TO PONDER

— Dark-green and yellow vegetables are rich in vitamin A.
— The depth of color is a fairly good index of carotene (pro-

vitamin A) content. Spinach and broccoli, for instance, have much more vitamin A content than lettuce, cabbage, or snap beans.

— Carrots are a very rich source of carotene, the amount increasing with maturity. Larger carrots have a much deeper color and consequently a much higher vitamin A value.

— Unless frozen peas are kept below 0 degrees F. there is progressive loss in the vitamin C content.

— Vitamin C is usually associated with citrus fruits and tomatoes, but cauliflower, cantaloupe, strawberries, cabbage, sweet potatoes, and brussels sprouts are also good vitamin C sources.

— Too much vitamin A or D can be toxic, but there is no danger in consuming too many of these vitamins from vitamin-rich foods like fruits and vegetables; in fact, natural food sources should be the only form of vitamins A and C you need, if you eat right, unless you smoke, live in polluted air, handle stress, or are approaching middle age and therefore don't absorb vitamins so well.

CHAPTER

FRUITS

MOST OF WHAT WE'VE ALREADY SAID ABOUT VEGETABLES goes for fruits, too. They are good sources of vitamins C and A, as well as potassium, calcium, phosphorus, and other minerals. Their high water content prevents these nutrients from being concentrated, however, which means that they should be eaten daily.

High water content makes fruit an excellent addition to protein-and-starch meals, and its enzymes can aid in digestion. Fruits also add texture and color to a meal. Their wholesome sweetness provides an ideal dessert and certainly a great nutritional bargain.

Fresh fruits are enormously superior to canned fruits. They are usually highest in quality and lowest in price when you buy them in season, locally grown. Their perishability demands, of course, that they be eaten as soon as possible.

Canned fruits are more convenient and have long shelf lives, but they suffer the same storage and processing abuses as canned vegetables. Many of the water-soluble vitamins and minerals are lost in canning, and the fruits canned in sugary, additive-soaked brine can tax your system.

Unfortunately, even fresh fruit has been tampered with before it reaches your supermarket or produce center: sprayed with pesticides, treated with chemicals to improve its looks and color, waxed to preserve its skin.

Below is a selective sampling of the more common fruits:

Apples. Peak season October to March. Fairly good source of thiamine; minor source of calcium, phosphorus, potassium, and vitamins A and C. Most of these nutrients are concentrated just below the surface of the peel. Many commercial varieties are waxed and should be peeled to remove the coating of wax and any residual pesticides. Select firm and crisp apples with no holes, soft spots or bruises. Should be bright and full in color, which indicates the apple's maturity. Store in a cool dry place, loosely wrapped but not in plastic.

Apricots. Peak season June and July. Excellent source of vitamin A and potassium. Substantial amounts of calcium, phosphorus, and vitamin C. Select ripe, firm fruits, juicy and plump with a bright orange-yellow color. Avoid green unripened and hard light-yellow fruit. Unripened apricots should be kept at room temperature. Once ripened, refrigerate. Ripe apricots are very perishable.

Avocadoes. Available year round from California and Florida. Good source of vitamin A, thiamine, riboflavin, and niacin, and potassium. Smaller amounts of calcium, phosphorus, and available iron. High fat content. For immediate use select avocadoes that yield under pressure; but squeeze gently—they bruise easily. Skin color should be dark purple (ripe) unless you're buying it unripened (rich green). Store in vegetable bin of refrigerator. Use quickly, for avocadoes are very perishable. Once ripened, they last for about a week.

Bananas. Available year round. Very good source of potassium and vitamin A; fair source of calcium, phosphorus, iron, and vitamin C. Select firm ripe fruit, sunny yellow, speckled with brown, closed at both ends. Ripen at room temperature. Don't store ripened bananas in the refrigerator.

Blackberries. Available July to September. Good source

of vitamin A and potassium; fair source of calcium, phosphorus, and vitamin C. Select firm, ripe, evenly colored berries. Avoid berries with caps (they were probably green when harvested). If the inside of the container is stained, the berries are likely to be overripe or moldy.

Remove overripe or spoiled berries, store in a well-ventilated container, and refrigerate.

Blueberries. Peak season May through September. Good source of iron and manganese. Small amounts of vitamins A and C, calcium, phosphorus, and potassium. Selection and storage: same as blackberries.

Cherries. Peak season June to August. Red sour cherries are a good source of vitamin A (ten times that of sweet cherries). All cherries are important sources of iron, copper, and manganese. They also supply calcium, phosphorus, potassium, and a small amount of vitamin C. Select firm, plump cherries, rich in color with no sign of surface or insect damage. Rinse and sort out damaged cherries, store in a well-ventilated container, refrigerate, and eat within a week.

Cranberries. Peak season September to December. Aid in digestion of carbohydrates and proteins, but offer very little nutritionally. Small amounts of vitamin C, calcium, phosphorus, and potassium. Select bright-colored berries (though color varies with different varieties), plump and well rounded. Avoid soft or bruised berries. Discard spoiled berries; do not wash before refrigeration because moisture will hasten spoilage. Will last four to eight weeks under refrigeration.

Coconuts. Available year round. The meat has fair amounts of sodium, potassium, and iron; small amounts of calcium and phosphorus. Select a nut that's heavy for its size; shake to make sure it's filled with milk. Once opened, refrigerate both liquid and meat.

Grapes. Available year round. Small amounts of vitamin A, potassium, calcium, phosphorus. Select plump and well-rounded grapes, brightly colored with frosted surface. Make sure stem is firm and green; stems of grapes during winter and spring months should be woody. Take home immediately after purchase and discard rotten, moldy, undeveloped grapes. Refrigerate in plastic bag. Highly perishable.

Grapefruit. Available year round. White and pink varieties are similar in vitamin C and mineral content, but pink grapefruit has over five times the amount of vitamin A as its white cousin. Both have small amounts of calcium, phosphorus, and potassium. Select firm fruit, heavy for size. Thin rind usually indicates juicier fruit. Juice from grapefruit harvested in September–October averages about 27 to 42 milligrams per 100 grams; spring harvest grapefruits average 33 to 35 milligrams. Defects and discoloration on the skin don't necessarily mean decay, but avoid wet spots and fruit with pointed ends. Will keep for five to six days at room temperature; several weeks under refrigeration.

Lemons and limes. Available year round. Excellent source of vitamin C; good source of bioflavinoids. Small amounts of calcium, phosphorus, potassium, and vitamin A. Select small-pored fruit with fine-textured skin, heavy for size. Slight greenish hue is sometimes desirable (the juice will be more acidic). Limes should have rich green color and be heavy for size. Avoid yellowish rinds; avoid dry, hard, blackened limes and shriveled, mushy, or hard lemons. Check stem ends for decay. Refrigerate in vegetable bin.

Mangoes. Available between May and September. Outstanding source of vitamin A; good source of vitamin C, iodine, niacin, and potassium; fair source of calcium, phosphorus, and sodium. Select plump fruit, with skin color ranging from unripened green to variations of orange-yellow, and a reddish tint when finally ripe. Ripe fruit should yield to slight pressure. Avoid mangoes with dark soft spots and other signs of decay. Unripened fruit can be left at room temperature for three or four days. Once ripe, refrigerate and eat as quickly as possible. Mangoes are highly perishable.

Melons. Available May to November. Melons are about

90 percent water, hence a good addition to a heavy meal. Low in calories. But because of their high water content they have a low concentration of vitamins and minerals. They are generally a good source of vitamin C. Vitamin A content escalates with richness of color: orangish-pink cantaloupes, dark orange Persian melons, and dark red watermelons are excellent sources of vitamin A. Cantaloupes should be firm and completely covered. Avoid overripeness and soft spots. For Persian melons, avoid soft spots and discolored, darkened netting.

Crenshaw should be larger with smooth skin and no netting; golden color. Casaba should be thick-skinned with rich yellow color. Honeydew should be large (five or 6 pounds) with a soft, slightly fuzzy surface that's oily or sticky. Avoid white and/or hard rinds.

General picking rules: avoid soft or noticeably overripe melons; avoid melons soft and soggy at the stem ends, for they are past their prime.

Once cut open, wrap in plastic, refrigerate, and use within a week.

Nectarines. Peak season July to August. Excellent source of vitamin A, good source of vitamin C and potassium, with small amounts of calcium and phosphorus. Select yellow-orange fruit with dabs of red. Run finger down the seam; if fruit yields under pressure, it's ripe. Avoid fruit that is hard, green, spotted, or bruised. Store in a cool, dry place.

Oranges. Available year round. Best known for vitamin C. Good source of vitamin A, potassium, phosphorus, calcium, and folic acid. California Navel are best oranges for vitamin C (60 milligrams of C per 100 grams edible portion). Florida late-season Valencias have low levels (37 milligrams per 100 grams). Early and midseason California Valencias and Florida oranges average about 51 percent. Vitamin C levels are always higher in the early part of the season. Frozen orange juice, prepared mainly from Florida oranges, averages about 45 milligrams per 100 grams. Loss of ascorbic acid during processing is negligible. Bright deep-orange oranges have probably been dyed. Look for orangish-brown rinds, firm, hefty weight, smooth surface. Avoid softness or sign of decay. Store in a cool, dry place.

Papaya. Peak season May and June. Aids in digestive disturbances because of its enzyme papain. Outstanding source of vitamins A and C and potassium. Small amounts of calcium and phosphorus. Select fruit with deep yellow-orange color; smooth unblemished skin that yields to slight pressure. Extremely perishable; eat quickly.

Peaches. Available July to October. Outstanding source of vitamin A, good source of niacin and potassium, fair source of vitamin C and other minerals. Select when firm with creamy yellowish color. Avoid hard green fruits (they've been picked early and won't ripen at home). Refrigerate without washing, which hastens decay. Highly perishable.

Pears. Available May to October. High moisture and fiber content; stimulates stomach action because of its fiber content. Low in vitamins A, C, and minerals. Select firm and unblemished fruit which is pale yellowish green or deep yellow to light brown with brownish russeting. Avoid soft, mushy fruit and watch for decay around the stem. Usually available unripened; will ripen within two or three days if kept in ventilated plastic bag. Ripe fruit should be refrigerated.

Pineapples. Available year round. A good source of vitamin C and potassium; generally low in most other vitamins and minerals. An enzyme, bromelin, aids in digestion; high moisture content helps to balance out heavy starch-and-protein meals. Select rich yellow to golden orange pineapples. Avoid green, bruised, or discolored fruit; avoid fruit with dried-out leaves. Eat when ripe; refrigerate leftover pineapple in plastic bag or tightly closed container to hold in moisture.

Plums. Available year round. High in moisture, low in calories. Dark-yellow pulp of some varieties a good source of vitamin A; other varieties poor sources. High in potassium, fairly high calcium and iron. Select richly colored plums; avoid hard, dull-colored, bruised or split ones. Can be bought firm and ripened at home. Keep unripe fruit at room temperature until soft, then eat; ripe plums are highly perishable.

Strawberries. Peak season spring months. Excellent source of vitamin C; good source of vitamin A, calcium, phosphorus, iron and potassium. Select firm, ripe, bright-red berries, solid in color. Look for berries capped with hulls. Avoid overripe, spoiled strawberries. Discard spoiled berries; don't wash or dehull before refrigerating. Will keep only a few days.

Tangerines, tangeloes. Available in winter; peak season near Christmas. Excellent source of vitamin C, good source of vitamin A and potassium. Small amounts of calcium, phosphorus. Select fruit with deep orange color, heavy for size. Avoid moldy, soft fruit. Highly perishable; refrigerate in vegetable bin.

FACTS TO PONDER

— Bananas and lima beans have the highest levels of carbohydrate among fruits and vegetables (about 23 percent). Lima beans are also relatively high in protein (about 6 to 8 percent).

— Apples can be a good source of vitamin C, depending on variety, season of maturity, and whether stored or peeled. For example, a large summer apple furnishes 22 milligrams of vitamin C per 100 grams if eaten whole, but only 14 milligrams if peeled. During long storage an apple's vitamin C content may drop as much as 50 percent.

10

WHOLE GRAINS, NUTS, AND SEEDS

THE PURPOSE OF THIS CHAPTER IS TO GUIDE YOU IN YOUR selection and preparation of whole grains, nuts, seeds, and produce. Most diets and meal plans are centered around meat, fish, or fowl, with potatoes and a few common vegetables (usually overcooked and tasteless) as side dishes. Therefore, by following the guidelines offered in this chapter you will be able to add dozens of tasty, as well as highly nutritious, foods to your family's meals.

The preparation of food is both an art and a skill. Using natural, whole foods in this process, you are assured of getting the broadest spectrum of essential nutrients. Since your body depends on a delicate interplay and balance of nutrients, you should concentrate on using untampered-with foods. Refined foods can upset and even destroy this balance, leaving the body unable to cope successfully with all the chemical pollutants, refined sugars, and starches they contain.

Our main objective in dealing with whole foods is to show you how to preserve their natural flavors and nutrients in preparation so they will be nourishing. Cooking and serving foods can become a truly creative, humble act as well as a means of understanding nature and her harmonies of taste, texture, aroma, and color. Eating whole foods in tune with the seasons and with the requirements of your own body will subtly improve your health and outlook. Whole foods can bring on a new awareness of the seasons as well as a realization of how much modern methods of cultivating, refining, preserving, and distributing foods have weakened our bonds with the earth and water around us.

Although natural foods and organically grown fruit and vegetables are often more expensive than supermarket fare, you will find when you compare what you actually obtain from these foods that the natural foods are by far the best buy.

If you're not going to eat your food raw, there are several basic ways of preparing it with heat. The methods for cooking vegetables are essentially the same as for the rest of our food, so these will be discussed first.

Vegetables may be fried in oil over a high heat, or sautéed. The most nutritious way to sauté vegetables is the quick stir-fry technique. You heat a wok or a heavy skillet, spread a little oil out evenly over the hot pan, add a pinch of salt, and wait a moment before dropping in the vegetables. Stir the vegetables in the hot skillet and lightly toss them about, coating them with salted oil. The oil will seal in their juices; the salt will tease out their inner moisture.

The sautéing may be the first cooking step in a series. After sautéing the vegetables, you may want to add a small amount of liquid, bring it to a boil, then lower the heat and let the vegetables steam for a short time. This method is especially effective with legumes like peas or beans, which often need extra moisture. Another possibility is to sauté the vegetables and then simmer in liquid. This gives them a toasted flavor, and takes less time than straight simmering. Vegetables may also be sautéed first and then added to casseroles for baking. The main idea is not to overcook any vegetable. When you're cooking more than one, sauté the tougher vegetables like carrots or green beans before dropping in the more tender zucchini or mushrooms.

Vegetables can also be simmered in liquid or stock without any precooking. The water is heated low enough to gently produce surface bubbles rather than to a rolling boil. This method is good when you add vegetables to bean soups after the beans have been cooked tender.

Vegetables are often cooked in a salted liquid with enough heat to produce a gently rolling boil. This method, however, is neither nutritious nor economical; many of the vegetable nutrients escape into the water. If you do boil vegetables you might drink the cooking liquid, use it for simmering other foods or for soup stock, or water your plants with it when cooled.

Steaming vegetables—whole or cut—in a closed container above boiling liquid is the easiest and most efficient method of cooking. You can use a collapsible steaming basket placed in a pan filled with a few inches of water, stock, or vegetable juices. Chinese-style bamboo steamers are also available in many natural food stores and Oriental markets. These consist of a large metal pan called a wok set on a ring to focus the heat at the base of the pan's rounded bottom. Set in the wok is a bamboo basket with a lid and with slats at the bottom which allow the steam to rise. Place the vegetables in the basket according to their toughness—first the tougher root vegetables, then the buds like cauliflower or broccoli, then the tender vegetables and greens such as kale or collards. Note that the manner in which vegetables are cut determines how they should be cooked. For instance, carrots cut in thin slivered coins will steam much faster than whole carrots.

Baking vegetables is a slower and gentler way to preserve natural enzymes and flavors. And you'll find that other cooking methods can be adapted to oven use. By slicing vegetables, brushing them with oil, and baking them, you actually oven-fry them. Or you can simmer or steam vegetables in the oven, placing them in liquid and covering them with a dish.

Vegetables can also be coated with a batter and deep-fried. This method, tempura, can be a truly artistic one which introduces unsaturated fatty acids from the cooking oil into the diet. Any unrefined vegetable oil can be used. A wok works very well for tempura, but a deep skillet will do nicely. Slowly heat the oil to 350 degrees F. and maintain it at that temperature by raising and lowering the heat. A number of batters can be used, some of the best combinations being buckwheat flour and rice flour, whole-wheat pastry with unbleached white flour, or whole-wheat flour in combination with corn or rye. To each cup of flour combination add ¾ cup of water and ¼ teaspoon salt. Many vegetables make beautiful tempura; try to use those in season. Carrots, burdock, squash and pumpkin, onion, mushroom, green beans, green pepper, broccoli, asparagus, and cauliflower are all possibilities for tempura cooking, as are more delicate foods such as parsley, carrot tops, celery leaves, and green leaves of many varieties.

You can use these various cooking techniques for vegetables when preparing grains and beans. The grain may be dry-roasted in a heavy skillet as a preliminary to cooking, or sautéed in a preheated, lightly oiled pan. In either case, you should toast the grain until it browns lightly and gives off a lovely fragrance. Simmering or pressure cooking—which is really simmer-steaming—is good for grains and beans. Pressure cooking is fast, conserves fuel, and allows for better control over the consistency of the food being cooked. But many people prefer the texture and taste of simmered grains and beans.

Both grains and beans can be baked in the oven with or without precooking.

Instead of using heat to prepare vegetables, you can salt them—to draw out excess liquid, mellow their taste, soften their texture, and preserve them. Once salted, you can leave the vegetables for several hours in a dish or for many months in a crock. First cut them into pieces, then sprinkle them with no more salt than you would use if you were going to eat them. Place them in a bowl, cover the bowl with a dish, and weight it down with a heavy pot or a jar filled with water. The plate will sink down as the vegetables soften and condense. Rinse the vegetables under cold running water before serving them. You can make a variety of crisp pickled vegetables by first salting the various components of the pickle and then layering them in a jar and adding a tamari-and-water solution. This can be weighted and left for several weeks before you sample the result. You can also pickle vegetables by burying them in miso (soybean paste) or mixing them in a rice bran paste and allowing them to age from several days to several months.

Vegetables lend themselves to beautiful presentation. The way a vegetable or fruit is cut affects the way it will taste and the manner in which it should be cooked. Long root vegetables such as carrots, parsnips, or burdock can be cut into irregular wedges, thick rounds, or thin-sliced diagonal slices. You can even cut them lengthwise and then slice them into half-moons. Long vegetables may be cut into rectangular pieces, matchsticks, or tiny diced pieces. Onions look especially beautiful in half-moon crescents: you cut the vegetable lengthwise into halves, laying the insides face down on the cutting boards and slicing crescent shapes along the length of the halves. Lettuces and varieties of Chinese cabbage can easily be cut into long strips by bunching the leaves of the head close together and cutting very thin horizontal slices. Shaving pieces or flakes from the vegetables is another possibility, as is grating; these are good techniques when you want to add tougher vegetables later to a soup. Tender lettuce and other greens may taste better if their leaves are simply torn into pieces rather than cut. Use your imagination, but let the shape and texture of the vegetable inspire your choice of cut. Quick, assured strokes with well-sharpened knives are best. If you use—and you should—dry whole herbs in cooking, crush them between the palms of your hands. You can also use mortar and pestle to crush dry herbs or pound fresh herbs, greens, and cooked grains into a paste.

OUTFITTING THE KITCHEN

You can cook a surprising variety of dishes over an open fire, in a fireplace, or even on a small hotplate. But if you have the opportunity to outfit yourself with a so-called modern kitchen, there is equipment which certainly can invite successful meals. Cookware is made of many materials, the best being cast iron, earthenware, stainless steel, and baked enamel. Not—please notice—aluminum. Just about anything seems to be made of aluminum these days, but studies have proven aluminum to be a toxic, highly reactive metal which combines with various elements in food, especially when the food has been cooked in or left to stand in aluminum for a long time.

Cast-iron skillets and heavy saucepans are indispensable for sautéing, dry-roasting and simmering. A large pot with a lid and outfitted with a foldable stainless steel steaming basket is fine for steaming vegetables; a Dutch oven or large soup pot will always come in handy for soups, pasta or simmered foods. A wok has many uses in addition to being a steamer basket base; it is perfect for stir-frying and deep-frying tempura. Essentials for baking include cookie sheets, bread pans, and casserole dishes. A stainless steel pressure cooker is a wonderful aid to fast cooking and may also serve as a soup-cooking pot when used without its lid.

Cast-iron skillets, woks, bread pans, cookie sheets, and even metal utensils should all be tempered to keep them from rusting and to prevent food from sticking to them. Here's how: when they're new you should first clean the implements thoroughly, then warm them in the oven at 300 degrees F. for about five minutes. Remove them from the oven and rub them with a thin even coat of vegetable oil, then replace them in the heated oven and bake for twenty minutes. Apply more oil, and rebake the utensils for five minutes. Don't use soap or scouring pads to clean them, just wipe them clean and dislodge any food particles with a tawashi brush (a natural palm-fiber bristle). If a pan's oil coating should become gummy, clean it with soap and retemper it.

Wooden spoons, tongs, and chopsticks don't tear or cut up vegetables and other foods as much as metal ones and won't scratch or chip the surface of pots and pans. Since wood is alive—constantly absorbing and losing moisture—don't overwash these implements; the soap and water can dry them out and crack them.

A wooden, unvarnished cutting board is best for all types of vegetable confrontations. If you are interested in preparing vegetables with some proficiency, try a heavy all-purpose Japanese knife called a hacho. It has a large rectangular blade and is available in stainless or carbon steel; though the carbon steel edge sharpens quite easily, it does not hold its edge and it reacts to the acidity in foods such as tomatoes and citrus fruits. One alternative to the Japanese vegetable knife is a heavier chef's knife with a curving blade. One of these plus a few small paring knives supplies enough cutlery for a small home kitchen.

Other kitchen needs include a metal or bamboo colander for draining washed vegetables or blanching noodles, a fine mesh strainer for washing grains and beans and sifting flours, a tawashi brush for scrubbing vegetables, a vegetable grater with several types of cutting sections, and possibly a suribachi—a serrated earthenware bowl—for grinding seeds and crushing or puréeing herbs and vegetables. A stainless steel or porcelain set of measuring cups and spoons with both English and metric capacities noted will come in very handy. If you are serious about baking and want to have the freshest possible ground flours and meals, perhaps you should consider the purchase of a small hand grinder. This grinder can be mounted on a countertop and used for nut meals and grinding beans as well as for producing fresh flour. Quaker City and Corona are both hand mills available for less than twenty-five dollars and come with either steel or stone grinding heads.

WHOLE GRAINS

To the vegetarian, grains are a particularly important food staple. Use a variety of them: each has a rich flavor to impart. But to enjoy these grains' true taste, choose those grown free of chemical fertilizers and sprays. And it goes without saying that the less whole grains are processed, the greater will be their nutrients.

Whole grains contain everything to nurture themselves from germ stage to sprout to mature plant. Plant a whole kernel of any grain and, given the right combination of earth, water, and air, it will sprout and grow to maturity. Not so with *refined* grains: bury a milled kernel and cultivate it as much as you like; nothing will grow because the kernel is already dead.

Milling the root of whole grains only refines away a wide range of trace minerals and vitamins in the outer layers which can make the grains bulkier and less healthy. Refined grains, robbed of the minerals and vitamins found in the discarded outer layers, strain the body's delicate mechanism of digestion. Nearly all of the B vitamins, vitamin E, unsaturated fatty acids, and quality proteins are found in whole grains, but refining removes most of these nutrients. Even in so-called enriched foods, only two or three B vitamins and iron are replaced; the remaining twelve or so B vitamins, as well as the minerals and proteins, are "refined" out.

There are three ways to prepare whole grains for eating: sprouting, soaking, and cooking until tender. All grains can be sprouted in two to three days, or until the sprout reaches the same length as the original seeds. You can reconstitute some semiprocessed grains such as bulgur wheat by soaking them overnight or pouring boiling water over them and allowing them to fluff up.

When you cook grains, rinse them first in a colander or strainer, pour the grain into a pot of water, and swirl it with your hands, removing hulls and bits of dirt which float to the surface. Drain the grain through a strainer, dry-pan-fry it in a heavy skillet, and add two parts boiling water. Cover the skillet, reduce the heat, and let the grain simmer for about half an hour (time varies with the grain).

Preparing grains in a pressure cooker is faster, conserves fuel, and requires less water. When using a pressure cooker, the proportion of water to grain is roughtly 1⅓ parts water for each part of grain. Add grain and water to the cooker and bring them rapidly up to full pressure. When the regulator on the lid makes a jiggling sound, the cooker has reached full pressure; reduce the heat to simmer and maintain the same pressure throughout the cooking. Allow the pressure to return to normal before loosening the lid, then open the pot and gently stir the grains, mixing the kernels toward the bottom with those at the top. Let them sit a few minutes, then mix them again.

All grains at least double in size from dry to cooked state. This means that 1 cup of cooked grain can feed two or three enthusiastic grain eaters or four or five eating grain along with other foods. To achieve a sweeter flavor and crunchier texture, you may wish to dry-roast the grain or sauté it before cooking. To dry-roast, start with a cold skillet, preferably cast iron. To sauté, you must first heat the skillet and then quickly and evenly coat it with oil. (If the oil smokes, it's too hot.) Whether dry-roasting or sautéing, stir the grain until a few kernels pop and a delicious aroma begins to rise.

Barley, a grain familiar to most people only as an ingredient in soups, actually has much to offer as a solo grain dish. Some of the best barley in the world—consistently high in protein and minerals—comes from the rich soil of the Red River Valley of North Dakota and Minnesota.

Since unhulled barley is almost impossible to cook, practically all barley available in food stores has been "pearled" so as to remove its tenacious hull. The factor to consider here is just how much pearling has taken place; too much results in a whiter product robbed of the nutrients in its outer layer. Look for the darker barley available in most natural-food stores.

When simmered barley is cooked with 2⅓ parts liquid (water, stock, etc.) to 1 part grain, allow 30 to 35 minutes for cooking. Barley can also be browned before adding it to the boiling liquid. Pressure cooking (2 parts water to 1 part grain) takes approximately 20 minutes. If the resulting grain seems too chewy, simply add ¼ cup more water, cover, and simmer until soft. You might also try cooking barley with other grains, such as brown rice and wheat berries.

Barley can be sprouted, but first it has to be dehulled (try seed houses and grain suppliers). Harvest the sprout when it's about the same size as the grain. Barley flour can be obtained already milled or ground fresh from the pearled grain. It is often pan-roasted before being used in breads, muffins, and cakes.

Buckwheat is actually not a true grain but a grass seed related to rhubarb. When raised commercially as a grain crop, buckwheat is unlikely to have been fertilized or sprayed. Fertilization encourages too much leaf growth; spraying stops the bees from pollinating. The best buy is whole, hulled, unroasted (white) buckwheat grains, known as groats. Roasted (brown) and cut groats are less nutritious, and the roasting can easily be done just before cooking without disturbing the flavor or the B vitamins.

Buckwheat cooks quickly, so it is rarely pressure cooked. Simmer for 15 to 20 minutes in the same saucepan or skillet you first roasted it in, using 2 parts water to 1 part buckwheat. If you prefer a porridgelike consistency, use 3 parts water. Cooked buckwheat can serve as a stuffing for everything from cabbage leaves and collard greens to knishes.

Buckwheat flour combined variously with whole-wheat, un-bleached white, and soy flours is a delight to fine pancake lovers. Whole-grain buckwheat flour is always dark; light-colored buckwheat flour is made from sifted flour rather than from unroasted groats. A Japanese pasta called soba (containing anywhere from 30 to 70 percent buckwheat flour) is now readily available in natural-food stores and Oriental markets. Its wonderfully subtle flavor and light effect on the stomach should encourage pasta enthusiasts to give it a try. It needs no heavy sauces; simply try a simple garlic or onion and oil topping.

You can prepare a buckwheat cream used for morning cereal from buckwheat flour sautéed in oil in a heavy skillet. You allow it to cool and then return it to the heat, gradually adding water and bringing it to a boil. This mixture is then stirred and simmered about 10 minutes or until it reaches the desired consistency.

Sprout buckwheat from the unhulled groats in half an inch of soil or on wet paper toweling and allow it to reach a height of 3 to 4 inches. The sprout or young grass, called buckwheat lettuce, can then be juiced or chewed. The bioflavonoid rutin, which is reported to cut short any type of external or internal bleeding and speed coagulation, is very high in sprouted buckwheat.

Corn, a staple food for some fifteen thousand years, has changed from a small shrub with only a few kernels to today's hybrid varieties with six-foot stalks bearing several ears that contain hundreds of kernels apiece. Both white and yellow varieties of dried corn are readily available, but in the American Southwest the blue and varicolored older types of corn are still grown. "Sweet" corn is normally boiled or steamed in water; field corn is likely to be ground into meals and flours. Field corn is allowed to dry out completely, which changes the simple sugars of the grain into starches.

Yellow cornmeal contains about 10 percent protein and is higher in vitamin A than the white variety. The only difference between a meal and a flour from yellow corn is the degree of coarseness. The germ of cornmeal starts deteriorating in a matter of hours, so you should grind your own meal or flour as you use it for corn breads, muffins, Southern spoon bread, johnnycake—whatever, you can try it in a pan and then cook it with 5 to 6 parts water as a hearty "mush." Adding cornmeal to whole-wheat flour in a tempura batter imparts a delicious crunchiness. One further favorite form of this versatile grain is creamed corn.

You can make creamed corn by cutting off the kernels just far enough down to allow the milky, sugary liquid to flow. Pour in enough water or milk to cover, a dash of salt, and cook the mixture gently for a few minutes. Corn flour can also be used in small amounts in whole-grain pastes. There is a variety of Texas Deaf Smith County sweet corn which can be sprouted successfully until the sprout is about ½ inch in length.

The many virtues of *millet* are often overlooked because of its reputation as poor person's rice. Being the only grain that forms alkaline, millet is the most easily digestible. It is an intestinal lubricant. Its amino acid structure is well balanced, providing a low-gluten protein, and it is high in calcium, riboflavin, and lecithin.

Millet is cooked the same way as most grains, with 2 parts water or stock to 1 part grain. Preroasting releases a lovely aroma and adds texture to the cooked grain. Leftover cooked millet is a highly versatile stuffing for anything from hollowed-out zucchini tubes to mushroom caps.

Millet meal and millet flour are quality protein additions to any bread recipe. Millet meal also makes a good hot cereal and sprouted millet makes an excellent base for morning cereal; just harvest the sprout when the shoot is the same size as the grain.

Oats must be hulled before they can be eaten; after hulling they are cracked or rolled into the familiar cereal forms. Rolled oats are shot with steam for a number of seconds and then passed through rollers; thus some loss of nutrients will occur. Rolled oats will cook faster than whole oat groats, but whole oat groats are the most beneficial. Known variously as Irish oatmeal, Scotch oats, or steel-cut oats, whole oat groats are soaked overnight before being cooked as porridge. None of these or any other cereals or porridges should ever be prepared in a pressure cooker: they tend to clog the vent on the lid of the cooker. Whole oats are wonderful in soups and you can add both rolled and whole groats to breads and patties of all sorts.

Oat flour, available at most natural-food stores, can be used in equal proportions with whole-wheat flour to bake up a tasty batch of muffins. Oat sprouts can be used in soups, salads, and baked goods; just harvest the sprout when it is no longer than the groat.

When it comes to rice, we are talking about brown rice—whole-grain rice which, unlike white rice, has not had its bran, along with much of its nutrition, removed. Brown rice is available in short, medium, and long-grain varieties, the difference being largely esthetic. The shorter the grain, the more gluten, which means that short-grain rice cooks up stickier and long-grain comes out fluffier. There's even a sweet rice grain, the most glutinous of all. Excellent-quality long- and medium-grain brown rice comes from southeast Texas and Louisiana; this rice is hulled by a special process that protects the bran layers.

Rice is traditionally simmered, the proportions of water to grain being as follows: short grain 2½ to 1; medium-grain 2 to 1; long grain 1½ to 1. All three varieties take from 25 to 35 minutes to cook fully. When the grains are done, stir up those that are slightly scorched and mix with the others for a few minutes before serving.

For pressure cooking, the proportion of water to grain is different: short-grain 2 to 1; medium-grain 1½ to 1; long-grain 1¼ to 1. When the rice is cooked, allow the pressure to return slowly to normal. Some of the cooling steam will add moisture to the grain.

Brown rice is a versatile grain aside from its variety of lengths. Rice cream is made commercially by a dry radiant roasting method, after which the grain is stone ground to a consistency somewhat coarser than rice flour. You can prepare it as a porridge from the whole grain itself, or from prepacked rice-cream powder. Combine the rice with 4 cups of lightly salted boiling water and stir constantly over a low heat to prevent lumping. Rice flour is extensively used in baking, especially by those on gluten-restricted diets. Rice flakes make quick additions to soups or casserole bases when no leftovers are available.

The flaking process for grains and beans was originally developed to improve animal nutrition. The grains are cooked for 15 to 20 seconds under dry radiant heat and are then dropped onto rollers and flattened into whole-grain flakes. Since no wet methods of processing are used, there is no leaching or modifying of nutrients. And flaked grains and beans cook in half the usual time. You can add them to breads and casseroles for protein, texture, or taste. In chili, wheat flakes complete the protein of the bean.

A rice-based grain milk called *kokoh* is available prepacked at natural food outlets. This mixture of roasted and ground rice, sweet rice, soybeans, sesame seeds, and oatmeal is good as a morning cereal or tea.

One further point: be careful about your source of brown rice. Commercially produced rice is among the most heavily chemicalized food crops.

Rye is mostly known in its flour form, used in loaves often flavored with caraway seeds. Especially in its sprouted form, rye is rich in vitamin E, phosphorus, magnesium, and silicon. Like wheat sprouts, rye sprouts sweeten as they lengthen because the natural starches turn to sugar. For salad purposes, use the rye sprout when it's the same size as the grain; allow it to lengthen up to 1 inch for a sweeter intestinal cleansing sprout and for cooking. Rye can also be harvested as a grass and chewed for its juice.

The whole rye berry is a good grain, adding chewiness and nutritious value, to combine with rice (use about 1 part rye to 2 parts rice). Rye flakes can be added to soups and stews, or used as a cereal if soaked overnight. Rye flakes, like wheat and oat flakes, make good homemade granolas. Or you might prepare cream of rye, somewhat coarser in texture than rye flour, by using 4 parts water to 1 part grain and simmering it over a low heat for about 15 minutes.

Triticale, a highly nutritious grain with a relatively high protein content (approximately 17 percent) and a good balance of amino acids, can be cooked whole in combination with other grains, especially rice (2 parts water to 1 part triticale). Sprouted, it can be used in salads or breads; flaked, in granolas and casseroles. Triticale flour has become a favorite of vegetarians because of its unusual nutty sweetness and high protein content. As a flour it must be mixed with other flours containing higher gluten, since its own protein has a low gluten content.

In today's world, **whole wheat** holds possibly the most eminent position among the grains because of its versatility and high nutritive qualities. Containing anywhere from 6 to 20 percent protein, wheat is also a source of vitamin E and large amounts of nitrates. These nutrients are distributed throughout the three main parts of the wheat kernel, or berry. The outer layers of the kernel are known collectively as the bran; there is relatively little protein here, but it is of high quality and rich in the amino acid lysine. The dietary fiber of wheat bran is also the home of about 50 percent of the eleven B vitamins found in wheat, as well as the greater portion of the trace minerals zinc, copper, and iodine. Next comes the endosperm, the white starchy central mass of the wheat kernel, which contains some 70 percent of the kernel's total protein, as well as the calorie-providing starch. Finally, there is the small germ found at the base of the kernel which, in addition to containing the same B vitamins and trace minerals as the bran, is the home of vitamin E and the unsaturated fatty acids.

If you use the wheat berry in conjunction with other grains such as rice, you're getting the entire nutritive value of the grain. Try pan-roasting ⅓ cup wheat berries with ⅔ cup rice and then simmering them with 2 cups water for 25 to 30 minutes until both grains are tender. You can also eat whole wheat as wheat flakes, cracked wheat, bulgur, couscous, sprouts, and flours (both hard and pastry). The flaking process preserves most of the nutrients of the original form. Wheat flakes lend themselves especially well to chili dishes, where their addition to the beans provides a completed protein. If added dry to the chili about 20 minutes before serving, they will break down into tiny pieces which coax admiring remarks from even ardent chili con carne aficionados. Cracked wheat (simple coarse-ground wheat) is most often appreciated as a morning cereal cooked with about 3 cups salted water to 1 cup wheat; it is often added cooked or uncooked to breads and muffins.

Bulgur is a variety of whole-grain wheat which is parboiled, dried (often in the sun) and then coarsely cracked. This Near and Middle Eastern staple has found its way to America in a distinctive salad called taboulie. Bulgur does not require cooking but is simply reconstituted by spreading the grain inch-deep in a shallow pan and pouring enough boiling water over it to leave about half an inch of standing water; once the water is absorbed, stir the grain several times with a fork until it's cool. Bulgur can then be chilled, combined with greens such as parsley, fresh mint and watercress, and marinated in a dressing of sesame oil, lemon juice and tamari.

What is generally known as couscous is a form of soft, refined durum wheat flour ("semolina") which has been steamed, cracked and dried. It can be prepared simply by adding 1 cup of couscous to 2 cups of boiling salted water with a teaspoon of butter or margarine if desired, reducing the heat and stirring constantly until most of the moisture is gone. Remove the couscous from the heat and let it stand covered about 15 minutes, fluffing it up several times with a fork.

Wheat also makes an excellent sprout, containing substantially larger amounts of all the vitamins and minerals found in the dormant kernel. The sprout, which sweetens as it lengthens, can be used in desserts.

Whole-wheat flour can be made from hard (high-protein, high-gluten) or soft (lower-protein and -gluten, high-starch) wheat or from spring or winter wheats. Hard wheats are excellent for making bread. The spring wheat contains a higher gluten content than the winter wheat. Soft wheat, either spring or winter, is known as pastry wheat because it yields a fine, starchy flour. Wheat flours are available at natural-food outlets in many pasta forms—alphabets to ziti—often combined with other flours such as buckwheat, corn, rice, soy, and Jerusalem artichoke.

Standard white flour is purely endosperm, with all the bran and germ removed, which means a loss of up to 80 percent of the essential nutrients of wheat. In addition, white flour may be bleached by chlorine dioxide, which completely destroys the vitamin E. "Enriched" flours are actually attempts at making up for these losses; only four of the nutrients—compounds of thiamine, niacin, riboflavin (vitamin B_2), and iron—are replaced. Most unbleached white flour has had its bran and germ removed, but at least it has not been bleached. Soft-wheat pastry flour, which can be substituted for unbleached white flour in any recipe, is a nutritionally superior whole, unrefined flour.

The problem of rancidity with whole-grain flours is handled best by storing them in a cool dry place immediately after milling. Rancidity occurs when the unsaturated fats in the flour are exposed to the oxygen in the air. The vitamin E in whole-wheat flour acts as a natural preservative, but within three months it is exhausted and rancidity takes place. Fortunately, there are a growing number of small natural-food companies which mill and distribute their fresh-ground flour, and home grinding machines are now available at many natural food stores.

Wheat gluten (kofu in Japanese cookery) has long been a popular vegetarian source of protein in many places around the world. It is prepared by mixing whole-wheat flour and water in a 2½-to-1 ratio and kneading it into a stiff dough. This dough is then covered with cold water and kneaded underwater; as the water clouds up with starch sediment, replace it and repeat the procedure about five or six times more until the water remains clear. Then steam or cook the remaining gluten dough in a double boiler for 30 minutes. Kofu may be eaten as is, flavored with soy sauce, or baked in casserole loaves combined with other grains, such as rice and beans.

BEANS (LEGUMES)

The members of the bean family are important inexpensive sources of protein, minerals, and vitamins. Legumes can be cooked whole, flaked like grains, sprouted, ground into flours, even transformed into a variety of "dairy" products.

As a general rule, 1 cup of dry beans will make about 2½ cups of cooked beans, enough for 4 servings. Some beans should be soaked, preferably overnight; these include adzuki beans, black beans, chick-peas (garbanzos), and soybeans. As an alternative to overnight soaking, you can bring the beans (1 cup) and water (3 to 4 cups) to a boil, remove the pot from the stove and cover, let the beans sit for an hour, then cook the beans by simmering after first bringing them to a boil or in a pressure cooker.

When using the beans for a soup dish, allow five times as much water as beans at the beginning of the cooking process.

Don't salt the water until the beans are soft (or after the pressure in the cooker has come down), because the salt will draw the moisture out of the beans.

Adzuki are small red beans which have a special place in Japanese cuisine as well as in traditional Japanese medicine, where they are used as a remedy for kidney ailments (when combined with a small pumpkin called *hokkaido*). Very high in B vitamins and trace minerals, adzukis should never be pressure-cooked because it turns them bitter.

After overnight soaking, simmer your adzukis with a strip of kombu (a kind of kelp) about 1 to 1½ hours until tender, in 4 to 5 cups water to each cup of beans. One favorite preparation: add 1 cup each of sautéed onions and celery to the tender beans and then purée them together in a blender. The resulting thick, creamy soup can be thinned with water or bean juice and flavored with a dash of lime juice, tamari, and mild curry.

Black beans and their close relative, turtle beans, have served as major food sources in the Caribbean, Mexico, and the American Southwest for many years. These beans should not be prepared in a pressure cooker since their skins fall off easily and may clog the valve. The Cubans achieve a smooth, rich black bean soup by cooking the soaked beans until tender, adding sautéed garlic, onions, and celery, and pressing the mixture through a colander (or, more easily, whizzing it in an electric blender). A small amount of lime juice may be added to lighten the taste.

Black-eyed peas, a Southern favorite, provide a delicious complete protein-balanced meal. Among the quickest-cooking of the beans, they become tender in 45 minutes to an hour. Eating this bean on New Year's Day is said to bring good luck throughout the year.

Chick-peas, or garbanzos, are so versatile that they have been the subject of entire cookbooks. High in protein, they are also good sources of calcium, iron, potassium, and B vitamins. They can be roasted, like peanuts, or boiled. After a very thorough roasting, chick-peas can even be ground and used as a coffee substitute. The preparation of chick-peas called hummus is a thick paste which combines mashed chick-peas, hulled sesame-seed tahini, garlic, and lemon juice. Bean pâtés using chick-peas as a base offer many creative opportunities for complete protein combining. Cooked grains, ground seeds and nuts, raw vegetables, herbs, and miso may all be combined with the cooked beans to produce a sophisticated, appealing pâté or paste.

Great northern beans and their small counterpart, **navy beans,** cook in less than an hour and require no presoaking. They are often used for hearty soups: cook the beans with 5 to 6 parts water or stock to 1 part dry beans. Firmer vegetables, such as carrots, rutabagas, or turnips should be added ½ hour before the soup is finished; other vegetables, such as onions, celery, and peppers, should be added 15 minutes later, either sautéed or raw.

Kidney beans, standard to all sorts of chilis, will cook in about an hour, after having been soaked for an hour. The fragrant brown bean juice produced in the cooking of the beans makes the addition of tomato actually unnecessary. Once the beans are tender, try dicing onions, garlic, and red and green peppers; sauté them lightly in sesame oil until the onions are translucent, then add them to the beans. Season to taste means just that, but rich Mexican chili powder seems to lend more flavor to the beans than does a scorching Indian one. Tamari, a dash of blackstrap molasses, fresh-grated ginger root—all can further enhance the beans. For a perfect final texture, add dry wheat flakes to the chili about 20 minutes before serving; this allows time for the flakes to cook and to fall apart, thickening the dish and complementing the protein of the beans.

Lentils come in a rainbow of colors, but generally only the green or brown and the red varieties are known in the United States. All of the varieties are inexpensive and nutritious sources of iron, cellulose, and B vitamins. Lentils require no presoaking and fall apart when cooked, leaving a smooth base to which you can add any number of fresh or sautéed vegetables (carrots, turnips, onions, and peppers lending themselves well). Lentils make very reliable sprouts which sprout well in combination with other seeds and produce large quantities. The uncooked flavor of the sprout is similar to that of fresh ground pepper on salad; when cooked it has a more nutlike taste. The sprouts should be harvested when the shoot is no longer than the seed.

Mung beans are probably best known in their sprout form, eaten raw or lightly sautéed with other vegetables. They can be cooked as a dry bean, using three times as much water as beans, and then puréed in an electric blender into a smooth soup. The result is rather bland and benefits from the addition of tamari and fresh or dried basil. But as sprouts, mung beans really come into their own. Mung sprouts are rich in vitamins A and C and contain high amounts of calcium, phosphorus, and iron, and the hulls are easily digestible and rich in minerals. Mung sprouts can be harvested anytime from the second day, when the shoot has just appeared, to the third or fourth day when the shoot is about 4 inches long. The beans make a good first choice for beginning sprouters.

Peanuts, though commonly grouped with seeds and nuts, are actually a member of the legume family. Their high protein content is well known, and in the United States eating peanut butter is virtually a national pastime. Peanut butter can—and should—contain 100 percent peanuts; sugars, colorings, stabilizers and preservatives are neither necessary or desirable. A single grinding under pressure extracts enough oil from the nut meal to give the peanuts a creamy texture.

Pinto beans are popular in American Southwest dishes and lend themselves especially well to baking. Naturally sweet in flavor, they adapt to many types of seasonings and, once cooked tender, can be used in casseroles. Pinto flakes cook quickly and reconstitute themselves into tender round beans in about 40 minutes (2 parts water to 1 part dry flakes). Cumin is a seasoning which blends nicely with these beans, if used sparingly.

Soybeans, unquestionably the most nutritious of all the beans, have been the major source of protein in Oriental diets for centuries. Soybeans are increasingly being viewed as the most realistic source of high-quality, low-cost protein available today on a large enough scale to meet worldwide human needs. In addition to high-quality protein, soybeans contain large amounts of the B vitamins, minerals, and unsaturated fatty acids in the form of lecithin that help the body emulsify cholesterol.

Thanks to their bland flavor after cooking and their high concentration of nutrients, soybeans can be made into an amazing array of foods. Western technology in recent years has focused upon creating a wide range of new synthetic soybean foods. There are protein concentrates in the form of soy powder containing from 70 to 90 percent moisture-free protein, isolates (defatted flakes and flours used to make simulated dairy products and frozen desserts), spun protein fibers (isolates dissolved in alkali solutions for use in simulated meat items), and textured vegetable proteins (made from soy flour and used in simulated meat products and infant foods). Most Western cooks have also come across soybeans in the form of full-fat soy flour, soy granules, and defatted soy flour and grits—all of which are available in natural-food stores. Full fat soy flour contains about 40 percent protein and 20 percent naturally occurring oils, makes a fine addition to many forms of baked goods. Soy granules contain about 50 percent protein, as do defatted soy flour and soy grits, which are basically by-products from the extraction of soy oil. Both of these are used in breakfast cereals, simulated meats, and desserts. Soybeans are also processed into flakes which, unlike raw soybeans, require no presoaking and only about 1½ hours of cooking.

In striking contrast to these highly refined products of the

West are the traditional East Asian products, tamari soy sauce, miso (fermented soy paste), and tofu. The first two fermented products will be discussed later. Tofu (soy curd or soy cheese) is a truly remarkable food. It is very inexpensive when purchased at Oriental markets or natural food shops and even more so if made at home.

You can make your own tofu by grinding soaked soybeans, cooking them with water, pouring the resulting mixture into a pressing sack, and collecting the soy "milk" underneath by squeezing as much liquid as possible from the sack, leaving the bean fiber behind. The soy milk is then simmered and curdled in a solution containing sea-water brine (called *nigari*), lemon juice, or vinegar. Any of these three solidifiers will work well, although commercial nigari is most often used for this coagulation process.

After the white soy curds curdle and float in a yellowish whey liquid, they are ladeled into a settling box, covered and weighted, and allowed to press into a solid cake which is then ready for immediate use as is—or for further transformation into a virtually unlimited variety of tofu products.

Tofu is high in quality protein and is excellent to use in combining protein, especially with grains. Tofu contains an abundance of lysine, an essential amino acid which many grains are deficient in; on the other hand, grains such as rice are high in the sulfur that contains methionine and cystine, amino acids which are absent in soybeans. These soy and grain proteins complement each other naturally.

Tofu is easy to digest, and low in calories, saturated fats, and cholesterol. When solidified with calcium chloride or calcium sulfate—as in most commercial American tofu—tofu contains more calcium by weight than dairy milk; it's also a good source of other minerals such as iron, phosphorus, and potassium. Since it's made from soybeans, tofu is free of chemical toxins.

Soybeans are an important feed crop for the beef and dairy

industries and the spraying of them is carefully monitored by the Food and Drug Administration.

In addition to tofu, the soybean can be enjoyed in many other ways. It's delicious when served as a fresh green summer vegetable, simmered or steamed in the pod. Roasted soybeans are now available in many varieties: dry-roasted, oil-roasted, salted, unsalted and with garlic or barbecue flavors. They contain up to 47 percent protein and can either be eaten as a snack or added to casseroles for texture.

When you cook whole dry soybeans, a pressure cooker can save you a great deal of time. Use 2½ to 3 cups of water over a low flame for each cup of dry soybeans. Once pressure has been reached, cook until tender—about 90 minutes. Before cooking soybeans by the ordinary simmering method, soak them overnight in 4 cups of water. Bring them to a boil in 4 more cups of liquid and simmer about 3 hours, adding more water whenever necessary.

A very interesting soybean preparation called *tempeh* is made from cooked dehulled soybean halves, to which a *Rhizopus* mold is introduced. The inoculated bean cakes are then fermented overnight, during which time the white mycelium mold partially digests the beans and effectively deactivates the trypsin enzyme, which could inhibit digestion. The soybeans have, by this time, become fragrant cakes bound together by the mold; you can either deep-fry or bake them into a dish which tastes remarkably like veal or chicken. Tempeh is rich in protein (from 18 to 48 percent) and highly digestible. In addition, like the other fermented soy products and sea vegetables, it is one of the few nonmeat sources of vitamin B_{12}. Tempeh can be made easily in any kitchen. The tempeh starter (*Rhizopus oligosporus* mold spores) is available from the Department of Agriculture, complete with an enthusiastic brochure.

A further use of this "queen of the beans" is as a sprout. Significant amounts of vitamin C, not found in the dried bean, are released in the sprouts, which are also rich in vitamins A, E, and the B complex, as well as minerals. The yellow soybean does well for sprouting, and the black variety can also be quite prolific. Rinse the sprouts two to three times a day and harvest them when the shoot is from ¼ to 1½ inches long. You may or may not prefer to remove the outer husk before using the sprout; it's simply a matter of taste. Steaming or boiling the soybean sprouts lightly before eating them will destroy the urease and antitrypsin enzymes that interfere with digestion. The sprouts can be ground and used in sandwiches and salad dressings, and they make a fine addition to any sauté of crisp Chinese-style vegetables.

Split peas, both green and yellow, make a simple soup full of protein and minerals. They do not require soaking. Start with 1 part dry peas and 5 to 6 cups water and cook quickly in about 45 minutes. Once the peas are cooked, the soup will continue to thicken; this leftover paste can be diluted several times in the following days for a quick hot soup. Sautéed onions, tamari, and ½ stick of soy margarine complete the soup.

NUTS AND SEEDS

Seeds and nuts are fine sources of protein, minerals (especially magnesium), some B vitamins, and unsaturated fatty acids. They can be eaten simply as a snack food or used with other foods to add interesting flavors, textures, and nutrition.

A general sprouting procedure for seeds and nuts: soak the dried seeds for about 8 hours (approximately 4 parts water to 1 part seed). Don't throw away the soaking water; use it as a cooking liquid, or water your houseplants with it. Rinse the seeds with cool water and place them in a sprouter.

Basically, the factors necessary for a successful sprouting are keeping the sprouts moist but never soaked, keeping them moderately warm, rinsing them as often as possible, and giving them enough room so that air can freely circulate around them. Actually, only about 5 minutes a day is needed for growing a successful sprout garden. Use the sprouts as soon as possible. They have a refrigerator life of 7 to 10 days. Sprouts can also be dried easily for use in beverages, nut butters, and spreads. Place the sprouts on cookie sheets for a few hours in a warm room, or keep them in a warm oven until they're dry. Then grind them in a blender and store this nutritious food concentrate in a jar and refrigerate.

Many people think of **alfalfa** as a barnyard grass, which it is. Because its roots penetrate deep underground to seek out all the elements it craves, alfalfa is one of the best possible fodders. But the fresh mineral-laden leaves of this plant are especially nutritious for humans when juiced. Alfalfa seeds purchased at a natural-food outlet may seem expensive, but a few of them go a long way—½ teaspoon of dry seeds yields an entire trayful of sprouts. The sprouts have a light sweet taste and are particularly rich in vitamin C, as well as in chlorophyll (when allowed to develop in light). They also have high mineral value, containing phosphorus, chlorine, silicon, aluminum, calcium, magnesium, sulfur, sodium, and potassium. Alfalfa seeds sprout well in combination with other seeds and have a high germination rate. They can also be used when dried.

Almonds will sprout only from the fresh unhulled nut after soaking overnight; they must be kept very moist until their sprouts reach a length of about 1 inch (4 days). They can be used to make almond milk: a combination of 1 cup of almond sprouts (or merely almonds soaked overnight) blended with 4 times as much water or apple juice. Almonds, which have an exceptionally high mineral content, are delicious raw or roasted with tamari. The raw nut can be sliced, slivered, or chopped in various ways, and can even be ground into almond butter.

Brazil nuts, like the other seeds and nuts, have a high fat content. But because they are also high in protein, they are actually not much higher in calories per gram of usable protein than are whole grains. Brazil nuts also offer unusually high amounts of the sulfur-containing amino acids. For this reason, you can serve them to good advantage as a chopped garnish for fresh vegetables, such as brussels sprouts, cauliflower, green peas, and lima beans. These vegetables are all deficient in the sulfur-containing amino acids but strong in the amino acid isoleucine which is lacking in Brazil nuts.

Cashews are another popular nut which can be added to many dishes. Use them as a layer in a casserole, or simply roast them lightly and toss them in a bowl of steamed snow peas. Cashew butter, from both raw and roasted nuts, is fast growing in popularity and is well suited for use in sauces, where it can be diluted with water and miso paste. You can mix yourself a nutritious soy "milkshake": blend 2 cups of plain or sweetened soy milk with ½ cup of cashew butter; add 2 tablespoons of carob powder, a pinch of salt, and a dash each of vanilla extract and nutmeg.

Chia seeds, now available in natural-food stores, have long been a staple of Mexican and American Indians, who used them to increase their endurance on long hunts and migrations. Though a member of the mint family, chia seeds have a mild flaxlike taste. They can be chewed raw or sprinkled into hot or cold cereals. Since they are among the mucilaginous seeds, which become sticky when soaked in water, their sprouting procedure is slightly different. Sprinkle the seeds over a saucer filled with water and allow to stand overnight. By morning, the seeds, having absorbed all the water, will be stuck to the saucer. Gently rinse and drain them, using a sieve if possible. Then, as with other seeds, rinse twice daily. Also try sprouting the seeds in a flat covered container lined with damp paper towels. Harvest the chia seeds when the shoot is 1 inch in length.

Clover, the red variety, makes a delicious sprout similar in taste to alfalfa. In its sprout form, this forage plant can be an excellent source of chlorophyll; when the primary leaves are about 1 inch in length, spread them out on a nonmetallic tray and dampen them. They should be covered with clear plastic to hold in the moisture and placed in a sunny spot for 1 to 2 hours.

Cress seeds are tiny members of the mustard family which add a zesty taste to salads when used in their sprout form. They are mucilaginous seeds and are sprouted as such (see chia). Harvest the sprouts at about 1 inch in length and use them in sandwiches instead of lettuce.

Fenugreek seeds were first used to brew tea in the Hellenic world. This strong tea is an excellent gargle, as well as a tasty and nutritious addition to soy or nut milk. The ground dry seed is one of the components of curry powder. When sprouted, fenugreek can be added to soups, salads, and grain dishes. The sprout should be harvested once it is ¼ inch long, for it will soon become very bitter.

Filberts, or **Hazelnuts,** are tasty nuts which, once chopped, make a delicious garnish for both greens and creamy tofu pudding. These nuts, however, contain too many calories for the amount of protein they provide.

Flax, also known as **linseed,** is a versatile plant. The fiber of the mature plant is used to make linen and pressed to extract its oil. As a sprout, flax has been used for centuries; it is recorded that at Greek and Roman banquets, flax sprouts were served between courses for their mild laxative effect. Though flax is sprouted as a mucilaginous seed, it sprouts very well in conjunction with wheat and rye kernels. Harvest when the shoots are about 1 inch in length and serve as a breakfast salad. Taken on an empty stomach, this sprout mixture cleanses and lubricates the colon.

Mustard. The small seeds of common black mustard will sprout quite readily and are usually available at herb and spice stores. Small amounts of these sprouts add a spicy flavor to salads and sandwiches. Harvest when the shoots are about 1 inch long.

Pecans are well-known nuts which are cultivated organically in Texas and New Mexico. Pecans, though high in potassium and B vitamins, are not good sources of protein; like filberts, they contain too many calories for the amount of protein consumed. Pecans are delicious as tamari-roasted nuts: dry-roast in a heavy skillet and, when they begin to emit a lovely fragrance, remove to a plate and sprinkle lightly with tamari.

Pignolias, or pine nuts, have an unusual flavor, but are a poor source of protein. Pignolias, found in the cones of the small piñon pine which grows in the American Southwest, have been used by many Indian tribes as a food staple. Most of the pignolias consumed in the United States, however, come from Portugal. Pan-roasted pine nuts are delicious with green vegetables such as peas and beans, and are also tasty in bread stuffings.

Pistachio nuts are familiar to many as an Italian ice-cream flavor. For snacking purposes, use the naturally grown pistachio rather than the dyed varieties. Like other nuts, pistachios should be consumed only in small quantities.

Pumpkin seeds, pepitas, and **squash seeds** are delicious seeds rich in minerals, and can be eaten as snacks or ground into a meal for use in baking and cooking. Eastern Europeans, who eat many more pumpkin seeds than do Americans, use them as a specific to prevent prostate disorders. Save the seeds from a pumpkin or squash and sprout them. Harvest when the shoot is just beginning to show (after 3 or 4 days); if allowed to lengthen any further, the sprouts will taste bitter.

Radish seeds, both black and red, make wonderfully tangy sprouts. They sprout easily and work well combined with alfalfa and clover seeds. They're relatively expensive compared to most sprouting seeds, but you don't need many of these peppery-tasting sprouts to perk up a salad. Harvest these shoots when they're about 1 inch long.

Sesame seeds, or benne, are popular around the world because of their taste and high nutritive content. Most sesame seeds available in the United States are grown in southern Mexico, where few sprays are used, and they are available hulled or unhulled. The unhulled variety is nutritionally superior since most of the mineral content is found in the hull. The seeds are an excellent source of protein, unsaturated fatty acids, calcium, magnesium, niacin, and vitamins A and E. The protein in sesame seeds effectively complements the protein of legumes, because both contain high amounts of each other's deficient amino acids. Therefore, an especially good addition to a soy-milk shake is tahini, or sesame butter.

Used extensively as the whole seed in breads and other baked food, in grain dishes, and on vegetables, the unhulled seeds can also be toasted and ground into sesame butter, which has a stronger taste and higher mineral content than sesame tahini. Tahini, made from toasted and hulled seeds, is a mild sweet butter. Tahini is used extensively in the Middle East, where the oil that separates from the butter is used as a cooking oil. Tahini is an excellent base for salad dressing and acts as a perfect thickener for all sorts of sauces.

The unhulled seed must of course be used when sprouting. The sprouts can be used, like the whole seed, in cooked food or blended into beverages. Harvest when the shoot reaches $1/16$ inch in length (usually within 2 days). At this stage, the sprouts are sweet, but become bitter with further growth.

Sunflower seeds are sun-energized nutritional powerhouses rich in protein (about 30 percent), unsaturated fatty acids, phosphorus, calcium, iron, fluorine, iodine, potassium, magnesium, zinc, several B vitamins, vitamin E, and vitamin D (one of the few vegetable sources). The high mineral content is the result of the sunflower's extensive root system, which penetrates deep into the subsoil seeking nutrients; the vitamin D is partially due to the flower's tendency to follow and face the sun as it moves across the sky.

Sunflowers were cultivated extensively by American Indians as a food crop. In their raw state, sunflower seeds can be enjoyed as snacks or included in everything from breads to salads. The seeds are also available from Erewhon in the form of a toasted, salted nut butter.

Sprouted sunflower seeds should be eaten when barely budded or they will taste very bitter. However, it usually takes 4 to 5 days for the shoot to appear. Unhulled seeds, or special hulled sprouting seeds, are used when sprouting, but the husk should be removed before eating.

Walnuts are a good source of protein and iron. Black walnuts contain about 40 percent more protein than English walnuts (also known as California walnuts in the United States). Walnuts will keep fresh much longer when purchased in the shell. This is true of all nuts and will also bring down the price considerably.

11

OTHER FOODS AND FLAVORINGS

SEAWEEDS

SEAWEEDS RANK HIGH AS SOURCES FOR THE BASIC ESSENTIAL minerals, as do green vegetables such as dandelion and watercress. All of these contain calcium, magnesium, phosphorus, potassium, iron, iodine, and sodium. Most Westerners dislike the idea of eating seaweed. If they were to sample what they're missing, though, they'd find a new world of taste and high-quality nutrients—especially trace minerals—in the six varieties of sea vegetables available in most natural food stores and food co-ops.

Agar, or **agar-agar** (called *kantan* in Japanese, also known as Ceylonese moss) is a translucent, almost weightless seaweed product found in stick, flake, or powder form. It is used like gelatin to thicken fruit juices or purées. Agar can also be used to make aspics and clear molds of fruit juices or of fruits or vegetables. One to 1½ sticks torn into small pieces and dissolved in one quart of liquid produce a puddinglike consistency, and more agar can be used for a jellied texture. When used in stick form, agar should be simmered in the liquid for 10 to 15 minutes, to ensure that all the pieces have dissolved. This simmering isn't necessary when using the flaked or powdered varieties.

Dulse is the only commercial sea vegetable which comes from the Atlantic Ocean (specifically, the Maritime Provinces of Canada). This ready-to-eat seaweed can be chewed in its tough dry state, but a short soaking to rinse it and to remove any small clinging shells is worthwhile. Dulse can be added to a miso soup.

Another Japanese seaweed is the jet-black **hiziki,** or Hijiki. This stringy, hairlike seaweed contains 57 percent more calcium by weight than dry milk, and has high levels of iron. Dried hiziki should be soaked in several cups of water for about 20 minutes, then strained in a colander and lightly pressed to squeeze out excess moisture. Once reconstituted, hiziki is best when sautéed together with other vegetables— especially onion and leeks—or cooked with beans and grains.

Kombu is the Japanese term for several species of brown algae. In English, these are usually referred to collectively as kelp. Kombu is especially rich in iodine, vitamin B_2, and calcium. When using the dried form of kombu, rinse it once and soak for 10 to 15 minutes. Note that all dried seaweeds increase greatly in size when reconstituted. For example, ¼ cup of dried hiziki would yield 1 cup when soaked. Save the water in which the seaweeds are soaked and use it as soup stock. Reconstituted kombu strips can be used whole in the cooking water for beans and grains, or can be cut into thin strips or diced for use in soups or salads.

Nori is the most popular Japanese seaweed, also known as dried purple laver. It's sold in the form of paper-thin purplish sheets, with 8 to 10 sheets per package. **Laver** has been used as a food by many peoples—including the American Pacific Coast Indians. The Japanese and Koreans are, however, the only people to cultivate these plants and dry and press their mature leaves into sheets. The nori sheets are toasted over a flame until crisp, during which time their color changes from black or purple to green. They are then crumbled or slivered and used as a condiment for noodles, grains, beans, and soups. Remarkably rich in protein, nori is also high in vitamins A, B_2, B_{12}, D, and niacin.

Wakame is a long seaweed with symmetrical and fluted fronds growing from both sides of an edible midrib. Although generally used fresh in Japan, it is only available dried in the West. It is reconstituted in the same manner as kombu: rinsed once, soaked, and pressed of excess moisture. If the midrib is particularly tough, it can be removed. When used in soups, wakame should be cooked no longer than several minutes and should therefore be one of the last ingredients added to miso soup. This delicious vegetable is rich in protein and niacin, and contains in its dried state almost 50 percent more calcium than dry milk.

FRUITS

Fruits are the culmination of a plant's energies in nature; they are enchanting foods with the full spectrum of delightful flavors, aromas, and colors. Although they are not particularly rich in protein—the chief exception being avocadoes and olives—they are packed with natural sugars, minerals, and vitamins.

The best way to enjoy their considerable pleasures is to make an entire meal of fruits alone, as their acids and sugars do not combine well with either protein or starch foods. Nor do the oils in avocadoes and olives combine well with protein. You risk digestive trouble by eating fruit along with most other foods, the chief exception being protein nuts, though not starchy ones such as coconuts or chestnuts. Not all fruits should be included in the same meal: very sweet fruits such as bananas, raisins, dates, figs, and prunes should not be eaten with highly acidic fruits such as oranges, pineapple, grapefruit, and strawberries. High-protein avocadoes, however, do combine well with acid fruits; an interesting salad would combine avocado slices with sections of grapefruits, oranges, and tangerines. Fruits are best—in season when possible and without added sweetener—as a snack, breakfast, or entire meal. It is not a good idea to drink large quantities of fruit juices between other meals; this can upset your digestive processes. Melons—cantaloupe, honeydew, crenshaw, watermelon, casaba, etc.—are best enjoyed alone since, as one of the simplest foods to digest, they proceed directly to the intestine and would quickly start to decompose and ferment if held up in the stomach by other foods being assimilated there.

Dried fruits are deceptively potent foods and should be eaten in moderate amounts. When selecting dried fruits, seek out untreated, unsulfured, and organically grown fruits whenever possible. Concentrated dried fruits contain concentrated amounts of whatever chemicals were used to grow and process them commercially. It is common knowledge among fruit growers that commercial raisins are one of the most adulterated crops, poisoned with some eighty pesticides and a fumigant called methyl bromide. Naturally grown fruit crops are not subjected to pesticides or artificial fertilizers and are either dried slowly in large dehydrators or by the sun. Once dried, the fruit is often rehydrated with steam to obtain the desired moisture content. Though naturally dried fruit appears drier than most commercial varieties, it is almost always more flavorful. Some dried fruits—notably pineapple, papaya, peaches, and pears—are "honey dipped." This is an unnecessary practice; the foods selected for this treatment are very sweet naturally. There are many types of dried fruits available in natural-food stores, from familiar varieties to bananas, cherries, and mangoes. If you feel a yen for fruit in the wintertime when not much is in season locally, a compote of dried fruits might be the solution.

Prunes are a favorite for stewed fruit compotes, but dried apples, apricots, peaches, pears, raisins, currants, and cherries can also be added. Soak the fruit for 15 to 20 minutes, until soft enough to be cut into smaller pieces. Place them in a saucepan, cover with several inches of water, bring the mixture to a boil, and simmer until the fruit is soft. Apricots and apples will cook the quickest; peaches, prunes, and pears will take about 20 to 30 minutes. During the cooking, you can add a few teaspoons of fresh grated lemon rind and sprinkles of cinnamon, dried or fresh ginger, cloves, and allspice. Fresh apple slices could also be cooked along with the dried fruit. The longer the mixture is simmered, the more homogenous it becomes, with all the fruit flavors blending into one exotic taste.

You can also make a compote of fresh fruit which is no longer perfectly fresh but not yet moldy or sour. Trim out any bad parts, wash and slice up the fruit and simmer it in a saucepan as you would dried fruit. If you want, add a few pieces of dried fruit for extra sweetness and if necessary, thicken the mixture with a little kuzu dissolved first in cold water.

FERMENTED FOODS:
MISO AND TAMARI

Miso and tamari, derived from soybeans and grain, deserve special consideration in any sensible vegetarian diet.

The fermentation process in the healthy human intestine isn't that different from what occurs in the production of fermented soy food. For example, maltose and glucose are broken down to form lactic acid, ethyl alcohol, and organic acids. The microorganic cultures responsible for these syntheses enter our own bodies when we digest them in fermented foods and help us to assimilate the nutrients we need.

Miso, a fermented soybean paste, has long been a staple seasoning in the Oriental kitchen. It is produced by combining cooked soybeans, salt, and various grains. Barley miso is made with barley and soybeans. Rice miso is made with both hulled and unhulled rice plus soybeans, and soybeans alone are used to make hatcho miso. These cooked and salted combinations are dusted with a fungus mold, *koji*, which produces the enzymes that start to digest the bean-and-grain mixture.

Tamari is a naturally fermented soy sauce. Originally considered excess liquid, it was drained off miso that had finished fermenting. Today it is a product in its own right and is made from a natural fermentation process of whole soybeans, natural sea salt, well water, roasted cracked wheat, and koji spores, all aged for twelve to eighteen months. Miso, like tamari, has a range of colors, textures, and aromas as wide and varied as that of wines and cheeses.

Miso and tamari contain between 9 and 18 percent complete protein; the higher the soybean content, the higher the protein. The protein in these products is "predigested": it is broken down into seventeen amino acids, which makes for easy digestion. Also, the digestion-inhibiting enzyme present in raw or poorly cooked soybeans is destroyed by fermentation. During the microorganic synthesis of these foods, the amounts of the B vitamins riboflavin and niacin are increased. In addition, miso and tamari are among the few vegetable sources of vitamin B_{12}, which is actually manufactured by the fungi and bacteria in the fermenting mixtures just as it is synthesized in the human intestine.

Miso and tamari are useful in all cuisines, but because of their high salt content—11 percent for the saltiest of hatcho miso and 18 percent for tamari—they should be used sparingly. Too much sodium is unhealthy for people with high blood pressure. Miso diluted with water can be used as a base for a sauce together with tahini; a dash of tamari brings out new flavors in familiar grains. Miso also makes a wonderful soup base, to which you can add tofu, mushrooms, seaweeds, and many fresh or cooked vegetables.

All of the natural miso and tamari available in the United States today comes from Japan. If the package of miso you purchase has started to expand, you can be assured that its contents have not been pasteurized and that the microorganisms are still alive and producing carbon dioxide gas.

In the coming years, the United States may begin production of its own fermented soybean foods. A lively market now exists and many people are acquiring the necessary technical know-how. Organic farmers are already producing the soybeans, wheat, barley and rice; the koji starter and engineering skills are always available from the Orient. As fermented soy foods play a larger role in American diets, we can start to develop and adapt our own distinctive varieties.

SALT: SOME ALTERNATIVE SOURCES

There seems to be some controversy these days about the virtues and dangers of salt. Some people consume large quantities of salt. Many others attempt to get their salt from the juices of celery, spinach, beets, or carrots; very little sodium, however, is derived from these supposedly sodium-rich foods. Still other people decide upon, or are prescribed, low-sodium or even "salt-free" diets. Those on low-sodium diets are often suffering from hypertension or kidney problems. Overconsumption of salt will lead to hypertension: the salt draws water out of blood cells and vessels, which in turn causes dehydration of the tissues and forces the heart to pump much too strenuously. Overconsumption of salt also clogs the kidneys and creates an excess of water which cannot be eliminated from the body.

On the other hand, moderate and intelligent consumption of salt helps the body retain heat by slightly contracting the blood vessels, which is why we tend to consume more salt in cold months. Sodium also helps maintain intestinal muscle tone. You should evaluate your own salt needs according to your physical activity, climate, water intake, and—above all —diet. People in meat-eating cultures seldom need salt per se, because they get all they need from the blood and flesh of the animals they eat; vegetarian or agricultural peoples, however, regard salt very highly and use it to cook, pickle, and preserve foods.

If you want to eat salt, though, you should use the natural sun- or kiln-dried variety which still contains trace minerals. Refined "table" salt is made fine by high heats and flash-cooling, and then combined with such additives as sodium silico aluminate to keep it "free-flowing." Kosher salt is an exception; it has larger crystals due to its milder processing, and there are no additives in the better brands. Natural salt—rock salt or sea salt—is not free-flowing, but some brands add calcium carbonate, a natural compound, to prevent caking. Incidentally, all salt is or once was sea salt, so the differences between salt obtained from inland rock deposits or from the sea are minor.

No natural salt contains iodine, which is far too volatile a substance to remain stable in salt without numerous additives. But there is an excellent source of iodine derived from the ocean: sea vegetables, the most common being kelp. These contain a natural, sugar-stabilized iodine—as well as about 4 to 8 percent salt. They are harvested, roasted, ground up, and marketed as salt alternatives.

Another healthful way of adding salt to your diet is to use sesame salt, sold as gomasio. This versatile condiment can be used in place of ordinary salt on cooked greens, grains, and raw salads. Gomasio can be purchased in most natural food stores, but the serious cook should grind his or her own at least once.

The ridged ceramic grinding bowl called a suribachi is needed to make sesame salt. A proportion of 15 parts sesame seeds (unhulled) to 1 part salt is recommended by Lima Ohsawa in her beautiful cookbook *The Art of Just Cooking*. She also suggests that this should be adjusted to fit the individual and the climate and advises a milder salt content for children. Start with 1 cup of sesame seeds, wash them in a fine strainer, and set aside to drain. Roast 1 level teaspoon of salt in a heavy skillet until the strong odor of chlorine is no longer released; then transfer the salt to the suribachi and pulverize it with the wooden pestle. Then roast the drained sesame seeds in the skillet over moderate heat, constantly stirring until they are light brown in color and release their characteristic aroma. Transfer these browned seeds to the suribachi and grind lightly with the salt until about 80 percent of the seeds are crushed. Store the mixture until needed in an airtight container. The making of such a versatile condiment as gomasio is a beautiful ritual well worth the effort.

Another alternative is salted umeboshi plums. These small Japanese plums are known for their high quality and quantity of citric acid. The citric acid in plums allegedly helps neutralize and eliminate some of the excess lactic acid in the body, helping to restore a natural balance. An excess of lactic acid in the body is caused by excessive consumption of sugar; if not converted to body energy, the sugar turns into lactic acid and combines with protein to cause ailments such as headaches, fatigue, and high blood pressure.

In Japan, these organically grown plums are available in a variety of preservative-free forms—from concentrates to salted plums. In most American natural-food stores, only the salted plums are available; these are a potent alkaline source, which is excellent for indigestion, colds, and fatigue. Umeboshi also has many culinary uses. Use them to salt the water in which grains will be cooked or use several in tofu salad dressings instead of tamari or sea salt.

SWEETENERS

Carbohydrate sugar is unquestionably essential to life, but obtain it in as unadulterated a form as possible. Common table sugar has been processed to 99.9 percent sucrose, devoid of the vitamins and minerals found in sugarcane or sugar beets. This refined sucrose taxes the body's digestive system and depletes its store of minerals and enzymes as the sugar is metabolized. For this reason and others, white sugar has earned a bad reputation and the label of "empty food."

In the carbohydrate category of nutrients there are many sugars. The best known is **sucrose,** or white table sugar, which breaks down in the body into the simpler sugars glucose and fructose. There are also starches found in the whole cereals (together with their own component enzymes, vitamins, minerals, and proteins) which break down uniformly in the body into simple glucose molecules once they have been cooked, chewed, and digested. Compared with these unrefined starches, refined sugars show their tendency to overstrain the body's digestive system. Therefore, it would seem wiser to get the sugars you need from the abundant natural stores in cereals, vegetables, and fruits. Eaten in moderate amounts, starches are not fattening, contrary to public opinion. In fact, according to Dr. Alfred Meiss, "the body's adaptation to starch is nearly perfect" since starch is the "biochemically most efficient" carbohydrate. Whereas "sucrose makes it harder for the body to produce energy over the long run."

When cooking with natural foods, you should simply replace the refined sugars with the richer flavors of naturally occurring sugars. **Maple syrup,** for example, or honey or fruit juice can substitute for sugar in almost any home recipe. Maple sugar is expensive and very sweet, so use it in moderation. Use ½ cup of maple syrup instead of 1 cup of sugar and either reduce the other liquids or increase the dry ingredients accordingly. Maple syrup has been noted by some authorities as a source of the trace mineral zinc. Be sure that the maple syrup you purchase has not been extracted with formaldehyde.

All **honeys** are basically the fruit sugar fructose, comprising varying amounts of dextrose, levulose, maltose, and other simple sugars. The flavor of honey—a wide variety from buckwheat to tupelo blossoms—depends on the source of the bees' nectar. All the honey you use should be unheated and unfiltered so that the natural enzymes and vitamins are still intact. When cooking with honey in a recipe originally calling for refined sugar, divide the amount of sugar called for in half and adjust the recipe with less liquid or more dry ingredients. Actually, not too much sugar of *any* kind should be used in cooking or baking, because heat can be destructive to protein in the presence of sugar. This is especially true when using honey or a refined glucose such as corn syrup. Try using fruit juices or purées made from soaked dried fruits to sweeten dishes; a little of these natural sugars will go a long way.

Granulated date sugar, available in many natural-food stores, is indispensable when your recipe specifically calls for a granulated dry sugar. This sugar has the distinctive flavor of whole dry dates. Another dry sweetener is **carob,** or St.-John's-bread. This powder comes from the dried pods of the carob tree and can be purchased roasted or unroasted. Use the unroasted variety and toast it yourself for a fresher taste. In addition to its natural sugars, carob is rich in trace minerals and low in fats. Not much of this strong sweetener is necessary; either mix with the dry ingredients or dissolve in a little water or soy milk before adding to the other liquids. Carob is also available as a syrup. If you are using carob as a substitute for cocoa or chocolate, the equivalent of 1 square of chocolate is 3 tablespoons of carob plus 2 tablespoons of water or soy milk.

From the starches, two grain sweeteners are available: **barley malt** (also made from other grains and containing the sugar maltose) and a rice syrup called *ame* in Japanese. These grain syrups are produced by combining the cooked grains—rice in this instance with fresh sprouts from whole oats, barley, or wheat. The combination is allowed to stand for several hours until it has reached the sweet stage, when the liquid is squeezed off through cheesecloth, lightly salted, and cooked to the desired consistency. This thick, pale-amber syrup works beautifully in pastries and in sauces. Its semisolid state can be softened to the consistency of thick honey by heating. It is also sold in health-food stores in the West as a chewy taffy.

For those who use dairy products, **noninstant dry milk pow-**

der is a versatile natural sweetener containing the milk sugar lactose.

So-called **raw sugar,** or turbinado, is available in many food stores, but is only slightly more nutritious than white sugar. It is 96 percent sucrose, compared with the 99.9 percent sucrose in white sugar. The only refining step to which it has not been subjected is a final acid bath which whitens the sugar and removes the final calcium and magnesium salts. This "pure" sugar was, as a juice from either sugar beets or sugarcane, only 15 percent sucrose; in its final form, all natural goodness has been lost.

Several sweeteners produced in the intermediate stages of sugar refining can be used somewhat more safely than white table sugar. Once the cane or beet juice has been extracted, clarified to a syrup form, and crystallized, it is then spun in a centrifuge where more crystals are separated from the liquid. This remaining liquid is **molasses,** which is then repeatedly treated and centrifuged to extract more and more crystal until the final "blackstrap" form contains about 35 percent sucrose. Blackstrap molasses also contains iron, calcium, and B vitamins. Another variety of molasses is known as Barbados. This milder, dark-brown syrup is extracted from the processes described earlier, resulting in a lighter-tasting product with a higher sucrose content. Sorghum molasses is produced by a similar process, but uses as raw material the cane from the sorghum plant. It has a distinctive, rather cloying, taste and is best used in baking, especially cookies.

UNREFINED OILS

For a healthful diet, you should obtain the necessary unsaturated fatty acids primarily from unrefined vegetable oils. Like other refined foods, these oils still contain all the nutrients present in the grains, beans, or seeds from which they were derived.

Nearly all cooking oils are made by first heating the grains, beans, or seeds; then, to produce "unrefined" oils, these heated vegetals are pressed with a centrifuge and thus expelled without the use of chemicals or solvents. No further processing occurs, but some firms filter their "unrefined" oils to remove the remaining particles of the germ. It is better, of course, to purchase unfiltered, unrefined oils with some sediment left in the bottle, for too much filtering removes the nutrients. Commercial processing also results in the loss of vitamin E, which is found naturally in the oil and is essential for the proper utilization of the important unsaturated fatty acids. Therefore, you benefit very little from refined oils, since they are a poor source of unsaturated fatty acids.

Refined oils also lack the natural odors and flavors that are noticeable in all the unrefined oils. The mildest of the unrefined oils are safflower and sunflower. Unrefined sesame oil imparts a unique nutty taste to sautéed food, whereas unrefined corn-germ oil gives a buttery taste to baked goods. Everyone has appreciated the full-bodied flavor of unrefined olive oil in salad dressings. Peanut and soybean oil are rather stronger in flavor and can be better utilized in sautéing, which reduces the intensity of their taste. Unrefined coconut and palm oil are also available in natural-food stores; these partially saturated oils are used extensively by southern cultures for all types of cooking.

A further reason for using unrefined oils is the fact that at high temperatures the chemical makeup of an oil is altered and possibly becomes detrimental to health. Many advertisements praise refined oils for their ability to be used at extremely high temperatures, but these high heats are neither necessary nor desirable. Unrefined safflower oil can be used for deep-frying at about 400 degrees, and can withstand higher temperatures than most other oils. Cooking temperatures above this simply aren't necessary. Overheating of unrefined, unfiltered oil causes the germ to scorch and most nutrients to be lost. When substituting unrefined oils for solid fats in recipes, reduce the amounts of other liquids slightly or increase the dry ingredients.

OTHER USEFUL FOODS

Bancha tea is high in calcium and is widely used in macrobiotic diets. The macrobiotic diet is not a regimen but simply an individual attempt to eat in harmony with one's daily activities in a given climatic and geographical area. Bancha is a coarse green undyed tea. The leaves, which must have remained on the bush for three years, should be roasted in the oven until browned. Bancha twig tea, known as kukicha, consists of the twigs of the tea bush and is generally available. One spare teaspoon of kukicha should be used for each cup of tea, which is prepared by simmering the twigs for about 15 to 20 minutes.

Baking powders are used to make "quick breads" which can usually be put together and baked in less than a half hour and which rise by virtue of the baking powder included. It's best not to use too many quick breads, but they occasionally lend themselves well to the use of concentrated nutrients such as seeds and nuts, and they can contain a mixture of flours such as whole wheat with fresh ground corn, millet, triticale, and soy flour. Never use "baking powder" (sodium bicarbonate) in making quick breads; its action is not only unnecessary but potentially unhealthy, destroying vitamin C and some B vitamins. The baking powder you choose should be low-sodium and aluminum-free; aluminum is known to be toxic. Potassium bicarbonate does not destroy vitamin D in the body. Most natural-food stores carry this type of low-sodium baking powder, but you can make your own by using 1 part potassium bicarbonate, 2 parts cream of tartar (potassium bitartrate) and 2 parts arrowroot powder. It may be necessary to obtain potassium bicarbonate through a chemical company because it is not generally available at pharmacies.

Nutritional yeast is a natural treasurehouse of proteins, vitamins, and minerals which can be used as a dietary supplement when added to juices or included in cooked dishes. Often called brewer's yeast because at one time it was only a by-product of the brewing industry, nutritional yeast is the tiniest of cultivated plants. The minuscule plants are grown on herbaceous grains and hops under carefully controlled temperature conditions. The yeast plant grows at an astoundingly fast rate. Once it has multiplied many times and matured, it is harvested and dried in a manner which preserves all of its nutrients. These yeast "flakes" are one of the most economical sources of the B vitamin complexes—B_1, B_2, B_6, niacin, B_{12}, folic acid, pantothenic acid, and biotin. In addition to these vitamins yeast flakes contain minerals such as calcium, phosphorus, iron, sodium, potassium and sixteen of the twenty amino acids, all working in conjunction with the B vitamins. Many people take several tablespoons of yeast daily. If yeast is to be used in a beverage such as a vegetable juice, the flakes should first be mixed with a small amount of the liquid and stirred into a paste, then added to the rest of the liquid and thoroughly mixed again; a blender will simplify this method. Yeast flakes may also be added to baked foods such as breads and casseroles or mixed in small amounts with nut butters or bean paste sandwich spreads.

Thickeners for smooth soups and sauces are usually based on a finely ground starch or flour, the most widely used being whole wheat, rice, and whole-wheat pastry. The thickness of a flour sauce is determined by the ratio of flour to liquid. One tablespoon of flour to 1 cup liquid yields a thin sauce; up to 3 tablespoons flour to 1 cup liquid, a thick sauce. Cornstarch, corn flour in its finest version, is used in the same way to thicken sauces. Arrowroot powder, or flour made from the arrowroot plant, produces a finer sauce than cornstarch.

The arrowroot starch should be dissolved in cold water before being added to hot foods to prevent lumping. Once the arrowroot has been added, simmer the thickened sauce to allow all the flavors to merge. Kudzu is another high-quality but rather expensive thickening agent. The kudzu plant grows wild in the United States as well as in Japan, where it has long been widely used in folk medicine, often prescribed for diarrhea and head colds. The crumbly white chunks should be dissolved first in cold water before being added to hot sauces to prevent lumping.

If **vinegar** is called for in a recipe, never use the white distilled or wine varieties; use an apple-cider vinegar made from whole, unsprayed apples, undiluted and naturally aged. Refined, distilled vinegar has few of the naturally occurring nutrients (such as potassium) and virtually none of the indefinable subtle flavors of slowly aged cider vinegar. Because of the predominance of acetic acid in white distilled and wine vinegars, use them sparingly. Apple-cider vinegar, on the other hand, contains a predominance of malic acid, which when wisely used is a constructive acid, naturally involved in the digestive system. Besides its culinary uses in preparing salad dressings and preserving foods, vinegar has long been used medicinally as an antiseptic and blood coagulant. Rice vinegar is also available at natural-food stores and in Oriental markets. It has a very distinctive aroma and taste; use it with utmost discretion, in pickling and salad dressings. Thanks to its natural fermentation it contains none of the questionable properties of commercial distilled vinegars.

12

COMBINING COMPLEMENTARY PROTEINS

THE BASIS FOR COMBINING INCOMPLETE PROTEIN FOODS TO create a complete protein mixture is simple: *as long as you get a proper balance of amino acids, it doesn't matter where they come from.* When you take money out of your bank account you don't ask which safe it came from; you're concerned only that it's the right amount. In your diet, it makes no difference whether the tryptophan comes from eggs or soybeans, the lysine from milk or black-eyed peas, or the isoleucine from sardines or black beans.

Once you know the principles of combining incomplete protein, you can see how combinations like rice and beans or bread and cheese have sustained underdeveloped nations for hundreds of years. These peoples did not need an understanding of biochemistry to realize, over generations, that these combinations provided enough of something to maintain life and promote growth. This something is the complementary mixture of amino acids necessary for protein synthesis.

In order for the body to make new protein, an adequate supply of carbohydrates and fats is required. Otherwise, your body will use the amino acids to produce glucose to burn as fuel rather than protein. In addition to adequate fats and carbohydrates, a steady supply of essential amino acids in just the right amounts and proportions—all at the same time —is needed to build protein. Since incomplete protein foods are deficient in some essential amino acids and have excesses of others, we simply combine them: a food weak in lysine but strong in tryptophan would complement a food deficient in tryptophan and abundant in lysine. This is not a matter of eating a bowl of rice at one meal and a piece of corn bread at another, but of putting these foods together in the same meal or recipe so that the essential amino acids will be right there at the same time.

The need for amino acids in the right proportions at the same time is like a recipe for baking several loaves of bread. The recipe calls for flour, shortening, honey, water, and yeast. You have several pounds of flour, a few cups of shortening, a big jar of honey, unlimited water, but only one dozen packets of yeast. With these ingredients you can only go on baking loaves of bread until you run out of yeast—the scarcest ingredient—and then you have to stop baking bread completely. Likewise, if you eat an incomplete protein food by itself, the amount of protein that it will cause to be synthesized will be limited by the amount of the essential amino acid most poorly represented, or the *limiting amino acid*.

The amino acid patterns of all protein foods are judged against that of the egg, which has the most nearly perfect pattern. A "perfect" amino acid pattern would be one that allowed 100 percent of the protein to be utilized; the utilization of the egg protein is 94 percent. All other foods contain protein that is less than 94 percent usable. Most incomplete protein foods do contain all of the essential amino acids, but one or more of them is present in only a small amount, which prevents the amino acid pattern from matching up with the one specific pattern (or recipe) your body can use. In this one specific amino acid pattern (represented by the egg) the eight essential amino acids always remain in the same proportions to one another, just like the ingredients of a recipe. Just as 100 percent of two cups of flour is needed to bake one loaf of bread, 100 percent of each of the specific proportions of the eight amino acids is necessary for protein to be synthesized. When you eat a food that contains 100 percent of the correct amounts of seven of the amino acids, but only 40 percent of the lysine necessary, you can use only 40 percent of the protein contained in this food to make new protein, and the rest of the amino acids will literally be wasted.

Incomplete protein foods mixed together never produce a combination of protein that is 100 percent usable. Remember that even the protein in egg is only 94 percent usable. But when you mix together two incomplete protein foods that complement one another, something remarkable happens. For example, soybeans and wheat each have an NPU of approximately 60, but when they are mixed together in the proportion of one part soybeans to six parts wheat, their protein usability is increased by 33 percent—which means that the NPU of the soybean-wheat mixture is now 80 instead of 60: 13 points higher than the NPU of beef.

There are eight essential amino acids, but when you begin complementing incomplete protein foods you really need to worry about only four of them: isoleucine, lysine, trypotophan and methionine. These are the amino acids in which grains, nuts and seeds, legumes, and vegetables are variously deficient. As you start combining incomplete protein foods in recipes, you will learn the limiting amino acid for each group. Eventually you will think of incomplete protein foods in complementary pairs and protein complementing will become as routine to you as knowing what herbs and spices go best with what kinds of foods.

While it is ideal to mix incomplete protein foods together in specific, scientifically tested ratios that complement each other's weaknesses, you will still be greatly increasing the NPUs of the incomplete protein foods you eat even if you don't follow the proportions exactly. If you remember that rice and soy are complementary but don't remember in what proportions, you'll still be better off putting them together in some proportions than eating one of them alone. We'll now evaluate the different nonmeat food groups according to their amino acid strengths and weaknesses, and then give you some simple guidelines to follow in creating your own complementary protein recipes.

DAIRY PRODUCTS

You can always count on dairy products to increase the NPU of any incomplete protein food. Milk, cheese, and yogurt have amino acid compositions that nearly equal the egg, and they also contain extra proportions of isoleucine and lysine. This means that they can really fill in the amino acid gaps of foods (e.g., nuts, seeds, grains) which are deficient in these two amino acids. Milk proteins need no complement so you needn't worry about combining too much of them with any one incomplete protein. More conveniently, only small amounts of dairy foods can multiply the protein usability of incomplete protein foods. Only one tablespoon of nonfat dried milk will increase the NPU of half a cup of whole-wheat flour by 45 percent. If you think for a minute, you can probably come up with a number of familiar foods and food combinations that make use of the great "complementarity" of dairy products. For example:

Milk + wheat:	Macaroni and cheese
	Bread and butter
	Pizza
Milk + rice:	Rice pudding
	Rice with cheese sauce
	Cream of rice cereal with milk
Milk + potato:	Potato soup
	Potatoes au gratin
	Potato pancakes
Milk + peanuts:	Peanut butter and jelly
	sandwich with glass of milk

GRAINS, NUTS, AND SEEDS

These food groups, generally deficient in *isoleucine* and *lysine*, can be complemented by small quantities of milk products, as well as brewer's yeast, which is also strong in isoleucine and lycine. You may have heard stories about the unpalatability of yeast, but actually very little of it is needed in a recipe to boost the protein usability of the food; also, yeast today is available in more forms—powder, granules, flakes—and has a greatly improved flavor. Brewer's yeast is barely noticeable when mixed into pancake batter and bread dough, and it adds a nice nutty flavor to vegetable-soup stocks. But the most common complement to grains is legumes (peas, beans, and lentils). Rice and beans, cooked with hundreds of seasonings, spiced with chilies and tart curry sauces, are the staples of many cultures. All legumes except black-eyed peas and mung beans are relatively strong in isoleucine, and all legumes are strong in lysine. They are weak in precisely the amino acids that grains are strong in: tryptophan and the sulfur-containing amino acids. Typical complementary food combinations for this group are:

Corn + legumes: Tortillas with refried beans
Rice + legumes: Stir-fried rice with bean sprouts, etc.; curried beans over rice
Wheat + legumes: Peanut butter on whole-wheat bread (peanuts are botanically classified as legumes); pea soup and whole-wheat bread (or sprinkled with bread crumbs)

Since nuts and seeds have the same amino acid deficiencies as grains, we can include them in this group. They are also complemented by legumes.

Nuts + legumes: Stir-fried rice with bean sprouts and cashew nuts, walnuts, or almonds
Seeds + legumes: Tahini (ground sesame seeds) and chick-peas, as in falafel and humus (Middle Eastern staple foods)

LEGUMES

Legumes are deficient in tryptophan and the sulfur-containing amino acids. Their NPU values can be increased by matching them with grains, nuts, and seeds, which are strong in these two amino acids and weak in those that legumes have in abundance—isoleucine and lysine. In the section on grains, nuts, and seeds, above, we explained how legumes can complement these foods; refer to the examples to see how legumes can be complemented by grains, nuts, and seeds.

VEGETABLES

Fresh vegetables are very weak in the sulfur-containing amino acids and are therefore best combined with foods strong in these acids: sesame seeds, brazil nuts, millet, wheat bran, mushrooms, wheat germ, and brewer's yeast. Sesame seeds ground into meal for better digestibility can be sprinkled over many vegetables and salads to complement them and spark up their flavor and texture. Millet would go well in vegetable soups, and wheat germ can be a topping for vegetable casseroles. Of course, fresh vegetables can always be complemented by milk and dairy products, such as green salad with Roquefort dressing, potato soup, and creamed corn.

COMPLEMENTING INCOMPLETES WITH MEAT AND FISH

The explosion of Chinese restaurants and cookbooks has probably made you aware of the scant yet creative use of meat and fish in Oriental vegetables. A typical main course contains five or six kinds of vegetables, and only an ounce or so of meat or fish per serving, cut into thin strips or tiny chunks and served over a bed of rice, unfortunately white. In these recipes, incomplete protein foods are satisfactorily complemented by meager quantities of animal proteins, so that the NPU of such a meal is equal to or greater than that of a whole plate of beef. Since animal proteins need no complements themselves, they can be used like milk in small amounts to increase the NPUs of incomplete protein foods. Studies comparing lactovegetarians and meat eaters show the value of even a very small amount of animal protein used in a basically nonflesh diet.

Mervyn G. Hardinge and Frederick J. Stare, two Harvard M.D.s, conducted an experiment using these protein diets to test their efficiency. They fed one group of people a diet containing 50 grams of protein daily, of which only 5 grams were animal (milk) protein; the second group ate 100 grams of protein, of which 60 grams were from animal sources; and a third group was fed a high-protein diet of 160 grams, nearly all of which was animal protein. After two months on these diets the participants were examined and the experimenters concluded, "No members of the low-protein group, not even the hardest worker, who averaged about 5000 calories expenditure on a working day, suffered measurable deterioration in physical vigor . . . it seems reasonable to conclude from this experiment that a daily protein intake of 50 grams, of which as little as 5 grams consists of animal protein, is perfectly adequate for good health and efficiency, providing, and this is a most important proviso, the diet is adequate in other respects, particularly calories and thiamine." [1]

Those gelatin supplements recommended for strong fingernails are not complements to incomplete proteins. Though gelatin is an animal protein, it is lacking in several essential amino acids and has an NPU of only 2. If combined with incomplete protein foods, gelatin may actually reduce, rather than increase, the NPUs of those foods.

You now know how to combine rice and beans for a high-protein meal. But despite the high protein and the low expense, you won't sit down to the meal with pleasure unless the food tastes good. Rice, beans, and other grains are bland in themselves, but *because* they are bland they can take on nearly any flavor. For beans, the variety of flavors includes the sweet Oriental bean-cake desserts, the beeflike taste of meat analogs made from soybeans, and the nutty, full flavors of Mexican frijoles (refried mashed beans). Aside from the various seasonings, the beans themselves have a subtle range of tastes, such as the porklike flavor of black-eyed peas, the buttery flavor of limas, and the richness of black beans.

How many ways can you fix a piece of meat? You can boil, fry, broil, sauté, marinate, bake, and smoke it; but regardless of the preparation, it will still taste like a piece of meat. The ways to flavor legumes and grains are endless. They can also be prepared in ways that give them textures, from crunchy to soft, from chewy to fluffy. If you cook with grains, legumes, and vegetables you will want to sharpen your culinary skills by learning about the condiments, herbs, and spices that make these foods delicious enough to eat day after day.

CHAPTER

13

AGRIBUSINESS
AND FOOD QUALITY

OLD MACDONALD HAD A FARM, BUT HE DID NOT HAVE FEED grinders, egg conveyor belts, vacuum milk pumps, artificially lighted laying barracks, and mass extermination facilities. Nor were his animals artificially inseminated, tranquilized, drugged, force-fed, and genetically manipulated. His grains weren't whisked off to be stripped naked, and his fruits and vegetables weren't pickled in preservatives. He had pride in his products, and you could be sure that when they looked good and smelled fresh, that's what they were.

Old MacDonald has become U.S. Agribusiness, which controls our whole planet, pollutes the food we eat, forces the cultivation of nonfood crops like coffee, sugar, and tea in place of food for people, and exhausts natural resources. The agricultural revolution has, in the name of progress, turned our food supply into a chemical cornucopia bearing cancerous fruits and a host of exotic diseases.

Americans consume so much beef that the feed we give to cattle constitutes *nearly the entire protein deficit of the world each year.* In America we feed about 20 million tons of edible protein to livestock each year, and only about 2 million tons get back to us as meat on our plates. Some of this 20 million tons of high-quality grain is bought at ridiculously low prices from underdeveloped nations; we don't even have to exhaust our own soil to pay for our expensive meat habit.

Just how big is agribusiness today? One out of every four jobs in private employment in the United States relates to agriculture in some way. Another 13 million people process or market farm goods, or provide farmers with supplies such as drugs, fertilizers, and feed. The food industry is the largest and fastest growing in this country. In 1971 its sales were $139.2 billion, up 63 percent since 1960. Food-industry trade journals attribute this remarkable growth to new convenience foods, created wholly or partly out of chemicals. Synthetic chemicals, being much cheaper to use than actual fruits and vegetables, bring enormous profits to companies that routinely use them. Every year, $500 million worth of food chemicals are sold to food processors, who in turn incorporate them into products which cost but a fraction of similar items produced from natural foods. Each year, about 5000 new chemically concocted foods are placed on supermarket shelves. In the early 1960s, there were about 1500 grocery items; today there are more than 32,000. Industry representatives gleefully predict that by 1980 the sales of food additives will reach $765 million, a 50 percent jump from the current $500 million a year.

If you think that the 32,000 grocery items give you an unprecedented range of product and price choice, you are wrong. You do not have the purchase flexibility that you may think. These thousands of products come from fewer and fewer sources, which have more and more power to establish prices and maintain questionable quality. Four manufacturers have over 90 percent of the cereal business; the Campbell company has over 90 percent of the soup business; the four largest canners sell 80 percent of canned fruits and vegetables; America's grain trade is dominated by six multinational corporations; it is estimated that Swift and Pillsbury own 90 percent of the chickens on the market; four companies control the U.S. meat-products industry.

A 1967 Census Bureau report showed that in many metropolitan areas, four or fewer food retailers own 51 percent of the supermarket business. For instance, in the Washington, D.C., metropolitan area, 60 percent of all grocery sales are controlled by Giant Food and Safeway stores. And these food-store companies are just the handle of the corporate umbrella of food- and nonfood-related subsidiary companies. For example, Safeway's $7 billion food empire owns more than 2400 supermarkets, 109 manufacturing and processing plants, 16 produce-packaging plants, 16 bakeries, 19 milk and 16 ice cream plants, four soft-drink bottlers, three meat processors, three coffee-roasting plants, a soap and peanut-butter and salad-oil factory, plus a fleet of 2100 tractor trailers.[1] Safeway's board of directors also shares members with the boards of such corporations as the Bank of California, General Electric, Wells Fargo Bank, Shell Oil, Pacific Gas & Electric, Caterpillar Tractor, and Southern Pacific Co.

Safeway also shares mutual money interests with Owens-Illinois manufacturers, one of the largest suppliers of shipping cartons, plastic and glass packaging, and with the AMFAC corporation, which in addition to being the largest producer of raw cane sugar in Hawaii, also has interests in food sales to hotel restaurants and resorts.[2] These food conglomerates make no attempt to disguise their profit motives. United Brands informed the federal government that it wanted to do with lettuce and celery what it had already done with bananas: control at least 50 percent of the market, to seize a "nonpreemptable position as leader in fresh and semiprocessed salad products" and boost the price of lettuce from 70 to 90 cents a carton. To achieve this end, United Brands in 1968 bought out at least six major lettuce and celery growers and shippers.

What are the consequences of this concentration of food production and marketing? Inefficiency and waste. The notion that bigness brings efficiency is a myth. How much sense does it make to grow food in Maryland, ship it to California for processing, and then ship it back to Maryland for sale? How much sense does it make to grow whole wheat, strip it of the vital nutrients contained in its hull and germ, and then make it into flour to which artificial vitamins must be added? How much sense does it make to color dog food with red dye, when dogs are color-blind? And how much sense does it make for plastic factories to pollute the air so that that you can have your slices of processed cheese individually wrapped? What is the ecological and financial price of "convenience"?

When food companies reduce competition, often the first thing to be affected is product quality. Agribusiness uses Henry Ford's mass-production, assembly-line principles to produce food. Generally speaking, most food companies employ cheaper materials and processes in food production when possible. For this reason, there is a spectacular array of food additives with a purely cosmetic function: to provide the *appearance* of freshness and natural ingredients. A partial list of these chemical deceivers includes artificial flavorings and colorings, preservatives, antioxidants, emulsifiers, stabilizers, thickeners, humectants (to keep foods marshmallow-moist for a long time), firming agents (to keep processed fruits and vegetables from becoming soft), anticaking agents (to keep powdered foods such as pudding mixes and dried milk free-flowing), clarifying agents (to remove minerals such as iron and copper which could make liquids cloudy).

And then there's price-fixing. "The high price of food is a direct consequence of the added costs imposed on the market by corporations whose economic control is unchecked by competition and largely unimpeded by the federal regulatory agencies." [3] This strong indictment is made by Carol Foreman, formerly executive director of the Consumer Federation of America, the country's largest consumer organization, now Assistant Secretary of Agriculture. She and her organization are fighting against the increasing concentration and decreasing competition among food producers and processors, the result of which is this: a family of four with an income of $9200 has to spend 38 percent of its disposable income on food, and poor families have to spend as much as 60 percent of their total earnings to feed themselves. When forty-three brand names of cereal sell for approximately the same price, it's obvious that competition has slowed to a standstill. Each year food prices are less related to traditional factors like the weather, and more dependent on conglomerate machinations that have nothing to do with food itself.

Profits lead to profits lead to profits . . . The profiteering of food conglomerates is an endless cycle. A bigger company can spend more on advertising to weaken the competition; the more it spends on advertising, the more you have to pay for its product. Advertising is a deductible business expense, and this should give you pause when you consider that companies like General Foods spend upwards of $200 million a year to promote their products. While grocery stores innocently apologize for their high prices, blaming them on the tight food supply or the high cost of labor, take a look at their profits: during the first nine months of 1974, Safeway increased its profits by 51 percent, Kroger by 94 percent, and Colonial by 37 percent. And food processors are raking it in as well: that same year, Del Monte, the largest producer of canned fruits and vegetables, increased profits by 43 percent, Pillsbury by 32 percent, American Can by 52 percent, and Continental Can by 35 percent. Iowa Beef Processors, the largest beef packer in the nation, was hindered by beef boycotts and internal strikes, and *still* produced profits of 50 percent that year; compared to their profits of the two previous years, 73 percent and 99 percent respectively, the 50 percent must have put them into a *desperate* squeeze.

Inefficiency, waste, and inferior quality are but a few consequences of this concentration of food processing and marketing. The virtual monopoly held by food conglomerates is a Pandora's box out of which pours a host of abuses. Competition is an untenable myth: large chains force rival super-markets out of business by slashing their prices—but only until the threat has ended. Thus the giants set their own price levels. Ralph Nader maintains that a secret F.T.C. staff report shows that if these conglomerates were broken up, food prices would drop by 25 percent.[4]

The food monopoly also enjoys a close relationship with the governmental agencies which were intended to monitor and regulate that very industry. Cases of bribery are common, and one fears that graft continues unabated. The power to influence these agencies is also due, in no small degree, to the two-way flow of personnel between government and private business. Instances which in other industries would be labeled conflicts of interest pass unnoticed in agribusiness.

A monopoly is by definition self-sustaining: the bigger the company is, the bigger it will get. An endless cycle of ever-increasing power and profit. As bleak as this may seem—and is—there are many ways out from the jungle of agribusiness. Our next chapters, which deal with the nutrient values, processing, and marketing of these consumer staples, show you how to beat the high prices and product hazards, with better health in the bargain.

ORGANIC VS. SYNTHETIC FARMING

Thanks to agribusiness, we have fresh tomatoes and corn on the cob all year round. But the winter tomatoes are pink-ish-gray, imitations of the sweet, juicy, seedy, vivid red summer tomatoes you enjoy eating saltless off the vine. And the winter corn is a dry, starchy, tough relative of the sweet, succulent late-summer corn on the cob you can eat by the plateful.

We buy these vegetables out of season just because they are there in the supermarket, and they are there in the super-market *because* we buy them. We unblinkingly accept produce that has been grown in chemically fertilized soil and artificially lighted, controlled-temperature environments, sprayed with pesticides, gassed with ethylene to artificially ripen them, coated with coal-tar dyes to give them appealing color, then waxed to retard water loss. And we've been conditioned to think that a mealy tomato is better than none at all.

Today there are only a few ways to obtain produce free of chemical fertilizers, pesticides, poisonous gases, and dyes. You can grow your own, buy from a local small farmer, or shop at a health-food store that stocks organically grown fruits and vegetables. Organically grown fruits and vegetables are raised in soil that has been fertilized with natural compost instead of chemicals. They have not been sprayed with herbicides, fungicides, or pesticides; they are simply grown by natural, preagribusiness farming methods used since our primitive ancestors first tilled the soil.

But broad, sometimes self-serving interpretations of the term "organic" by some health-food stores and other commercial concerns have made it generic, scientifically vague, possibly misleading, and of questionable significance to the consumer. After all, *all* foods are "organic" substances: how can one apple be more organic than another? Are these organically grown fruits and vegetables better than the grocery-store varieties? Are they more nutritious? And are they actually free of chemical residues? These questions are at the center of a controversy, over the value of organic vs. synthetic farming methods, which has involved representatives of consumer groups, the health-food movement, major food processors, and the federal government in fierce debate.

The F.D.A.'s disclosure that some health-food-store owners have been duping consumers by selling them inorganically grown produce labeled "organic" may make you skeptical about health-food-store produce. After all, how do you know that your organic greengrocer didn't simply whisper "organic" over the cucumbers before placing them on the higher-priced shelf? How are you to know that the organic produce has no pesticide residues, unless you chemically test them yourself? Is it really possible nowadays for any produce grown on this polluted planet to be free of chemical residues? Tests have shown that even the produce of the most conscientious organic farmer may contain airborne and water-borne pesticide residues.

In 1971, Dr. Elmer George, director of the New York State Food Laboratory of the Department of Agriculture and Markets, tested some 55 organically grown produce items taken from health-food stores in the New York City area and found that 30 percent of them contained pesticide residues. In his analysis of beets, he found .03 parts per million of DDT, about the same as beets grown by inorganic methods. Among other organic vegetables with detectable residues, the levels were comparable to the levels of chemically grown produce.

The New York State Food Laboratory has been conducting analyses of food samples for pesticide residues since the mid-1960s at the rate of 1500 to 1800 samples a year. Dr. George reports, "Today we find pesticide residues in only 15 to 25 percent of all the samples we test, organic and inorganic, and generally these levels are only a tenth of what the allowed tolerance is. This is due to the fact that more biodegradable and less powerful pesticides are being used on today's crops." [5]

Even if the vegetables in your health-food stores are truly organically grown and contain only a bare trace of chemical residues, are these vegetables nutritionally superior to ones grown by conventional methods? This question is at the heart of the organic-vs.-synthetic controversy. An advocate of synthetic farming methods, Dr. Frederick J. Stare, chairman of the Department of Nutrition at Harvard University, maintains that "Fertilizers, regardless of the type, do not influence the nutrient composition of the plant in regard to its content of protein, fat, carbohydrate, or the various vitamins . . . Foods from any good grocery store will produce just as good nutritional health as any and all natural foods, at half the price." And others who feel the same way point out that since plants absorb nutrients from the soil in their inorganic form, it doesn't matter whether the nutrients are from organic or synthetic sources, except that the synthetic sources are much cheaper.

Proponents of organic farming methods, like botanist Dr. Bargyla Rateaver, insist that the nutritional difference between chemically fed and organically grown plants is considerable. A book she is writing will include scientific studies showing that organic farming methods have produced rice with a higher protein content, spinach with a higher iron content, and cereals with a higher trace-element content.

Over the last fifty years scientists have conducted long-term studies using organic and inorganic farming methods to evaluate the quantity and quality of yields from both methods. These studies have consistently shown that regardless of method of farming, three factors affect the biological composition of plants: genetics, climate, and soil.

Each plant is invested with a genetic code which determines to a large extent the proportion of minerals it will absorb from the soil and the proportions of vitamins it will synthesize. For example, alfalfa always contains more calcium than corn, even when the two grow side by side in the same soil, because the genetic code of the alfalfa plant instructs it to absorb more calcium than does the genetic code of the corn plant. A plant's genetic code influences the plant's level of proteins, carbohydrates, vitamins, and minerals, and a plant can absorb or synthesize no greater quantity of these nutrients than its genetic code prescribes.

The second factor which influences a plant's nutrient composition—climate—is a complex of environmental factors including the amount of sunlight, temperature and moisture content of the air and soil, and wind. The amount of vitamin C in a ripening tomato depends on the amount of sunlight that strikes the tomato. If foliage shades the tomato or if cloudy weather persists, the vitamin C content will be less than usual.

The third factor, soil, is the one most subject to debate. Agricultural scientists can manipulate soil far more easily than they can manipulate genetics or climate. There are hundreds of varieties of soil, each with a different acidity, alkalinity, mineral composition, density, texture, capacity to hold moisture, and organic-matter content. These soil characteristics determine the kinds of plant life that can grow in the soil, the quantity of the yield, and the mineral content of the plants. If you follow your way up the food chain— from tiny microorganisms in the soil to the plants that feed on their nutrients to the animals that feed upon the plants to the humans that feed upon the animals that eat the plants— you can appreciate the ultimate influence of the condition of the soil on human health. The incidence of the iodine-deficiency diseases goiter and cretinism provides a dramatic example of the relationship between soil and human health. Less than a hundred years ago, goiter in adults and cretinism in children were prevalent in many regions where the soils and waters were low in iodine. The introduction of iodized salt corrected this problem.

Agricultural scientists studying the relationship of soil to human health have focused on the effect soil fertility has on the nutrient concentration of a given plant. This scrutiny led them directly to the importance of trace minerals. Research on these is still in its infancy, as was vitamin research in the 1930s, but more and more clinicians suspect that many of our modern maladies such as heart disease may be related to subclinical (undetectable) deficiencies of essential trace minerals, due either to depletion of trace minerals in our food supply, drinking water, and soil or to contamination of soil and water by trace minerals that are toxic. Though trace minerals are present in the body only in minute amounts (they are measured in millionths of a gram), they can produce profound biological effects because they function primarily as catalysts in the enzyme systems of the cells. Diets that are deficient, imbalanced, or excessively high in particular trace minerals can create physiological disorders, some of which can be fatal.

The purpose of fertilization is to restore to the soil the trace minerals it has been depleted of, so that a new cycle of crops can be grown on the land. But many agricultural scientists are concerned that through fertilization, which is itself an artificial process, we are adding trace minerals to the soils in improper amounts and proportions, and thereby tampering with the nutrient content of the plants grown in them. Agricultural scientists have cause for concern when the U.S. Geological Survey discovers that cardiovascular mortality rates in neighboring counties in Georgia correspond to trace mineral levels in the soil. Such correlations between soil and human health bring greater urgency to the question of whether there is or is not a difference between organic and synthetic-compound fertilization.

The organic method of farming involves building the soil with a community of living organisms that breathe, retain moisture, and decay slowly, releasing essential nutrients into the soil in a gradual process. Soil with a high content of organic material from crop residues, farmyard manure, mulches, composts, peat, straw, and dead leaves stimulates the growth of microscopic fungi which grow around the roots of plants and help them absorb nutrients from the soil through the plants' tiny root hairs. They help to erode rocks in the soil, thereby making rock minerals more readily available to the plants. They also help to nourish the plants by converting organic forms of nutrients to their soluble inorganic components such as potassium, phosphorus, and nitrogen. When these microorganisms die, the proteins from their decaying tissues are passed on to the plant through the root hairs, providing further nourishment. If you were to remove a plant from organically composted soil, you would see these dead and alive microorganisms in a type of gooey gel around its root hairs.

Advocates of the organic method explain that soil with a high content of organic material is easier to till because rain soaks into it rapidly, improving the crumb structure and ability to hold water, which in turn ensures against drought. Organic farmers also point out that soil with a high content of organic material provides plants with a slow, steady supply of nutrients throughout the growing season because of the gradual decomposition of the microorganisms. And because the release of nutrients is slow and gradual, fewer nutrients are lost to the leaching of heavy rains.

Two significant scientific experiments conclude that organic fertilizers produce greater increases in mineral content of plants than do inorganic fertilizers. Over the twelve years from 1960 to 1972, Dr. Werner Schuphan conducted experiments that compared the yields and nutritive values of plants grown with four different types of fertilizer: stable manure, NPK (nitrogen, potassium, calcium), a mixture of stable manure and NPK, and a biodynamic compost. The biodynamic method of gardening and farming and the organic method have the same goals: to improve the humus content of the soil. The two methods differ, however, in that the biodynamic gardener mixes carefully proportioned amounts of raw materials to form compost, whereas most organic gardeners don't differentiate between varying materials in the compost. The biodynamicist is concerned with losing as few nutritional elements as possible in making compost. Schuphan discovered that the organic fertilizers, as a rule, produced plants with significantly higher mineral content. The spinach he grew with organic fertilizers had 18 percent more potassium, 10 percent more calcium, 13 percent more phosphorus, and 77 percent more iron than spinach grown with NPK. The organically fertilized spinach also contained 23 percent more dry matter, 18 percent more protein, 28 percent more ascorbic acid, 19 percent more total sugars, and 23 percent more methionine, an essential amino acid. Further, the organically fed spinach had an increased resistance to aphids, due to stronger cell walls and a decreased water content, and contained significantly smaller amounts of undesirable constituents like nitrates (93 percent less), free amino acids (42 percent less), and sodium (12 percent less). Dr. Schuphan's findings have been substantiated by experiments conducted by William S. Peavy and J. K. Grieg at Kansas State University.

Both studies produced negative results as well. The organic fertilizers drastically reduce yields. In the Schuphan study, the organic yields were from 20 to 56 percent less than those of synthetic fertilizers, depending on the soil type and the climatic conditions during the growing season; the Kansas State studies produced similarly low yields. This, say proponents of synthetic farming, is the major drawback to organic farming. Yields from organically fertilized soil would be too small to feed our hungry population. Former Secretary of Agriculture Earl Butz estimated that if organic farming were the sole agriculture method of this country, 30 million people in the United States alone would face starvation. Whether or not that figure is an exaggeration, it is true that organic farming is not practical today on a vast scale. Organic waste is very bulky in volume and proportionately lower in nutrient content than are synthetic fertilizers; it therefore presents greater problems of transportation and application. Most farm manure has only one twentieth the nutrient content of an equal weight of synthetic fertilizers and an undesirably low proportion of phosphorus, which must be supplemented with quantities of inorganic phosphorus.[6]

Another practical problem is that organic wastes need to be processed to balance trace-mineral deficiencies or excesses and to remove toxic inorganic compounds and harmful microorganisms such as salmonella bacteria and gastrointestinal parasites. While some manures may be deficient in phosphorus, others, like poultry manure, may contain too much nitrogen and potassium. Sewage sludge may contain residues of heavy metals like lead, cadmium, and mercury, as well as gastrointestinal parasites that can cause roundworm, hookworm, and other parasitic diseases. The sterilization of organic wastes, necessary to remove these parasitic organisms, is a complicated, expensive process.

The cost of sterilizing and transporting organic waste can increase the price of organic fertilizers to a hundred times that of their synthetic counterparts. For example, the cost of nitrogen from garbage compost is $12 a pound, from dried cow manure $5 a pound, and from commercial chemical fertilizers, 7.5 to 15 cents a pound.[7] Each person in the United States today generates hundreds of pounds of organic waste a year, and farm-animal waste amounts to nearly 2 billion tons annually. As these mounting wastes make the recycling of organic wastes an ecological necessity, agricultural technologists will have to develop new, inexpensive, and efficient methods of processing them.

Since the first chemical fertilizers were applied to European soils around 1750, world crop yields have increased tenfold. It is estimated that the application of 30 million tons of nitrogen fertilizers produces an additional crop yield equivalent to about a thousand calories a day for each person in the world.[8] These chemical fertilizers, which cost pennies to produce and can be transported easily anywhere in the world, have made possible the cultivation of an unprecedented variety of crops, regardless of the original condition of the soil. And chemical fertilizers, because of their readily absorbed inorganic form, do provide growing plants with nutrients. Chemical fertilizers have undeniably been responsible for increasing the abundance and variety of the world's food supply.

But there are potential problems involved with the use of such fertilizers. Fertilizing the soil with chemicals is not as gradual a process as it is with steadily decomposing matter. Chemical fertilizers provide more nutrients than the plants need at one time; consequently, some nutrients may interfere with the absorption of others, and the plant may get an excess of certain nutrients. When, for example, there is too much nitrate in the soil, the plant accumulates more nitrate than it needs and retains the excess in its tissues. Plants containing large quantities of nitrates are potentially harmful to the animals and humans that eat them.

Dr. Rateaver and other soil scientists maintain that chemical fertilizers, particularly those containing sulfur and gypsum, destroy most of the microorganisms living in the soil. This interrupts the steady nutrient flow and deprives the plants of the other useful functions served by the microrisa. The higher alkaline salt content of chemically fertilized soil affects plants much as salt does humans. These thirsty plants require more water than usual and accumulate a high water content.

The discoveries of the insecticidal properties of DDT in 1939 and the herbicidal properties of 2,4-D in 1941 began the chemical revolution in agriculture. Prior to that, farmers throughout the ages battled endlessly with the 10,000 species of insects, 600 species of weeds, and 1500 diseases known to afflict plants. In the United States today, we annually use some half billion pounds of 900 chemicals in about 60,000 formulations for pest control. But despite these pesticides and fungicides, pests and disease still destroy a considerable proportion of the world's food output. Fungus diseases alone destroy enough food each year to supply 300 million people with 2500 calories a day.[9] Rats and spoilage destroy enough food grains to supply another 350 million persons with a daily 2500 calories. Dr. Norman E. Borlaug, a Nobel Prize-winning agriculturist, claims that if pesticides were banned in the United States, our plant food supply would diminish by half, and food prices would increase four or five times.[10] The abundance of our food supply is due largely to pesticides. Unfortunately, this abundance has at times been at the expense of our environment.

Once they are sprayed on the crops and soil, what becomes of these pesticides? Depending on the characteristics of the pesticide and the climatic conditions, any number of biological fates are possible. Some chemicals vaporize into the atmosphere without chemical change and are redeposited in the soil by rain. Others are washed into the soil and are lost through leaching of the rains. Certain pesticides undergo chemical reactions on or within the surface of the soil, whereas others are broken down by soil microorganisms.

Many pesticides now in use are not readily biodegradable. Over the years, many pest organisms have developed strong resistance to the chemicals used to kill them. In turn, farmers sprayed higher doses of these chemicals, and manufacturers developed new chemicals to which the pests weren't resistant. Many of these chemicals are so prevalent in the environment that residues of them have passed through the plants up through the food chain. We now have pesticide residues in the butter and cream of cows from sprayed pastures and in fish from waters contaminated by runoffs. Pesticides have become so pervasive that scientists recently found traces of DDT in the flesh of Antarctic penguins.

One example of how pesticides can tilt the ecological balance occurred in California in the 1950s. The pesticide DDD, similar to DDT, was used in heavy doses to kill off the black gnats of Clear Lake, California. The plankton and larvae in the lake absorbed the chemical, and fish in the lake fed on the plankton. A Western bird, the grebe, fed on the fish. At the end of one year, the local grebe population fell from a thousand to twenty pairs.[11]

The longevity of pesticides depends on their biodegradability, volatility, and absorbability. Chlorinated hydrocarbons such as DDT, aldrin, dieldrin, and heptachlor may persist upwards of fifteen years. The organophosphate pesticides, which are generally biodegradable within a few days, are much more toxic to humans, and tremendous caution is required in their application. The carbamates are the most popular among environmentalists because of their rapid biodegradability and low mammal toxicity.

The search for safer methods of pest control has been extensive. One such method involves the use of "botanicals," natural poisons extracted from plants rather than mineral sources. Botanicals, however, are limited in their effectiveness, and the farmer must spray crops with an expensive variety of botanicals to deal with the different pests. Yet another method is "biological control," in which male insects are raised in a laboratory, sterilized by radiation or chemical treatment, and then released over an infested area. Their female mates produce fewer or no eggs, and the pest population is decimated. This method, unfortunately, is also time-consuming and expensive.

The chemical revolution in agriculture illuminates the delicate balance of our planet's ecology: one form of life cannot be altered without disturbing another. Manipulation of the soil has perhaps the greatest consequences to the environment, for these chemicals not only work their way up the chain into the food we eat but also infiltrate the air we breathe and the water we drink. Dr. William Albrecht sees clearly the central issue: "All too few of us have yet seen the soil community as the foundation in terms of nutrition of the entire biotic pyramid of which man, at the top, occupies the most hazardous place." [12]

Agricultural scientists have a tremendous responsibility to develop methods that are both ecologically sound and financially realistic. Ideally, these methods would combine the best of both organic and inorganic farming practices. At present, the organic-synthetic controversy remains unsettled, for neither method alone can meet the world's food needs and yet maintain the precarious balance of the world's ecology.

FACTS TO PONDER

— Many of the commercial farms in the United States and Europe use both organic and synthetic fertilizers.
— The primary function of green plants in the food chain is to transform inorganic compounds into organic materials.
— The presence of smog can reduce the amount of vitamin C synthesized by growing plants.

— Nitrate toxicity in cattle has been a serious problem where pastures are extensively fertilized with poultry manure.
— The direct effect of soil composition on human nutrition is much less than that on the nutrition of farm animals.
— In 1970, more than 1 billion pounds of pesticides were used in the United States, with half of that amount devoted to agriculture.
— Pesticides have been a prime factor in the agricultural revolution, which has made it possible for less than 6 percent of the American population to feed the other 94 percent and export tons of plant foods to other countries.
— The higher the organic content of the soil, the more readily pesticides are absorbed.
— Americans generate hundreds of pounds of domestic organic waste per person per year.
— The average person's mercury intake is now estimated at 350 micrograms per week, some 10 times greater than it was 35 years ago.
— Pesticide residues are distributed throughout the plant and cannot be removed by washing or peeling.
— These chemicals sprayed on root crops such as potatoes and onions to prevent sprouting are suspected carcinogens and have caused sterility in pigs.
— Some 42 growth-regulating chemicals are approved by the U.S.D.A. for more than 100 different uses in crop production.
— In November, 1969, the World Health Organization reported that defoliants, used extensively in Vietnam, are suspected causes of birth defects.
— Physicians at Johns Hopkins Hospital estimate the yearly consumption of mineral oil from treated fruits and vegetables at nearly 50 grams per person.
— The waxing of fruits and vegetables seals in whatever residue of pesticide, dye, or gas may remain on the produce.
— In the period from 1940 to 1969, the protein content of Kansas feed wheat declined 44.7 percent.

— Trace-mineral deficiencies in the soil have been reported in all fifty states of the United States.

— Tobacco is frequently sprayed with arsenic, which some scientists suggest is the cause of lung cancer in smokers.

— Trace-mineral researchers point out that some of the trace elements we now consider nonessential may in fact have important functions in the body's processes.

— Zinc is the trace element most often lacking in soil worldwide. In the United States, zinc deficiency has been reported in 32 states, and over 40 different crops are weak in this trace element.

— It is projected that sales of organic food will reach $3 billion by 1980.

— It is a genetic fact that, regardless of fertilization, the amount of vitamin C in an apple cannot be made to equal that of an orange.

— For every dollar you spend on food, 37.6 cents goes to farmers, 32.2 cents to retailers, 18.3 cents to processors, 7 cents to wholesalers, and 4.9 cents to transporters.

— Conglomerates recently blamed rising food prices on grain shortages, and then exported a record $20 billion worth of food overseas.

— In most of the nation's six metropolitan areas, just two to four chains control the majority of grocery sales.

— An analyst in the U.S.D.A. estimates that 20 percent of the total increase in food prices during 1973 to 1974— the big food-inflation year—was due to the rise in the price of sugar.

— In 1974, about 13.6 million Americans were getting food stamps. A year later, the figure jumped to nearly 19 million.

— Surveys have shown that shoppers who buy groceries primarily when they are hungry spend an average of $10 more on food per week.

— According to the U.S.D.A., today's cheapest source of protein is peanut butter.

— According to one National Cash Register Company survey, supermarket cashiers make mistakes in almost 80 percent of all orders over $9.

— A company that spends $500,000 on advertising reaps benefits in excess of 100 times those of a company that spends $5000.

— Today, 1.06 billion pounds of additives are added to our food supply, or five pounds per year per person.

— A price survey of supermarkets in Newark, New Jersey, showed that over 90 percent of some 5000 items were priced identically by the four major supermarket chains.

— A U.S. Justice Department strike force has alleged that some New York city supermarket executives have received from $8500 to $90,000 in bribes from certain suppliers.

PART II

NUTRITIONAL REQUIREMENTS FOR THE HEALTHY VEGETARIAN

CHAPTER
14

LIPIDS

"CHOLESTEROL IS BAD FOR YOU!"

"Polyunsaturates will save you from heart disease!"

"Lecithin can unclog your arteries!"

From the message on the margarine wrapper to the late-night TV commercials, you are saturated with so many "facts" about dietary fats that the function of fats in human nutrition may seem thoroughly confusing. You might even believe that you should avoid them completely. However, fat requirements are as important to your diet as protein needs, and an understanding of lipids—the group of compounds which includes not only fats and oils but waxes, fatty acids, phospholipids, lipoproteins, sterols, and the fat-soluble vitamins—is essential to a sound diet.

Fats and oils are the lipids most often discussed in human nutrition. You probably think of fat as the greasy white substance in animal meat and of oils as the clear liquid squeezed from vegetables, grains, seeds, and nuts. Chemically, however, fats and oils are basically the same substance, with properties common to other lipids: they are insoluble in water but soluble in alcohol, benzene, or chloroform, and they can be utilized by animal organisms. Oil is actually a fat with a melting point low enough to remain liquid at room temperature. The melting point of fat depends upon its chemical makeup. All fats—liquid and solid, animal and vegetable —are composed of fatty acids which are either saturated or unsaturated. Unsaturated fatty acids, such as those in corn oil, are liquid at room temperature, whereas saturated fatty acids, such as those in beef fat, are solid.

What determines whether a fatty acid is saturated or unsaturated? Its molecule consists of a chain of carbon atoms to which hydrogen atoms are linked. Chemically, a fatty acid is considered saturated when its molecule is filled with as many hydrogen atoms as the carbon chain can hold. The distinction between the two varieties of fatty acids is quite simple: a saturated fatty acid molecule is saturated with all the hydrogen atoms it can contain, and an unsaturated fatty acid molecule is not. Fats containing a large proportion of short-chain (twelve or fewer carbon atoms) unsaturated fatty acids are liquid at room temperature, and those containing a large proportion of long-chain (fourteen or more carbon atoms) saturated fatty acid molecules are solid. Polyunsaturated fatty acids are fatty acids with two or more double bonds.

Liquid oils can be transformed into solid fats by adding hydrogen atoms to the unsaturated fatty acid molecules. This process, hydrogenation, is widely used by the food industry to manufacture margarine and shortening and to keep oil from separating out of processed peanut butter and other products. Hydrogenation can be carefully controlled to get the desired degree of hardness.

All the fats in your body and in the food you eat are combinations of saturated and unsaturated fatty acid molecules. But a fat is saturated when it contains a greater proportion of saturated fatty acids and, similarly, unsaturated when unsaturated fatty acids are predominant. The fat of herbivorous animals is harder (more saturated) than that of carnivores, and the fat of land animals is harder than that of sea creatures, and the fat saturation of these animals varies according to their diet. Beef and sheep fat is more saturated than either pork or chicken fat, and fats from all these animals are more saturated than fish fat, which contains a high proportion of polyunsaturated fatty acids.

A well-known function of fat is to supply a concentrated source of energy to the body. Fats supply 9 calories per gram, compared to the 4 calories per gram provided by protein and carbohydrates. Fat, with a high density and low solubility, is the best biological package in which to store this energy. When the body has enough fat stores to burn for energy, proteins will be conserved for their important body-building functions. Carbohydrates and proteins in excess of your daily needs are converted into fats and stored for later use as energy.

Fat also provides the necessary protection for internal organs and nerves. Approximately 45 percent of the abdominal cavity is filled with fat, which is distributed around the internal organs to cushion them from physical damage. In addition, fats regulate temperature by acting as an insulator against the loss of body heat in cold weather. They are needed to absorb and transport the fat-soluble vitamins and to facilitate the digestion process. Unsaturated fatty acids are important in fat transport and metabolism, and are essential to the proper formation of a group of compounds that regulate blood pressure, heart rate, and functions of the central nervous system.

The polyunsaturated fatty acids required for the body's proper growth and the maintenance of healthy cellular membranes are called *essential fatty acids*. These are linoleic acid, arachidonic acid, and linolenic acid. They function in every cell of your body and are involved directly or indirectly in nearly all its chemical reactions.

The insolubility of fats in water may lead you to think that fats are hard to digest. The digestive system, however, has a variety of emulsifiers and acids that, under normal conditions, easily digest and absorb at least 95 percent of dietary fats. The fat content of a meal determines how long the meal will remain in the stomach, for enzymes must separate fat from the protein and carbohydrates before the food can pass through the digestive tract. A meal with a high fat content may remain in the stomach four or five hours before it is transported to the small intestine, where fat is digested and absorbed. On its way, the fat passes through the duodenum and stimulates the intestinal walls to secrete the hormone that signals the gall bladder to force its bile into the intestine. Bile is necessary for the proper absorption of fat from the gastrointestinal tract, and it stimulates intestinal *peristalsis,* the wavelike muscular contractions that move the food along the digestive tract.

Once the bile has emulsified the fat and lowered its surface tension, a principal fat enzyme breaks the fat down. The smaller-carbon-chain fatty acids are separated from the bile salts and travel directly to the liver, where they are distributed to other tissues via portal circulation. The longer-carbon-chain fatty acids remain in the intestinal walls until synthesized, at which time they penetrate the membrane wall and are carried through the bloodstream to the liver.

The rate and efficiency of fat digestion and absorption are influenced by several factors. Generally, unsaturated fats are absorbed more quickly and efficiently; thus, vegetable fat is more readily digested than animal fat, and fish fat more readily digested than beef fat. While normal cooking heat has little influence on a fat's digestibility, heat too high or too prolonged reduces a fat's digestibility. High temperatures speed up the oxidation of fatty acids and produce an irritant in the gastrointestinal membrane which interferes with digestion. This is one reason to avoid eating restaurant fried foods such as french fries and onion rings, which are often boiled in grease that's been cooking for hours. Quantities of calcium can also reduce your digestion of saturated fats. Age is a further influence on digestion and absorption: young children and older people digest and utilize unsaturated fats more easily than saturated fats.

The liver can completely alter the physical properties of fatty acids: it can change one acid to another simply by adding double bonds on the carbon chain. The liver can also synthesize fat from carbohydrates and protein and convert glycerol, a fat compound, into glucose for energy.

Because lipids are insoluble in water, they must be chemically altered before passing from the liver to the cells. The lipid molecules, therefore, combine with protein molecules to form lipoproteins. Once converted into lipoproteins, they proceed to the cells and are used for energy or to perform specific cell functions, such as permeability regulation. Lipoproteins may also pass into the adipose tissue, where they are stored for future use as energy.

Your unsaturated fat consumption influences the hardness of your body fat. The predominant constituents of vegetable oil are linoleic, linolenic, and oleic fatty acids, and it is the proportion of linoleic and linolenic acids that determines the degree of hardness.

The relationship between unsaturated fat consumption and quality of body fat became obvious in the 1920s, when hogs on a diet high in soybean and peanut oils developed fat so soft and shapeless that it was unmarketable. When this pork fat was tested it was found to contain as much as 30 percent linoleic acid; normal pork fat contains only about 2 percent linoleic acid. Dogs fed a diet of highly unsaturated linseed oil developed bodies high in unsaturated fats, but when switched to a high saturated fat diet, their bodies became abnormally hard. Carbohydrates also influence the hardness of body fat. Lab animals kept on a diet high in carbohydrates and low in fats develop markedly harder body fat.

Fat metabolism is an ongoing process in the adipose tissue. Regulated by hormones secreted by various glands, fat is constantly synthesized, stored, and released for energy as it is needed. How do hormones regulate your body's fat metabolism? Suppose you skip breakfast and lunch: since your body can't maintain a glucose supply for more than thirteen hours, your blood glucose level is low. This low level causes the endocrine glands to secrete insulin and other hormones, which increase the rate of fat utilization and mobilization by releasing fatty acids from the fat cells. Concurrently, these hormones signal your liver and adipose tissues to stop synthesizing fat and start converting it to fuel. The glycerol stored in the adipose tissue is then transported to the liver and converted to glucose to fuel your nervous system. The fat stored in the adipose tissue is then broken down into free fatty acids for use in muscle tissue as energy.

All of your body's cells, except those in the central nervous system, can oxidize fatty acids for energy. This chain reaction of hormonal secretions and fat mobilization will continue until you eat again. Given an adequate carbohydrate intake at your next meal, hormonal secretions will signal the liver and adipose tissue to halt the mobilization and resume the synthesization and storage of fat.

An excess of lipids in the adipose tissue and liver places an unhealthy strain on the liver and the rest of the body. Abnormal fatty deposits enlarge the liver and impair its functions. These deposits generally result from a low-carbohydrate diet: the liver is forced to mobilize large quantities of fat to meet the body's energy needs. Lipid deposits in the liver are also caused by an imbalanced diet with too many refined foods and too few calories. A fatty liver condition is further aggravated by the consumption of too much saturated fat.

Approximately 41 percent of the calories in the American diet are in the form of fats, which amounts to about 110 pounds of fat per year for each adult. Although meat and eggs account for the largest proportion of fat in the national diet, many Americans react to the heart-disease epidemic by turning to unsaturated-fat foods such as margarine, vegetable oil, and fish. All vegetable oil is classified as unsaturated fat with the exception of coconut oil, which is nearly solid at room temperature. Linoleic, linolenic, and oleic acids are the primary constituents of vegetable oils, although the proportions of these fatty acids vary. Olive and peanut oils contain as little as 15 percent linoleic acid, whereas safflower and sunflower oils contain 75 percent and 67 percent, respectively. Other common vegetable oils are sesame seed, cottonseed, and corn.

Phospholipids, strong emulsifying lipids essential for the proper digestion and absorption of fats, are found in every cell of the body, though concentrated in the liver, brain, and nervous system. Small amounts of them are found in most foods, but the major dietary sources are liver, egg yolks, and raw vegetables. Some nutritionists, however, note that many phospholipids are processed out of our foods and that we may not be getting an adequate supply.

Public concern over the amount of fat in the American diet often overlooks the quality of that fat. The issue is not simply one of saturated versus unsaturated fats. Fat-processing methods affect your health as well. Hydrogenation is popular with the processed-food industry because hydrogenated fats are resistant to deterioration and rancidity, and therefore have a longer shelf life. The baking industry uses hydrogenated fats because of their shortening effect, creaming quality, and resistance to odor absorption.

Unfortunately, hydrogenation destroys many vitamins and minerals contained in the original vegetable oils and alters their protein structure. And hydrogenation either destroys the essential fatty acids or changes them into an abnormal and unhealthful form.

Hydrogenated oil bears no resemblance to the original oil: it is dark and foul-smelling, and must therefore undergo further cosmetic purification. The hydrogenated oil is bleached, filtered, and deodorized into a white, odorless, and tasteless fat. This fat is then processed further to make shortening, margarine, or lard.

Even unhydrogenated oil is refined and bleached to prolong

its shelf life. Vegetable oil is refined by treating it with caustic soda, lye, or other strong alkalis which destroy some of the proteins, phospholipids, and carotenoid pigments and lower the vitamin E content. The oil is steamed or mixed with water to remove other impurities and then filtered. The filtered oil is bleached with fuller's earth or clay, which reduces the chlorophyll content, and filtered again. Since refined and bleached oils have an unpleasant flavor and odor, they are usually deodorized at high temperatures in a steam distillation process which increases their resistance to oxidation in the body. To guarantee an even longer shelf life, some manufacturers add phosphoric, citric, or tartaric acids to the refined and bleached oil.

Mayonnaise is heavily processed. In addition to being refined, bleached, and filtered, its oil may be "winterized" to keep it from solidifying when refrigerated. The oil is cooked slowly for a long period, its solids removed, and the remnants filtered again.

Margarine is a hydrogenated fat adulterated with stabilizers such as sodium benzoate, benzoic acid, and citric acid. These chemicals have been known to cause severe reactions in certain individuals.

Commercial vegetable oils are suspect in other ways. Many oil-bearing crops are heavily sprayed with pesticides, and the residue may contaminate vegetable oils. Other harmful residue results from the process which extracts the oil from the seed: the seeds are crushed, cooked, and exposed to a petroleum solvent commonly found in gasoline. Residues such as these *can* make their way into the final product on your grocery shelf.

Widespread fear of cholesterol is evidenced by the decline in the egg industry and the burgeoning market for egg, milk, and butter substitutes, polyunsaturated fat products, and low-cholesterol cookbooks. Our cholesterol consumption has declined—butter and egg consumption is half what it was thirty years ago. After all these years of anticholesterol propaganda, generated largely by the polyunsaturated-food industry, many investigators and cardiologists now suspect that cholesterol has little direct effect on heart disease. Though they recognize that cholesterol is a major component of the atherosclerotic plaque, the researchers point out that it has yet to be demonstrated that cholesterol *caused* the plaque or that the cholesterol in the plaque came from a dietary source. The cholesterol theory of heart disease conflicts with too many long-standing observations: that heart disease attacks American men three times more often than American women, that it attacks both the sedentary and the active, the obese and the lean, smoker and nonsmoker, and people with both high and low cholesterol levels. Nor does the cholesterol theory take into account the fact that cultures with high-cholesterol diets, such as the Eskimo and the Masai of Africa, have little or no incidence of heart disease.

Cholesterol, regarded popularly as a poisonous substance, is actually a natural and necessary part of every cell of your body. It is a waxlike solid alcohol, a phospholipid that belongs to a group of compounds called steroids. Found in all animal cells, it provides the framework of support for each cell. Cholesterol comprises most of the dry weight of your brain and serves as the conductor for nerve impulses throughout your body. The liver uses about 80 percent of the cholesterol in your body to produce bile salts, which are transported to the small intestine for use in fat absorption. The remaining 20 percent is central to a number of important processes, such as biosynthesis of steroids, adrenocortical hormones, and sex hormones. Cholesterol is also necessary for your body's synthesis of vitamin D.

Cholesterol in your diet is derived only from animal sources, the richest being organ meats, dairy products, egg yolks, and animal fat. But to avoid animal foods is not to avoid cholesterol; even without dietary sources, your body supplies its own cholesterol. It is produced primarily in the liver, but also in the muscles, skin, intestinal walls, testes, and aorta. In fact, cholesterol can be synthesized in nearly all of the body's cells. The average person synthesizes 1500 milligrams of cholesterol daily, whereas the amount provided by his diet is usually less than 200. The body balances the amount of cholesterol absorbed through the diet and the amount produced in the body: if you reduce your intake of cholesterol, your body will compensate by producing more.

Cholesterol is found throughout your body, but heart-disease researchers are concerned only with the cholesterol in the blood. The cholesterol content of the blood usually depends on four factors: how much cholesterol the body synthesizes, how much is broken down and excreted in the bile, the balance maintained between the cholesterol level in the tissues and the level in the blood, and the amount absorbed from the diet. It is the last factor that attracts so much attention in discussions of heart disease.

Tests have shown that the level of dietary *fat* intake, particularly saturated-fat intake, affects the serum cholesterol levels of humans. In these tests, a diet heavy in saturated fat caused blood cholesterol levels to rise. Scientists believe that high fat consumption causes the liver to increase both its rate of fat metabolism and, in its cells, the amount of acetyl-coenzyme A, which is used to manufacture cholesterol. On the other hand, diets rich in cholesterol have little effect on the blood cholesterol level: fat, not cholesterol, influences the serum cholesterol level.

Cholesterol has been a public enemy ever since it was isolated as a "risk factor" in the development of heart disease, along with high blood pressure and cigarettes. To call cholesterol a risk factor simply means that the incidence of atherosclerosis may be higher in persons with elevated serum cholesterol levels than in those with lower levels. There are people with low cholesterol levels who do have heart attacks, and many people with high cholesterol levels who do not. There are strict vegetarians, with no dietary cholesterol, who do have heart attacks, and heavy meat eaters who do not. What, then, are "high" and "normal" cholesterol levels?

Heart-disease researchers cannot agree on a normal level of serum cholesterol. The average level of adult Americans is between 150 and 250 milligrams of cholesterol per 100 milliliters of blood. Some researchers believe that an abnormally high serum cholesterol reading is anything above 275 milligrams and others place the figure at 175 milligrams. Even if scientists could define a high serum cholesterol level, a simple test is impossible: your blood cholesterol level fluctuates wildly throughout the day. A "high" cholesterol reading may reflect only anxiety—even anxiety over the results of the cholesterol reading itself. Stress, emotional or physical, raises your blood cholesterol level. Moderate to strenuous exercise affects cholesterol levels, as do kidney disease, sleeping patterns, malnutrition, infection, gallstones, pancreatic irregularities, diabetes, excessive alcohol, low blood proteins, pregnancy, and the use of certain drugs. Dr. Meyer Friedman of San Francisco claims that high cholesterol levels too often are blamed on dietary factors rather than on behavioral patterns. Dr. Kenneth Rose of the University of Nebraska conducted a series of experiments which supports this view: the laboratory animals subjected to various forms of stress and frustration suffered an increase in the blood cholesterol levels.

The results of the many experiments testing the relationship of serum cholesterol to heart disease point in dozens of directions. The food industry, however, has zeroed in on the tests that incriminate cholesterol as a cause of heart disease. Companies producing chemical copies of eggs, butter, bacon, sausage, and cream spend millions of dollars on slogans like "the change will do your heart good" and "Brand X can help lower your cholesterol." They even peddle their products at annual meetings of the American Heart Association.

The mass media have also spread the cholesterol panic by its cholesterol-focused reports on heart-disease research, with the result of a drastic change in our national diet. The American Heart Association is now concerned that we might be overdosing on polyunsaturates. In a recent policy statement on the cholesterol–heart-disease question, the American Heart Association advised the federal government of the potential dangers of an overreliance on polyunsaturates. This report further states that no conclusive evidence justifies a change in the type of fat people eat and that polyunsaturates have not been shown to prevent heart trouble.

There is a parallel dispute over the ability of polyunsaturated fats to reduce the cholesterol in the blood level. Those nutritionists who feel that they do claim that the essential fatty acids contained in polyunsaturated fats, which are necessary for the efficient transport and metabolism of cholesterol, help to keep cholesterol in the blood at a safe level.

On the other side, much evidence indicates that polyunsaturates cause disease rather than prevent it. Researchers at both Tulane and Duke universities have demonstrated that a diet high in polyunsaturated fatty acids can result in a depletion of vitamin E. Scientists have observed that animals fed solely on polyunsaturated fats suffer hair loss, diarrhea, a reduced capacity for growth, and an earlier death. One experiment established that the liver's detoxification function was inhibited in animals fed on corn oil for long periods of time. Similar effects have been detected in humans: a number of people developed severe liver damage after increasing their intake of polyunsaturated fat.

Polyunsaturates have also been linked with the blood condition known as *sludging,* a syndrome in which the red blood cells stick together in clumps. Due to sludging, the blood cannot flow evenly through the blood vessels at a rate consistent with the oxygen needs of body tissues. The effects of this syndrome are most noticeable in lung tissue, especially if the person lives in a high smog area: the combination of sluggish blood and air pollution can be extremely dangerous.

Dr. Denham Harman of the University of Nebraska College of Medicine has shown that excessive use of polyunsaturates can increase the possibility of cancer, atherosclerosis, and other diseases. His experiments have also linked polyunsaturates to premature aging and a shortened life-span.

The connection between polyunsaturated fat and cancer is under current study by a number of researchers. The Mayo Clinic reports that many patients with breast cancer also have a high level of polyunsaturated fats in the breast tissue. These results concur with the University of Western Ontario's discovery that animals fed large quantities of polyunsaturated fats had a higher incidence of cancer than did animals on a normal diet. A similar experiment, conducted by Dr. Daniel Melnick, revealed that the incidence of breast cancer in female rats increased by 127 percent when they were fed a diet of heated corn oil. Dr. David Kritchevesky of the Wistar Institute also fed animals heated corn oil and found that it helped to induce the development of atherosclerosis.

It is believed that the danger of polyunsaturates stems from their highly reactive chemical composition. A saturated fatty acid reacts poorly with the chemicals around it because its molecules are composed of a stable formation of atoms. The molecules of an unsaturated fatty acid, however, contain loosely bound atoms prone to react with the molecules of other compounds. A *poly*unsaturated fatty acid is even more unstable because it has an even greater number of potentially reactive atoms in its molecule.

Their unstable nature causes polyunsaturated fatty acids to be easily oxidized, and this oxidation is detrimental to the body. Polyunsaturated fats are oxidized by the heat of normal cooking, by reacting with X rays, sunlight, and trace metals such as iron. Oxidation of polyunsaturates produces toxic lipid peroxides capable of converting normal cells into ceroid pigments, or dead cells with a burned appearance. The cumulative effect of this cell destruction is premature aging.

Heat increases the toxicity of polyunsaturates by converting them into polymers, the chemical compounds that produce varnish, shellac, and plastics. The longer a polyunsaturated fat is heated, the more toxic it becomes. Consider this, too, before you order french fries prepared in restaurant grease that's been heating all day.

Lecithin is as celebrated today as vitamins C and E were a couple of years ago—a miracle solvent. Health-food stores now stock lecithin tablets, granules, liquid, and powder. Lecithin, it is claimed, reduces blood cholesterol levels, dissolves cholesterol plaques already laid down in artery walls, lowers the blood pressure, fights infection, corrects certain skin disturbances, serves as a brain food and a natural tranquilizer. Hundreds of scientific articles have been written about lecithin. What is it?

Lecithin is a phospholipid made from phosphorus, nitrogen, fatty acids, and glycerol. Every cell in your body contains phospholipids and, consequently, lecithin. It is the most widely distributed phospholipid in the body, and is necessary for the proper digestion and absorption of fats. Lecithin also improves the absorption of both carotene and vitamin A.

Through a series of complicated chemical reactions, lecithin combines with proteins and cholesterol to form the membrane which encloses each living cell. If this membrane is imperfect in structure, the contents leak and the cell dies. And if enough cells die, the body dies. The health of the cell membranes is so vital that each cell is equipped to produce its own supply of phospholipids, including lecithin.

Through another chemical reaction, lecithin is converted to myelin, a fatty protein substance that sheathes the major nerves of the body, including the spinal cord. This sheath must be in good health if nerves are to function correctly. Damage to the sheath interferes with a person's mental processes and contributes to neurological disorders, among them multiple sclerosis.

Lecithin can be manufactured in the body in the presence of the B vitamins, particularly B_6, but is also found in many foods, including liver, egg yolks, and raw vegetables. Cholesterol foods also contain lecithin, and this fact has led many researchers to believe that lecithin is the compound which keeps cholesterol soluble in the blood. Scientists are now investigating the ability of lecithin to control the level of cholesterol in the blood and the accumulation of fatty plaque on the artery walls. Tests have indicated that lecithin rich in unsaturated fatty acids interacts with cholesterol more readily than does lecithin high in saturated fatty acids. Scientists have found an additional correlation between the proportion of unsaturated fatty acids in lecithin and the permeability—the characteristic which allows the cell wall to be penetrated by nutrients and other fine particles or molecules—of the cell membrane. Cholesterol, when tested by itself, greatly reduced the permeability; when combined with lecithin, cholesterol's effect on cell-membrane permeability was not so dramatic.

Biochemist Dr. Jacobus Rinse is well known for the "lecithin breakfast" he recommends for heart patients. He believes that this breakfast diet assists in the prevention and cure of atherosclerotic complications such as high blood pressure, angina pectoris, and obstructions in the arteries of the neck, legs, and arms. Dr. Rinse recommends a daily dose of the following concoction: first mix up an elixir of one part each of soybean lecithin, debittered yeast, raw wheat germ, and bone meal. Mix 2 tablespoons of this mixture with 1 tablespoon dark brown sugar or honey, 1 tablespoon safflower or soybean oil, and enough milk to dissolve the sugar and yeast. Add yogurt to increase the consistency, cold or hot cereal such as granola or oatmeal, and, if desired, fruits.

Even those scientists who consider high serum cholesterol levels dangerous recognize that heart disease is caused not by cholesterol alone but by a complex of factors. Researchers generally agree that heart disease begins early in life and develops over several decades. Because of its epidemic nature in industrialized countries, heart disease is attributed largely to environmental and cultural factors, which in turn are influenced by a wide range of dietary, hereditary, and pathological factors. Many studies of these other risk factors have yielded impressive statistical results, but at this point are just as controversial as the cholesterol theory.

One diet-related theory of heart disease proposes that atherosclerosis is the result of nutritional deficiencies. Vitamins E and C and nicotinic acid have been singled out as nutrients lacking in the American diet. Richard Passwater, a biochemist, writes in *Supernutrition*: "The relationship of vitamin E to heart disease covers many areas, including preventing the formation of active sites for cholesterol plaques in the arteries, preventing blood clots, utilizing heart energy, improving blood circulation and blood-oxygen efficiency and reducing scar formation in the heart due to infarcts."

Researchers all over the world are studying the role of vitamin C—plentiful in the vegetarian diet—in the prevention of heart disease. A British pathologist, Dr. Constance Spittle, conducted experiments on humans in which vitamin C reduced the serum cholesterol level by 10 percent. In the United States, Dr. Ralph Mumma reports that a high intake of vitamin C reduced the cholesterol in laboratory rats. And Dr. Carl Shaffer's experiments with guinea pigs indicate a link between vitamin C deficiency and the development of arteriosclerosis. He observed that an animal, when deprived of vitamin C, develops arteriosclerosis, and that the condition reverted to normal when vitamin C was reintroduced into the animal's system.

The most revealing of these studies was conducted by Drs. Ginter and Onizer of the Institute of Human Nutrition Research in Czechoslovakia. They recorded the vitamin C intake of numerous families over a year. This intake followed seasonal variations, depending on the access to sources, and there seemed to be a corresponding seasonal fluctuation in the cholesterol level. The highest concentration of serum cholesterol occurred during the period of minimal vitamin C intake;

a daily supply of 300 milligrams of vitamin C had, for a period of 47 days, little effect on the cholesterol levels of the subjects. But once their cells were saturated with vitamin C, this same intake was found to lower the cholesterol blood level. Ginter and Onizer theorized that during the winter months the cells contain a very low level of vitamin C and the highest level cholesterol. During the other seasons, when vitamin C is sufficiently abundant for the cells to build up their reserves, the cholesterol level drops.

Numerous studies substantiate the well-known contention that stress and sedentary life contribute to heart disease. And while the importance of vitamin C is reassuring, especially to the vegetarian, the wide variety of experiments and results illustrates the complexity of heart disease vis-à-vis dietary fats. Nor does it help when one doctor prescribes a low-cholesterol diet, another says that dietary cholesterol consumption is irrelevant, a third tells you to cut down on polyunsaturates, and a fourth fears you may have a deficiency of essential fatty acids. What *is* a rational fat consumption?

A rational fat consumption allows enough fat intake for the proper absorption of fat-soluble vitamins and other nutrients, balances saturated and unsaturated fat (a ratio of one to three), and avoids highly processed fats. Because hydrogenation reduces the linolenic content of a fat, buy small quantities of chemical-free cold-pressed oils and keep them refrigerated and airtight. Use a low temperature when frying, as high heat speeds up oxidation. Discard oil which is smoking or burned, as it is hard to digest and irritates the gastrointestinal lining. Avoid fried foods in restaurants because they are fried in grease that has been heated for hours. Prepare the variety of foods which are low in saturated fats, such as non-creamed cottage cheese, lean meats, and seafoods; and instead of frying your foods, broil, boil, bake, roast, steam, or poach them. As a general rule, keep your fat intake down to no more than one fourth of your total calories.

FACTS TO PONDER

— Triglycerides account for 98–99 percent of the fat intake of most Americans. The phospholipids lecithin and cholesterol account for a tiny percentage of our fat intake, but receive more attention than all the rest.

— Regardless of labels and advertising, liquid fat is more saturated than solid fat, and the temperature at which a fat melts will clearly indicate the degree of its fatty-acid saturation.

— Fats containing a high proportion of unsaturated fatty acids are vulnerable to oxidation when exposed to air and high temperatures.

— Only linoleic acid is considered essential to the diet. In the presence of vitamin B_6, the body is able to synthesize the other important fatty acids from the dietary linoleic acid. The richest source of linoleic acid is safflower oil.

— The liver is the control center of fat metabolism.

— The hardness of body fat depends on the proportion of linoleic acids in the diet. A diet high in unsaturated fatty acids produces soft body fat.

— Extreme heat reduces a fat's digestibility.

— In general, vegetable and fish oils are highly unsaturated; animal fats are highly saturated.

— All fats and oils contain both saturated and unsaturated fatty acids.

— Concentrated feeding and confinement of animals have converted the soft, partially unsaturated animal fat into a hard, white, highly saturated fat.

— Nickel, a catalyst agent used in the hydrogenation of fats and oils, is a suspected carcinogen.

— Imported olive oil is usually less refined than domestic olive oil.

— Pesticide residues concentrate and can be retained in the fatty portions of grains.

— Seeds and nuts are good sources of unsaturates.

— Coconut oil is a highly saturated fat and is used extensively in commercial candies and baked goods because of its preservative ability.
— Americans eat over 235,000 tons of peanut butter a year.
— Margarine is made from palm, coconut, peanut, and soybean oils.

CHAPTER
15

CARBOHYDRATES

CARBOHYDRATES ARE PLENTIFUL ORGANIC COMPOUNDS FOUND in the cellulose of plants, in roots, grains, nuts, seeds, fruits, and vegetables. About half the calories in your diet are derived from carbohydrates. Carbohydrates are comprised of carbon, hydrogen, and oxygen atoms—the hydrogen and oxygen proportions being the same as in water. A carbohydrate is simply a "hydrated" carbon, a carbon atom linked to a water molecule.

The group of carbohydrate compounds includes starches, sugars, and celluloses. Starches and sugars, regardless of sources or chemical complexity, are always broken down by the body into its main fuel, glucose. Cellulose, on the other hand, is passed through the digestive tract as a fibrous mass and provides the roughage necessary for proper digestion of other foods. If we were able to absorb the sugar contained in cellulose, our food energy supply would be unlimited: grass, flowers, and leaves—nearly any form of plant food—would fill the carbohydrate needs of our bodies.

Sugars, according to the complexity of their molecular structures, are classified into monosaccharides (simple sugars), disaccharides (double sugars), and polysaccharides (complex sugars).

The monosaccharide molecular structure is a single-sugar unit which cannot be hydrolyzed, or broken down, into smaller units. These simple sugars have the greatest nutritional importance and include glucose, fructose, galactose, and ribose. Glucose, fructose, and galactose are six-carbon sugars present in fruit juice, plant sap, and honey. They differ from one another primarily in their physical properties, such as solubility and sweetness. All are easily absorbed through the intestinal lining and carried directly to the liver, where fructose and galactose are converted into glucose.

Glucose—also known as dextrose, grape sugar, and blood sugar—is the major source of energy for the brain and nervous system and the most important of the sugars. All carbohydrates except cellulose are transformed into glucose before being absorbed into the bloodstream and used directly by the cells for energy. This extremely soluble compound, the least sweet-tasting of all the monosaccharides, occurs naturally in sweet fruits such as grapes, berries, and oranges and in vegetables such as corn and carrots.

Fructose, or fruit sugar, is found in fruits, honey, certain vegetables, and the sap of many plants. It is much sweeter than glucose and for that reason is one of the main constituents of table sugar.

Galactose, the third of the monosaccharides, does not exist in a free state in nature. The sole source of galactose is lactose, the sugar found in milk. Galactose must also be converted into glucose before it can be used for energy.

Disaccharides, more complex sugars, contain two monosaccharides. The most common disaccharides are sucrose, lactose, and maltose. Sucrose is found in maple, cane, and beet sugar, as well as in molasses and sorghum, and has equal parts of glucose and fructose. Sucrose, the most widely used commercial disaccharide, is commonly found in refined-carbohydrate products such as baked goods, pastries, candies, sodas, and other sweet foods. The transformation of sucrose into a useful form is, however, a wasteful process: the distillation of glucose and fructose from sucrose requires certain minerals and the B vitamins niacin and riboflavin. If you eat too many sucrose-rich foods, your body's reserve of these vitamins is lowered.

The disaccharide lactose is found only in milk. Human milk contains 5 to 8 percent lactose and cow's milk only 4 to 6 percent, which explains the slightly sweeter taste of the former. Lactose is less soluble than other sugars and is therefore retained in the intestines long enough to encourage the growth of bacteria which promote the synthesis of some B vitamins. Many people can't digest it at all; it has, in fact, been recorded that 70 percent of the world's adult population is lactose-intolerant.[1] These people lack the enzyme lactase, without which lactose cannot be hydrolyzed. They experience diarrhea after drinking milk because the lactose passes into the large intestine and, instead of being digested, ferments.

Maltose, or malt sugar, is a by-product of starch digestion and is not found in a free form in nature. This disaccharide is often included in infant-feeding formulas.

Polysaccharides, including starches and complex sugars, are the most common carbohydrates in our diet. Polysaccharides are heavy and complex carbohydrate molecules containing ten or more monosaccharide units. They are neither sweet nor soluble in water, and their conversion to glucose is a multiple-step process. Starch, cellulose, and glycogen are the most important polysaccharides in human nutrition. Starch is found in grains, roots, vegetables, nuts, seeds, and legumes. Complex sugars are found in fruits.

The chief function of carbohydrates is to provide energy: each gram of carbohydrate supplies four calories. All carbohydrates except cellulose are ultimately converted to glucose, the sole form of energy for the brain and nervous tissue. Glucose must constantly be available to these tissues to ensure their proper function. A thirteen-hour supply of glucose is stored, in the form of glycogen, in the liver, muscles, and adipose tissue. At any given moment, about 100 grams of glycogen are stored in the liver and 200 grams in the body's muscle, a sum sufficient to half a day's energy needs.

Carbohydrates are the primary fuel of muscular exercise. An adequate supply of carbohydrates spares the proteins for their important body-building functions.

Carbohydrate is a more efficient fuel for muscular exercise than either protein or fat. Protein and fat as a muscle fuel yield less than their total caloric value because they must first be converted into glucose, and in the process some of their molecules are lost. Carbohydrates also act as body regulators by taking part in the synthesis of vital body compounds and help the body resist infection. (A group of polysaccharides called *immunopolysaccharides* are part of the body's defense mechanism.)

Of all the organs and tissues in your body, the central nervous system is most dependent on a continuous supply of glucose. Nervous tissue contains very little glycogen—which can be converted to glucose—and is therefore dependent on glucose in the blood, the level of which is maintained by a steady intake of carbohydrates. Otherwise, hypoglycemic symptoms will develop. Although the cells of the central nervous system can, during a prolonged fast, use ketone bodies (fats used for fuel) in place of glucose for energy, you cannot afford to deprive your body of a daily supply of carbohydrates. Without an adequate carbohydrate intake, your body will metabolize fat for use as an alternate fuel, breaking it down into free fatty acids for muscular activities and ketone bodies for brain cells. Usually, the rate of fat breakdown and ketone-body formation is such that ketone bodies are promptly disposed of by peripheral tissues. However, when fatty-acid breakdown becomes excessively rapid and the formation of ketone bodies in the liver is more than the peripheral tissues can handle, ketone bodies accumulate in the blood and are excreted in the urine—a condition known as *ketosis*. An intake of carbohydrates can usually correct a mild state of ketosis, but for diabetics ketosis is severe, and coma or even death may result if insulin is not administered.

Once the fat stores are consumed, your body will then burn its protein for fuel. The conversion of protein to fuel taxes the body, and protein can be used only for a limited time before starvation begins. The daily protein intake *must* be accompanied by an adequate intake of carbohydrates and fats if proteins are to perform their body-building functions.

An adequate carbohydrate intake protects the liver by providing it with adequate glycogen, the substance it stores for conversion into glucose. A liver adequately stocked with glycogen is more resistant to poisonous substances such as alcohol, arsenic, and toxic bacteria. A high glycogen level in the liver is, in fact, necessary for the health of the entire body, for one of the chief liver functions is to filter toxic agents before they poison other vital organs. Glycogen is also needed in the liver for the regulation of the synthesis of hormones and for the disposal of steroid substances that might be carcinogenic.

Carbohydrates also facilitate digestion. The carbohydrates cellulose, hemicellulose, and pectin are indigestible, but their bulk stimulates the wavelike peristaltic movements of the gastrointestinal tract which moves the food through the digestion process. These three carbohydrates, known as fiber or roughage, are found in the skins of fruits and vegetables and in the outer coating of cereal grains. They undergo no chemical changes in the digestive tract. Tough fibers may be broken into smaller pieces by muscular contractions of the stomach and intestines and softened by stomach acids, but they are not dissolved. For most people, a daily diet of raw vegetables, fresh fruits with skins, and cooked fruits and vegetables will provide sufficient fiber. Those with digestive problems may need to increase their fiber intake by including bran, wholegrain cereals, or bread. Vegetarians normally get three or four times the fiber of nonvegetarians.

Carbohydrates are digested by breaking down the complex

sugars, disaccharides and polysaccharides into simple sugars (monosaccharide). Monosaccharides require no additional digestive action.

Carbohydrate digestion begins in the mouth. As the food is chewed, the parotid glands near the ear secrete saliva containing amylase. Amylase contains ptyalin, the enzyme which triggers the conversion of starch, glycogen, and dextrin into maltose. This conversion action continues until the hydrochloric acid secreted in the stomach halts the amylase activity. The by-products of maltose—glucose, fructose, and galactose —are then absorbed through the walls of the small intestine. These monosaccharides are absorbed according to the rate at which the food travels through the stomach and intestine; the higher the fiber content of the meal, the more quickly it will pass through the digestive tract, and the healthier the digestive and bowel actions will be.

After the carbohydrates have been absorbed through the wall of the small intestine, they are carried to the liver, the control center for fuel metabolism. There the glucose is converted into either adipose or glycogen; it may be stored, sent to the muscle walls for low-blood-sugar emergencies, or sent via the bloodstream to the cells for energy. The liver's use of the glucose is determined largely by the level of glucose already in the blood and by the cells' demand for fuel.

If you consume large amounts of carbohydrates during the day and place little stress on your body, your liver's glycogen reserves will probably be converted to fat. If carbohydrate intake is low and stress or exercise high, the glucose will immediately enter your bloodstream to nourish the cells. Once your cells are adequately nourished, the excess glucose is converted to glycogen for storage in the liver and adipose tissues.

It is vitally important that your blood maintain an adequate glucose level because your brain and central nervous system can use *only* glucose as its source of energy. Your nervous system can store only a low level of glycogen for emergencies —a thirteen-hour supply. But glucose is so important to your body as a fuel that even when your carbohydrate diet is poor, adaptive reactions in your body assure the cells a steady glucose supply. Your body will convert fat to glucose until your fat reserves are exhausted, and then convert protein to glucose until the point of starvation. These adaptive reactions take place because the cells' energy needs take priority over all bodily functions.

The body also regulates its glucose level through hormonal action. When the blood-glucose level is too high, the pancreas maintains a proper level by excreting insulin, which facilitates the synthesis of glycogen and the conversion of glucose into fatty acids. When the blood-glucose level is too low, the pancreas secretes a hormone called glucagon, which raises the level by increasing the conversion of glycogen into glucose. Many carbohydrate foods are rich, sweet, and high in calories, so are often considered fattening. That most of our body fat comes from carbohydrates does not necessarily make carbohydrates fattening. Once your daily quota of calories has been filled, any excess calories—whether carbohydrates, fats, or proteins—are deposited as fat in your body's adipose tissue. It is therefore illogical to label any one type of foodstuff as fattening—*all* foodstuffs are fattening if taken in sufficient quantities.

SOURCES OF DIETARY CARBOHYDRATES

Carbohydrates are the most abundant of all organic compounds. Cellulose, for example, is the main constituent of all plant cells and fibers. Carbohydrates are concentrated in grains, roots, nuts, seeds, vegetables, and fruits. The primary sources in the human diet are grains and vegetables and fruits.

Grains and legumes are all excellent sources of carbohydrates, as well as vitamins and minerals. So important were these foods to many cultures that the seed was often worshiped as a deity. North American Indians revered corn as the "giver of life" and cooked with it in innumerable ways. For thousands of years grains have been baked into breads, leavened and unleavened, ground into gruels and porridges, and even sprouted. Since 3000 B.C. the Chinese have known that sprouted seeds are even more nutritious than cooked seeds. During sprouting, seeds increase their vitamin A content by 300 percent and their vitamin C content by 500 to 600 percent,[2] and the sprouting process converts starches to simple sugars, which makes sprouts more easily digested than the grains and seeds they come from.

Potatoes have been the staple of European nations for hundreds of years, and now the world potato crop is second only to the world wheat crop. Of the nearly 293 metric tons of potatoes grown in the world in 1967, 85 percent were grown in Europe.[3] Some historians associate the eighteenth-century European population explosion with the efficiency of the potato as a food staple. Potatoes are a good source of protein and carbohydrates, and historically have been more productive and less expensive than grain crops. Yams and sweet potatoes are other tubers which contain carbohydrates. Root vegetables have a longer season than vegetables grown above the ground, and they are often more nutritious.

We must not forget fruits, of course. Fruits are a good source of cellulose and sugars. Dates, figs, prunes, sweet grapes, apples, bananas, and raisins are excellent sources of glucose.

Pouring instant potatoes from a box instead of peeling the genuine article is routine procedure for many Americans. Breakfast tables display cereal boxes boasting of wheat and corn shot by guns, puffed up, flaked, checked, made with alphabet letters, stars, or doodles—most of them laced with sugar. A familiar companion to these convenience carbohydrates is the loaf of soft, spongy, white bread with its nine shelf lives. Carbohydrate foods compete heavily for the consumer's attention in an extraordinary variety of forms. In processed potatoes, grains, breads, and other carbohydrate foods, the fiber, vitamins, minerals, and essential amino acids have been replaced by synthetic vitamins and minerals, preservatives, and sugar. The result: a longer shelf life.

American consumption of carbohydrate foods over the past several years has steadily remained at about 50 percent of the total caloric intake, but the nature of these carbohydrates has changed drastically. The heavy processing of carbohydrate foods has caused a shift from starch to sugar. From 1909 to 1913, starches constituted 56.1 percent of America's carbohydrate consumption, with sugar providing 21.5 percent. Fifty years later, from 1960 to 1964, sugars provided 35.7 percent and starches 37 percent.

Since foods high in carbohydrate content are relatively inexpensive compared with those rich in protein and fat, the working class relies heavily on these carbohydrates for its calories. Its diet includes a larger proportion of carbohydrates than do the diets of the middle and upper classes. Unfortunately, most of these carbohydrates are highly refined and, consequently, fill the body with "empty" calories and dull the appetite for nutritious foods.

How have carbohydrate foods been devitalized? White flour, the basis for many refined carbohydrate foods, has been produced by the ton since 1874, when the invention of the steel rolling mill made possible the large-scale conversion of whole-wheat flour into white flour. Whole-wheat flour consists of the germ (the heart of the wheat grain) and the bran (the first six outer layers of the wheat berry), both of which contain protein and fat. Whole-wheat flour, however, is vulnerable to rancidity and unless refrigerated has a short shelf life. Milling strips away the germ and bran portions, leaving a white, starchy flour with a longer shelf life.

A famous study conducted in 1943 revealed that rollermilling reduces the whole-wheat content of manganese by 98 percent, iron by 80 percent, magnesium by 75 percent, phosphorus by 70 percent, copper by 65 percent, calcium by 50 percent, potassium by 50 percent, thiamine by 80 percent, niacin by 75 percent, riboflavin by 65 percent, pantothenic acid by 50 percent, and pyridoxine by 50 percent.[4] The study also reported that processing reduced the B vitamins inositol, folic acid, choline, and biotin, as well as the para-aminobenzoic acid content of wheat.

White flour has, since 1935, been "enriched" with synthetic thiamine, riboflavin, and niacin, and with iron, calcium, and vitamin D. Most people, however, are not aware—and food companies don't advertise—that many nutrients removed from whole wheat are *not* restored: the vitamins biotin, pyridoxine, and pantothenic acid, the minerals phosphorus, potassium, manganese, and copper, and the essential amino acids lysine and tryptophan.[5]

White flour has been prized for centuries by the upper classes, who considered it more delicate and refined, and by the bakers, who depended upon it for elegant tarts, pastries, and cakes. Millers then discovered that the baking qualities of flour could be improved by further bleaching. Bleaching also allowed them to sell inferior and high-quality flour together; no one would be the wiser.

Processed flour today is bleached with chlorine dioxide, which—according to trade literature—"not only oxidizes the flour pigment but also has a valuable bleaching effect on the coloring matter of the bran, which makes it particularly valuable for bleaching very low grade flours." An article in the *British Journal of Nutrition* claims that chlorine dioxide destroys whatever vitamin E survived the milling process. Further, this chemical may react with the amino acid methionine to form an unhealthful substance.[6]

The average American eats approximately 92 one-pound loaves of bread a year, most of which contain additives he or she is not aware of. Although federal law requires bakeries to proclaim on bread labels the presence of calcium or sodium propionate, it places no demands on bakeries to list the 80 chemical ingredients used to flavor, preserve, and color bread. In fact, America's bread industry uses over 16 million pounds of chemicals per year, primarily leaveners and preservatives.

Chemical emulsifiers are substituted for milk, nitric acid is used as a yellow coloring in place of egg yolks, artificial butter flavoring supplants the genuine article, and dough conditioners are added to ensure a product which is consistent despite the variations in flour characteristics. These compounds render bread dough drier, more elastic, and easier to machine; and, as cheap substitutes for more expensive raw ingredients, they increase bread volume and profits. Oxidizing agents, to keep air in the dough while it bakes, and shortenings with emulsifiers increase the volume of the loaves. These additives are added not only to bread, but to almost all processed baked goods. Use of additives has become so extensive that the average bread loaf contains as little as 50 percent flour and the average cake only 25 percent.

Wheat is not the only grain to suffer nutritionally from processing. Corn, refined into cornmeal, is depleted in protein, fiber, fat, niacin, riboflavin, thiamine, phosphorus, iron, and vitamin A. Brown rice is converted into the convenient white, "minute" variety: the hull, embryo, and outer layers of the rice, all of which are rich in nutrients and the essential amino acid lysine, are removed; the rice which remains is high in starch and low in protein. Grains such as rye and buckwheat are processed for use in pretzels, pancake mixes, and breakfast cereals. Only oatmeal survives refinement with any integrity. Oat milling removes only the hull. Most of the bran and germ remain, as do the proteins, lipids, and vitamins.

The next time you find yourself in a supermarket, try counting the number of cereal brands. More than 70 of them compete for an annual sales volume of $600 million; about 12 percent, or $72 million, is allocated to advertising and promoting these cereals. Cereals are big business, and of late have come under heavy indictment thanks to their nutritional inadequacy and heavy coatings of sugar and artificial sweeteners. Robert B. Choate, Jr., a former government adviser on hunger, testified before a Senate Consumers Subcommittee that the nutritional content of ten leading breakfast cereals is so low as to be justifiably called sources of empty calories. Mr. Choate charged that these cereals "fatten but do little to prevent malnutrition." Some cereals contain more sugar than grain, and are much more expensive than unsweetened brands.

The potato, once sold with dirt still on the skin, has gone the way of the burlap bag of whole wheat—to the processors for transformation into convenience food. Now available are potato flakes, precut hashbrowns, french fries, potato pancakes, potato puffs, potato chips, diced potatoes, potatoes au gratin, and frozen baked potatoes complete with sour cream or cheese toppings. In 1950, the average American consumed 6.3 pounds of processed potatoes per year; by 1969 that figure had risen to 49.4 pounds, almost half of the total consumption per person per year. Proportionately the number of fresh cooked potatoes steadily declined.[7] Processed potatoes contain preservatives, synthetic vitamins, emulsifiers, antioxidants (which stretch the shelf life of potato chips from three days to twenty-six days), stabilizers, and thickeners.

Of what consequence is this processing to you? Many nutritionists and laboratory investigators believe that processed carbohydrate foods contribute heavily to the epidemic proportions of gastrointestinal disorders, obesity, diabetes, hypoglycemia, tooth decay, and heart disease. Dr. T. L. Cleave has published numerous articles on this connection and considers refined carbohydrates a prime cause of obesity, peptic ulcers, diabetes, varicose veins, *Escherichia coli* infections, and urinary-tract infections. He has traced the rise of these diseases to the wide-scale introduction of refined carbohydrates. His theory is supported by studies of primitive tribal cultures that suddenly developed new diseases once exposed to a Western diet of refined carbohydrates.

Dr. Denis Burkitt, a former medical missionary in Uganda, and currently on Britain's Medical Research Council, has studied extensively the relationship of a highly refined, low-fiber diet to cancer of the bowels, the most common form of the disease after lung cancer. Dr. Burkitt noted that Ugandans, who live on a high-fiber banana diet, have the lowest rate of colon-rectal cancer in the world and that residents of Connecticut, with one tenth the fiber intake of the Africans, have the highest. The Ugandans have a daily intake of about 25 grams of fiber; the Connecticut residents have an intake of only 2¾ grams. In a thesis recently published in the *Journal of the American Medical Association*, Dr. Burkitt and two colleagues (Drs. Neil Painter and A. R. P. Walker) observe that populations with a high incidence of colon-rectal cancer consume greater amounts of fat and that the intestinal bacteria are consequently altered. The intestinal bacteria of persons in high-risk populations reduce bile salts into substances which may cause cancer. And when such people are on a low-fiber diet, their intestinal contents move slowly through the digestive tract, giving harmful bacteria more time to multiply. When fiber is added to the diet, however, the breakdown of bile salts is less frequent and material passes through the digestive tract twice as quickly. Dr. Burkitt is convinced that fiber deficiency, while not the sole cause of colon cancer and other diseases, is a primary factor.[8]

A change to a high-fiber diet involves substitution of whole-grain products and fresh raw fruits and vegetables for refined carbohydrates and processed fruits and vegetables. A diet including whole-wheat bread, rolled oats, brown rice, bran, and vegetables and fruits—with seeds, skins, and strings intact—is high in fiber and valuable nutrients. If you prefer a more gradual increase of fiber, begin by adding a few grams of wheat bran to your daily cereal, or by mixing it with fruit juice, yogurt, or soups. Bran is five times as effective in restoring roughage to the body as is whole-wheat flour, so a small amount is sufficient.

Dr. David Reuben and others have pointed out that a high-fiber diet encourages weight loss. High-fiber foods must be well chewed: the more you chew, the more saliva and gastric juices are produced. These liquids mix with the food in the stomach, swell up the food fibers, and increase the feeling of fullness. A high-fiber meal is likely to satiate you before you eat too much.

Other researchers are investigating the relationship of dietary fiber to heart disease. Studies involving pectins, indigestible carbohydrate substances derived from fruits and vegetables, have been conducted at the University of Iowa. During an initial four weeks, three healthy men were fed according to the average American diet; during the second five weeks, the men were fed the same diet, supplemented by 20 to 23 grams of pectin per day. Once the pectin was added, the serum cholesterol levels of the men decreased by 13 percent, and more fat was excreted in their stools.

It is theorized that pectins and other fibers may reduce serum cholesterol levels by reducing the body's absorption of cholesterol by altering the intestinal environment or by increasing the elimination of bile acids.[9]

Refined carbohydrates have been linked to the high incidence of dental problems. Tooth decay results from bacterial production of acid which, if allowed to remain on the tooth surface, dissolves the enamel and causes a cavity. The frequency of carbohydrate intake, not the total amount consumed, influences tooth decay. Carbohydrates, particularly sugar, also interfere with the maturation of tooth enamel, which makes children on high-carbohydrate diets particularly susceptible to cavities. Powdered sugar is especially cariogenic.

Some 5 million Americans are diabetic, and of that number over 35,000 die every year. It is estimated that by 1980, 10 percent of all Americans will have the disease or carry it in their genes. As diabetes reaches epidemic proportions, more and more researchers are examining the American diet for its cause; their conclusions increasingly support our overconsumption of refined carbohydrates—particularly sugar—as a factor in the development of diabetes, and other diseases involving glucose-level imbalance.

The average American's carbohydrate diet is 50 percent

sucrose, which is devoid of nutrients. The conversion of sucrose into glucose is a process that taxes the body's nutrients —B vitamins in particular—and vitamin B deficiency has been identified as a cause of depression. The average adult consumes 126 pounds of sucrose per year: in the form of table sugar, or hidden in soft drinks, desserts, baked goods, sauces, etc. In the six-to-twenty age bracket, sugar consumption averages 150 pounds a year.

The diabetes syndrome may result from the overstimulation of the insulin response and the impairment of the insulin-producing system caused by excessive amounts of sugar. Insulin is secreted by the pancreas to control the level of glucose in the blood. If your pancreas fails to produce and excrete this hormone appropriately, your blood glucose reaches a dangerously high level.

Hypoglycemia, or low blood sugar, attracts greater media coverage as more and more people discover they have it. Hypoglycemia is a syndrome, rather than a distinct disease, that causes a glucose deficiency in the blood, which in turn impairs the function of the nervous system. Hypoglycemia is chronically found in people diagnosed as schizophrenic, alcoholic, or prone to migraine headaches, hyperactivity, obesity, fatigue, trembling, anxiety, depression, allergies, cold sweats, dizziness, fainting spells, forgetfulness, and other disorders.

Such symptoms are common to all of us: we experience traces of hypoglycemia each day. Hypoglycemia brings on the late-morning and afternoon cravings for coffee or snacks, midmorning or midafternoon drowsiness, mild depression, and that trembling feeling. "Hunger pangs" indicate a low blood-sugar level, not an empty stomach. For most people, these symptoms are ephemeral; for others, however, hypoglycemia causes persistent physiological and emotional depression. The vegetarian, fortunately, is less susceptible to the hypoglycemia syndrome, as fewer refined carbohydrates are part of a vegetarian diet.

In the chronic syndrome of hypoglycemia, the pancreas

secretes too much insulin, which causes the glucose level of the blood to fall to an abnormally low level. This depressed level starves the brain and nervous system, and in extreme cases results in coma. Hypoglycemia is often induced by over-indulgence in sweets and refined carbohydrates: coffee, cola, strong tea, and nicotine.

But how, you ask, can eating a lot of sugar *lower* one's blood sugar? Isn't sugar a source of quick energy? When you eat a candy bar or a rich dessert, your intestine quickly absorbs the sugar, and your level of blood glucose shoots up rapidly; this is the "energy lift." Unfortunately, it's only temporary. But once your pancreas detects the high blood-sugar level, it pumps insulin to normalize this level. The sugar burns off rapidly by itself, leaving you with suddenly low blood sugar; the insulin then further lowers that level. To compensate, the liver converts its stored glycogen to glucose in order to raise the blood-sugar level to normal. When the liver's glycogen stores run low, however, the last tiny amount of glycogen is reserved for a physiological emergency. At this point, glucose production simply stops. A few candy bars or heavy sweets a day will cause this taxing cycle to repeat itself and the chronic overdumping of insulin depletes the liver's glycogen stores with the result of an insufficient blood sugar level.

Hypoglycemics must either avoid or drastically reduce refined sugars, as well as caffeine, nicotine, and alcohol. A person prone to hypoglycemia is usually told to eat up to six small high-protein meals a day—to provide a steady flow of energy throughout the day—and to snack on protein foods like cheese and nuts instead of carbohydrate foods like potato chips and pretzels. Once the hypoglycemic cycle is broken with a regular high-protein/moderate-carbohydrate diet, the craving for sugar ceases, and the blood maintains a normal level of glucose.

J. Daniel Palm, of St. Olaf College in Minnesota, reports that he has successfully treated hypoglycemics with fructose. In two years of testing, hundreds of hypoglycemia patients were administered 100 grams of fructose per day as a supplement to their carbohydrate-free diets; the symptomatic hunger, fatigue, and anxiety were alleviated. Palm believes that fructose combats hypoglycemia symptoms simply because it is a form of energy for the nervous system which does not trigger the secretion of insulin as does glucose.[10]

Refined sugar is another suspected factor in heart disease and is thought by some researchers to be a greater risk than a high intake of saturated fat or a high serum cholesterol level. According to Dr. John Yudkin and his colleagues at the University of London, the person who consumes four ounces of sugar daily—from any and all sources—is five times as likely to develop heart disease as someone eating only half that amount. He concludes from his studies that sugar is the principal cause of heart disease, diabetes, and other killers.

Professor Richard A. Ahrens, of the University of Maryland, thinks that refined sugar contributes to circulatory problems by increasing the concentration of blood solids, thereby producing hypertension. In an article published in the *American Journal of Clinical Nutrition*, he argues that sucrose can cause a significant rise in blood triglyceride (fat) levels, reduce urine output, and elevate the blood cholesterol level.

Obesity is a less dramatic but equally fatal consequence of a high-carbohydrate diet, particularly one of refined carbohydrates. Refined sugar is an "empty food"—very high in calories but utterly void of vitamins, minerals, essential amino acids, and fatty acids. Worthless nutritionally, sugar can only tax the body's nutrients as it is converted to glucose. Sugar also kills the appetite for foods which do contain the essential nutrients. Since sweets and starches satisfy the body's hunger for only a short while, a large amount is required to satisfy the hunger craving. The unavoidable upshot is obesity. One out of every four Americans is overweight, one out of two improperly nourished.[11] Of course, too many calories in any form (fats, protein, carbohydrate) and too little exercise are also prime factors in overweight.

Processed carbohydrate foods are easily recognized: slickly packaged, they either boast of their ability to "cook in minutes" or are premixed with all the necessary ingredients. Their cost is also special: about three times more than you'd pay for the raw ingredients. Their packages list the synthetic vitamins, preservatives, and other less familiar ingredients. Nearly all the breakfast cereals consist of refined grains coated with refined sugar—even "back-to-nature" cereals contain refined brown sugar. The solution to this problem is a delicious one: buy your own oats, wheat flakes, buckwheat, or millet; cook them singly or together as a hot cereal, or roast them with honey and oil to make your own dry granola cereal. If you like, add dry fruits, nuts, or seeds.

You can also buy and refrigerate whole-wheat bread free of preservatives, emulsifiers, and stabilizers—if there's a local bakery you can trust. The best guarantee of purity and freshness is, of course, to bake your own bread. If you do, bake several loaves at a time and freeze the extra.

If you like brown rice, buy it with hulls intact and refrigerate until ready for use. This rice requires an additional twenty to thirty minutes of cooking, but has the wonderfully chewy texture, nutty flavor, the vitamins and minerals that white rice lacks. As for potatoes, cook with real ones and leave the skins on whenever possible: they contain about 20 percent of the nutrients.

Stay away from refined sugar and products that contain it. Even raw sugar and brown sugar should be avoided, though they contain some trace of vitamins and minerals. Neither light nor dark brown sugar succeeds in making "enriched" bread enriched; they have been stripped of their nutrients and treated with molasses to restore their original dark color. These sugars are essentially sucrose and can overstimulate insulin reaction, lower the blood sugar, and tax the body's energy supply.

Honey, while just as likely to cause obesity, tooth decay, and other ailments as sugar, is probably the least damaging sweetener. It consists of fructose and glucose, neither of which requires conversion; both can be absorbed directly into the bloodstream through the stomach wall. Honey is relatively free of pesticidal contamination and artificial flavors, colors, and preservatives. Honey contains the enzyme inhibine, which prevents molding and renders preservatives superfluous. You can use honey to replace table sugar in cooking and baking, to sweeten tea, coffee, and cereals.

Remember that most soft drinks and many fruit juices contain sucrose or artificial sweeteners. Drink pure fruit juice and sweeten your own lemonade and iced tea with honey. Avoid packaged mixes of these drinks. When you eat fruit, also eat the peels—they are important sources of cellulose and vitamins. Vegetables cooked lightly retain both their fiber content and their vitamins, minerals, and enzymes. Make a habit of cooking with whole-wheat flour instead of bleached white flour; though lumpy, it is preferable because of its nutty flavor and abundant nutrients.

FACTS TO PONDER

— Out of the average American family's food budget, at least $200 a year goes for the packages that contain the food itself.
— Historically, light-colored bread has been a sign of wealth and prestige.
— Although bread labels may list only one chemical additive, up to 60 other chemicals may be present in the loaf.
— During the past 70 years, carbohydrates have accounted for about 50 percent of the total caloric intake in the American diet.
— Highly refined grains and sugars are the cheapest sources of calories.
— Cellulose is found in the skeletal structure of plants, the skins of fruits, the coverings of seeds, and the outer layers

of grains. Its dietary function is to provide bulk for the intestines.

— Glycogen is the form in which monosaccharides are stored in the liver and muscle tissue of humans and animals.

— All carbohydrates must be converted into glucose before they can be used by the body.

— Refined sugar is stripped of its B vitamins, vitamin E, and trace minerals copper, manganese, zinc, and iron.

— Sugar, like salt, is found in nearly all processed foods.

— The average American consumes one quarter pound of sugar daily.

— By 1967, the annual per capita consumption of candy in the United States had reached 19.6 pounds.

— The annual consumption of soft drinks in the United States amounts to 243 eight-ounce bottles per person.

— Cirrhosis of the liver has been discovered in teenagers who drink large quantities of soft drinks.

— The body prefers carbohydrates over fats or proteins for its energy needs. Proteins will be converted to glucose only when the supply of carbohydrates is insufficient.

— A healthy person stores about 13 hours' worth of glucose and glycogen in the liver.

— The brain and nervous system require a steady supply of glucose to function properly.

— A liver with a high concentration of stored glycogen is more resistant to toxic substances.

— Dietary fiber contains no nutrients, but it stimulates the wavelike movement of the intestinal tract necessary for regular elimination.

— Carbohydrates cannot supplant fat in the diet since they lack essential fatty acids and fat-soluble vitamins.

— Excess calories—whether in the form of carbohydrate, protein, or fat—are deposited as fat in the adipose tissue. It is therefore inaccurate to label any one of these fattening, because all of them are fattening if taken in large quantities.

— Carbohydrates are the most efficient body fuel for muscular exercise.

— Carbohydrates and fats are both fuel material; the former are indispensable, the latter are not.

— The pituitary gland of a person under emotional stress secretes the hormone epinephrine, which triggers the liver's conversion of glycogen into glucose.

— When violent exercise is preceded or accompanied by a large carbohydrate intake, the body works somewhat more efficiently.

— In developing countries of the tropics, carbohydrates may account for up to 90 percent of the diet.

— Carbohydrates from cereal grains represent the primary source of energy for the world's population.

— Carbohydrates are compounds synthesized by living organisms and have as their common elements carbon, hydrogen, and oxygen.

— Pectins and agar, both indigestible polysaccharides, are used in the processing of jellies, jams, and preserves because of their ability to absorb water and make substances gel.

— In 1880, the average American consumed 8.1 grams of fiber per day, as compared to 3 grams today.

— Epidemiological studies of different populations indicate a strong correlation between high-fiber diets and low serum cholesterol levels. New Guinea males on an unrefined native diet had serum cholesterol levels of 109 milligrams, whereas those on a refined diet averaged 183 milligrams.

— The milling of rice both removes vitamins and proteins and changes the quality of the remaining protein by reducing its percentage of lysine, an essential amino acid. Minute Rice undergoes the heaviest processing of all: it is soaked, steamed, and dried quickly to produce a puffy quality.

16

VITAMINS

THE TERM *vitamin* APPLIES TO THOSE ORGANIC COMPOUNDS which are not proteins, carbohydrates, or fats. Though found in extremely small quantities in foods, vitamins are necessary for various bodily functions. Because many vitamins can't be manufactured in sufficient amounts by the body, they must be supplied by the diet.

Polish scientist Casimir Funk, of the Lister Institute of London, isolated a B-vitamin in 1912 and called it "vitamine" —*vita*, the Latin word for life, plus *amine*, an organic substance containing nitrogen. Though we now know that not all vitamins are amines, the name has persisted.

Vitamins were originally given names which reflected their curative abilities or simple letter designations. Nowadays, we often use chemically descriptive names, although the letter names remain in common usage.

Vitamins are divided arbitrarily into two categories: fat-soluble and water-soluble. This classification does not imply any similarity of nature and function of vitamins within the categories.

FAT-SOLUBLE VITAMINS

Scientists didn't identify **vitamin A** until the twentieth century, but its function has long been understood. An Egyptian medical treatise circa 1500 B.C. prescribed liver of ox—a rich store of vitamin A—for night blindness, an affliction we now recognize as a primary symptom of vitamin A deficiency.

In 1913, two separate teams of scientists discovered that rats whose sole fat source was lard ceased to grow and developed eye disorders. When the researchers added butterfat, extract of egg yolk, or cod-liver oil to the diet, these symptoms were corrected. One researcher labeled the organic complex responsible for his improvement "fat-soluble A."

Vitamin A is soluble in fat and fat solvents, but insoluble in water. Stable when exposed to heat, acids, and alkalies, vitamin A is easily oxidized unless in the presence of vitamin E. Ultraviolet irradiation quickly destroys it.

The carotene synthesized by plants is the ultimate source of vitamin A. A large proportion of the carotene consumed by animals and humans is converted into vitamin A and is, therefore, called provitamin A or precursor of vitamin A. The availability of these carotenes varies widely; not all of them in a particular food are absorbed by the body, and not all of the absorbed carotene will be converted to vitamin A. Researchers for the World Health Organization estimated that half of the carotene you absorb is transformed into vitamin A and that only 32 percent of that is eventually utilized.

Because vitamin A, in both pure and carotene form, is absorbed in the same manner as fat, it requires bile. If your diet is low in fat or if the bile tract is obstructed, the absorption of vitamin A and carotene is seriously impaired. If mineral oil is present in the intestinal tract, it will hold the vitamin A and carotenes in solution and cause them to be lost through excretion; mineral oil, therefore, should neither be substituted for other fats in cooking nor be used as a laxative near mealtime.

In the intestinal mucosa, carotenes are converted into retinol and transported in large fat molecules through the bloodstream to the liver. Though a quantity of vitamin A is absorbed directly into the portal circulation, the largest proportion is carried to the liver for storage. Some nutritionists believe that the average healthy adult stores enough vitamin A to meet the body's needs for as long as a year.

As mentioned before, the best-known function of vitamin A is the prevention of night blindness. The retina of the eye has two receptors: rods, for dim light, and cones, for bright light and color vision. When the purple pigment of the rod and the violet pigment of the cone are exposed to light, they split into two parts: vitamin A and protein. The pigments regenerate in the dark, but only if the blood provides sufficient retinol.

Vitamin A is necessary for healthy epithelial tissues—the tissues of the skin and of the passage linings in the hollow organs of the respiratory, urinary, and digestive systems. A vitamin A deficiency leads to shrinking, hardening, and eventual degeneration of these tissues and makes you more susceptible to infections of the eye, ear, sinuses, nasal passages, lungs, and urinary tract. The epithelium of the eye can be irreversibly damaged by a vitamin A deficiency.

Vitamin A deficiency is one of the two major nutritional problems found throughout the world (the other is protein deficiency). Since it usually occurs when the diet lacks other nutrients as well, a pure vitamin A deficiency is hard to find. Scientists have long known that a deficiency of vitamin A retards growth; sadly, it is prevalent among children, whose vitamin A supply is easily depleted during the growing process.

On the other hand, too much vitamin A results in an overdose called hypervitaminosis. Vitamin A, being fat-soluble, is not excreted as readily as water-soluble vitamins. The most common symptoms of hypervitaminosis A are intermittent pain in bones and joints, insomnia and fatigue, hair loss, dryness and cracking of the lips and other skin areas, appetite and weight loss, and enlargement of the liver. Excessive amounts of vitamin A taken by a pregnant woman can have harmful effects on the fetus. Some nutritionists, however, feel that the toxicity factor of vitamin A has been greatly exaggerated. They contend that this vitamin is toxic only in amounts of 100,000 milligrams or more.

Your chances of experiencing hypervitaminosis are slim, and it is more important that your diet provide enough of all vital nutrients, including vitamin A.

The daily recommended dosages of vitamin A are:	
Children up to 12	1500–3500 I.U. (international units) per day
Children over 12	4500–6000 I.U. per day
Adults (moderately active)	5000 I.U. per day
Pregnant women	6000 I.U. per day
Nursing mothers	8000 I.U. per day

Good sources of vitamin A include spinach, asparagus, cooked carrots, apricots, pumpkins, cantaloupe, kale, collards, sweet potatoes, turnip greens, mustard greens, watercress, broccoli, peaches, sour cherries, dark lettuce, tomatoes, egg yolk, milk, butter, cod-liver oil, and halibut-liver oil. Liver and kidneys are the best meat sources.

The Greek historian Herodotus noted the connection between healthy bones and the sun in the fifth century B.C. In the Middle Ages, cod-liver oil was prescribed for rickets. In 1919, Dr. Edward Mellanby of England discovered that the skeletons of growing dogs were affected by a specific fat-soluble substance in the diet. Dr. Alfred Hess of New York found in 1924 that foods exposed to ultraviolet rays could prevent rickets. In 1930, **vitamin D** was isolated in its pure, crystalline form. It was called calciferol.

Though generally considered a single vitamin, vitamin D is actually a group of chemically distinct sterol compounds produced when a provitamin D, or precursor of vitamin D, is exposed to ultraviolet light. The pure forms of vitamin D are white odorless crystals which are soluble in fats and fat solvents and stable in heat, alkalies, and oxidation.

The intestines absorb vitamin D and fat together. Bile salts are required for its absorption. Most of the body's vitamin D is stored in the liver, and the remainder is found in the skin, brain, spleen, lungs, and bones.

As any schoolchild knows, vitamin D is the sunshine vitamin. The sun's ultraviolet rays produce vitamin D on the skin: the vitamin is then absorbed through the skin.

Vitamin D regulates the important absorption of calcium and phosphorus from the intestinal tract. Scientists believe that vitamin D renders the intestinal mucosa more permeable to calcium and phosphorus and facilitates the active transport of calcium across the cell barriers. Vitamin D also controls the deposit of calcium in bones and teeth.

A vitamin D deficiency can eventually result in skeletal malformations. Improper absorption of calcium and phosphorus and mineralization of bones and teeth cause the bones to soften: the skeletal structure cannot carry the body's weight.

Rickets is a vitamin D deficiency disease that affects children. Widespread use of fortified milk and cod-liver oil has made rickets relatively rare in America, but it does occur in northern areas, where there is less sun, and in overcrowded urban areas, where the sun's ultraviolet rays barely penetrate the soot and smog. The most noticeable symptom of this disease is bowleggedness, caused by the softness and fragility of the bones.

The corresponding bone disease in adults is osteomalacia, in which the calcification process falls behind the other metabolic processes of the body. It is sometimes an indirect result of inadequate or otherwise faulty fat absorption. Both rickets and osteomalacia are treated with high doses of vitamin D. Some nutritionists believe that insufficient vitamin D consumption in adults can also lead to pyorrhea, a condition in which the gums and bones around the teeth recede until the remaining bone structure is too weak to hold the teeth in place.

Like vitamin A, vitamin D can be toxic if taken in large amounts. Being fat-soluble, it is not readily discarded by the body. Since vitamin D aids calcium absorption, an excess supply can lead to hypercalcemia—an overabundance of calcium in the blood—which results in the calcification of soft tissues, especially those of the kidneys. The most common symptoms of this condition are loss of appetite, weakness, and constipation.

Fortunately, the range of tolerance for vitamin D is wide. Among children, even a consistent intake of 1800 I.U. is only mildly toxic. The National Research Council recommends a mere 400 I.U. a day, as compared to the 2000 I.U. suggested by some nutritionists. The latter explain that because of our clothing and the poor atmospheric conditions in many parts of the country, we cannot rely on the sun's rays as a consistent, reliable source of vitamin D.

Unfortunately for vegetarians, there are no good plant sources of vitamin D. The best sources are fish oils, especially cod-liver and halibut-liver oils; next best are milk, salmon, tuna, butter, and eggs. For meat eaters, liver is an excellent source.

Vitamin E was discovered at the University of California in 1922 by Drs. Herbert Evans and Katherine Scott Bishop. Since its deficiency caused sterility in rats, they called this vitamin tocopherol, from the Greek *tokos*, meaning childbirth, and *phero*, to bring forth. In 1938 Dr. Karrer of Zürich succeeded in synthesizing it.

Of the four forms of tocopherol—alpha, beta, delta, and gamma—the most active is alpha. Vitamin E is stable in heat and acids, but oxidizes rapidly in the presence of rancid fat and lead or iron salts and is destroyed by ultraviolet light.

Vitamin E is crucial to the proper maintenance of muscles and red blood cells. Its second important function is as an antioxidant. During oxidation in the cells, toxic by-products called peroxides may be released to form free radicals which are responsible, at least in part, for the aging process. In other words, vitamin E might be able to slow down aging. Linus Pauling, the two-time Nobel Prize winner, has postulated that a combination of vitamin E, the principal fat-soluble antioxidant, and vitamin C, the principal water-soluble antioxidant, may currently be the best means of staying youthful.

The most vociferous advocates of vitamin E are Drs. Evan and Wilfred Shute of Canada, who have used it to treat heart disease, rheumatic fever, high blood pressure, varicose veins, thrombophlebitis, diabetes, kidney disease, and burns. Their therapeutic doses range from 50 to 2500 I.U. per day. Dr. Alton Ochsner reports successful treatment of varicose veins and hemorrhoids with vitamin E. Unlike most anticoagulants, vitamin E does not promote hemorrhaging.

While a connection between vitamin E and a woman's ability to conceive is unlikely, the vitamin does seem to help women with histories of miscarriages and premature birth; vitamin E can enable these women to sustain a normal, full-term pregnancy. It also improves the quality of sperm and may prevent congenital deformities.

Vitamin E is a favorite among athletes because of its antioxidant effect: it keeps pure oxygen available to the tissues and provides for a high level of energy, stamina, and endurance. Strenuous endeavors deplete the body's supply of vitamin E much more rapidly than does normal activity. The antioxidant effect also improves red blood cell survival; consequently vitamin E is central to the treatment of hemalytic anemia, a disease frequent in premature babies which destroys red blood cells.

Processing and storage destroys much of the vitamin E in our foods. The daily recommended allowance is 30 I.U., and although vitamin E is not toxic like vitamins A and D, people with high blood pressure, hyperthyroidism, or chronic rheumatic heart disease are cautioned against taking large amounts.

Vitamin E, in about 33 percent of the cases, worsens the condition of those who suffer high blood pressure.

Excellent sources of this vitamin are vegetable oil, dark green leafy vegetables, fruits, butter, and eggs. There have been several studies that show vitamin E in large doses (300 I.U. up) can produce weakness and fatigue.

In 1929, Henrik Dam of the University of Copenhagen observed that a group of chickens suffering from a hemorrhagic disease returned to normal once liver fat and alfalfa were added to their diet. He called the unknown substance in alfalfa a "*K*oagulation Vitamin." Ten years later, **vitamin K** was isolated.

Vitamin K is fat-soluble and resists heat well, but is easily destroyed by acids, alkalies, and irradiation. The vitamin takes several forms, all belonging to a group of chemical compounds called quinones: K_1 found in green plants, K_2 synthesized by intestinal bacteria, and a synthetic and biologically active compound called menadione.

Vitamin K is usually synthesized by bacteria in the lower intestinal tract, unless you've taken medications of sulfa drugs or antibiotics. It is most likely that only a small proportion of this synthesized vitamin K is actually utilized, for large amounts are excreted in feces. Being fat-soluble, K requires bile for its absorption. A limited amount of vitamin K is stored in the liver, where its function is to stimulate production of prothrombin and other blood-clotting proteins. Most surgeons recommend that a patient be given vitamin K prior to surgery.

Because of individual variations in the intestinal synthesis of vitamin K, no recommended daily allowance has been set. Vitamin K deficiency is relatively rare.

WATER-SOLUBLE VITAMINS

B vitamins are the most important of the water-solubles. Vitamin B is not a single vitamin, but rather a group of compounds now called the **vitamin B complex.** Although the various roles played by these vitamins in metabolism have yet to be fully understood, we do know that the B vitamins are vital to the metabolic changes common to all cells. Basically, these vitamins combine with specific proteins to facilitate the breakdown of proteins, fats, and carbohydrates.

The B complex vitamins are so interrelated that an insufficient supply of any single B vitamin can impair the usefulness of the others. Thus it is unwise to take supplements of an individual B vitamin, for an imbalance may lead to deficiency of the other members of the complex.

Since the B vitamins are refined out of white bread, white flour products, white sugar, and polished rice—and since you must get B vitamins elsewhere to utilize these carbohydrates properly—the more refined carbohydrates you eat, the more B vitamins you need. Because they are water-soluble, B vitamins are also lost in cooking water. Intense heat, prolonged cooking, light, baking soda, and baking powder destroy them as well.

In 1926, Jansen and Donath isolated vitamin B_1—*thiamine*—from rice bran. The primary function of thiamine is to act as a coenzyme in carbohydrate metabolism; it also plays an important part in the oxidation of the cells, especially nerve cells. Without sufficient thiamine you'll become irritable, jumpy, and tired. Researchers recently discovered that supplemental thiamine can significantly improve the learning ability of children.

Thiamine deficiency occurs mainly among drinking alcoholics. Their diets are generally poor, and the thiamine they do consume is used up in metabolizing alcohol. Thiamine deficiency may also result from severe diarrhea or vomiting.

Prolonged deficiency leads to indigestion, constipation, insomnia, headaches, rapid heartbeat, weakness and cramps in the legs, burning and numbness in the feet, and eventually beriberi, which is marked by severe emaciation and cardiac failure. In the Far East, many mothers don't get enough thiamine, and their low-thiamine milk leaves their infants susceptible to fatal beriberi.

The best source of both thiamine and the entire B vitamin complex is brewer's yeast; grain germs, such as wheat and barley, are nearly as good. Other sources are whole grains, nuts, soybeans, peas, lima beans, turnip greens, asparagus, collards, kale, sweet corn, cauliflower, mustard greens, spinach, broccoli, and brussels sprouts. Egg yolks contain thiamine, as do lean pork and organ meats.

By the late 1800s, scientists had noted that milk, liver, yeast, and certain other foods contained yellow-green, fluorescent pigments. These pigments were called flavins. In 1932, two scientists in Berlin, Warburg and Christian, isolated from yeast a yellow enzyme necessary for cell respiration; they also discovered that this enzyme consisted of protein and the pigment flavin. Then, in 1935, the vitamin *riboflavin* was synthesized.

It was so named because of its structural similarity with the sugar ribose and its relation to the flavin group. In its pure state, riboflavin is an odorless, bitter compound which is stable to heat, acids, and oxidation.

Riboflavin is vital to proper growth and general health, central to the function of the gastrointestinal tract, and necessary for the assimilation of iron. The body guards closely its supply of riboflavin, more so than it does thiamine. Alcohol, fats, and minerals deplete it.

Some nutritionists believe that Americans are more deficient in riboflavin than in any other vitamin. Alcoholics are again the prime targets. The usual signs of riboflavin deficiency are cracked lips, purplish tongue, burning and dryness of the eyes, sensitivity to light, hair loss, eczema, spinal pain, and weight loss. The central nervous system may also be impaired.

The Food and Nutrition Board of the National Research Council recommends 2.3 to 3.3 milligrams of riboflavin for an adult per day. Infants require about one third the adult allowance, and children up to age ten about one half.

The main sources of this vitamin are brewer's yeast, soybeans, wheat germ, peanut butter, turnip greens, collards, kale, broccoli, mustard greens, asparagus, spinach, watercress, brussels sprouts, cauliflower, and squash. Milk and eggs are good sources of riboflavin. Meat eaters get their supply from organ meats such as liver.

During the early part of the twentieth century, pellagra was one of the most prevalent causes of mental illness and death in the United States. In 1912, Dr. Joseph Goldberger claimed that the diet of poor Southern families encouraged pellagra and theorized that the cause was B vitamin deficiency. In 1937, it was discovered that nicotinic acid was a cure for blacktongue in dogs, a condition similar to human pellagra. The name *niacin* was suggested, as it distinguished between the *ni*cotinic *ac*id vitam*in* and the nicotine in tobacco. Pureform niacin is a white crystalline substance which is stable in heat, light, oxidation, acids, and alkalies.

Niacin is absorbed from the small intestine and then converted into its active form, nicotinamide. The essential amino acid tryptophan is a precursor of niacin. Thus a diet high in tryptophan will provide sufficient niacin, so long as the B_6 supply is adequate.

Niacin deficiency usually takes months to develop. Pellagra affects the skin, the gastrointestinal tract, and the nervous system. Its early symptoms are listlessness, headache, backache, weight loss, vomiting, and diarrhea. The mouth and throat become sore; the tongue and lips turn red. Patches of skin appear sunburned and, if untreated, become cracked and scaly. As the disease progresses, symptoms such as dizziness, confusion, irritability, and persecution delusions are common. The final stages of pellagra are often referred to as the four Ds: dermatitis, diarrhea, dementia, and death.

The daily requirement of niacin is 23 milligrams for men, 18 for women, 23 for nursing mothers, 20 for teenagers, 18 for all others.

Brewer's yeast and wheat bran are excellent sources, as is

peanut butter. Whole-wheat flour, dried beans, mushrooms, peas, kale, collards, sweet corn, asparagus, potatoes, rutabaga, squash, peaches, watercress, and broccoli are other vegetable sources. Mackerel and salmon are good fish sources. Meat eaters get niacin from liver, pork, beef, beef heart, lamb, veal, chicken, and turkey.

Vitamin B_6 is an odorless white crystalline substance which is stable to heat and acid but destroyed by light. There are three forms of vitamin B_6: pyridoxine, pyridoxal, and pyridoxamine. Of the three, pyridoxine is the most resistant to processing and storage and is by far the most common B_6 in our food.

B_6 is a necessary coenzyme for a number of metabolic functions, particularly the metabolism of amino acids. It is also required for the conversion of tryptophan to niacin.

In animals, the primary characteristics of vitamin B_6 deficiency are skin lesions, nervous symptoms, and blood disorders. However, no such clear-cut symptoms have been found in humans. Extreme deficiencies result in seborrheic dermatitis around the mouth and eyes, depression, nausea, and abnormalities of the central nervous system. In 1950, doctors discovered that infants fed a formula depleted of its pyridoxine experienced nervous irritability, convulsions, weakened coordination, and abdominal pain. More recently, scientists have linked chronic B_6 deficiency to multiple sclerosis and retardation in children.

Women who are either pregnant or taking birth control pills require large supplements of vitamin B_6. Some doctors suggest that the mental depression experienced by many women taking oral contraceptives is due to mild B_6 deficiency. Adequate vitamin B_6 is also considered crucial to the proper brain development of fetuses, because the placenta contains high concentrations of the pyridoxal phosphate form of B_6.

The daily recommended dosage of B_6 is from 1.5 to 20 milligrams, depending on individual requirements. Some nutritionists recommend that pregnant women take from 15 to 20 milligrams per day. Because of the relation of B₆ to amino acid metabolism, people with a high protein intake should also take a higher dosage of B₆.

Brewer's yeast, wheat germ, peanuts, lima beans, peas, bananas, sweet potatoes, cabbage, and molasses are good B₆ sources. Meat eaters get this vitamin from organ and muscle sources.

Pantothenic acid is present in every living cell. As a free acid, it is unstable and soluble in water. Little of it is lost in cooking, except in acid or alkaline solutions. As the crystalline compound calcium pantothenate, it is bitter-tasting and thoroughly stable.

Pantothenic acid is essential to the intermediary metabolism of carboyhdrates, fats, and proteins. It is also necessary for the synthesis of cholesterol, steroid hormones, hemoglobin, and phospholipids. Its highest concentration is in areas with the greatest metabolic activity—the liver, kidney, brain, adrenal, and heart tissues.

Since pantothenic acid works in conjunction with the other B vitamins, a lack of it reduces the body's production of *all* the vitamins in this complex. Pantothenic acid is a relatively recent discovery and consequently daily requirements and deficiency symptoms have yet to be determined. A daily allowance of 5 to 10 milligrams is considered sufficient for adults and children. Chronic fatigue, depression, and low resistance to infection are suspected symptoms of a deficiency. Pantothenic acid is important to your body's vitality and can aid recovery in many illnesses.

The best sources are yeast, peanuts, peas, wheat germ, egg yolk, and, for meat eaters, liver.

The B vitamin *biotin* is so potent that no cell of your body contains more than a minute trace. Liver, one of the richest sources, has less than one part per billion.

Biotin is a necessary coenzyme for the synthesis of fatty acids and for other metabolic processes, including the movement of carbon dioxide to and from active compounds and the oxidation of carbohydrates. Your intestinal bacteria can synthesize biotin.

Biotin is an effective antidote for skin rashes and hair loss caused by the avidin in egg whites; the harmful effects of avidin are countered by the biotin in the yolks. Eczema is frequently treated with daily 5 milligrams injections of biotin. Since biotin is so potent, a deficiency is rare. Unpolished rice, brewer's yeast, soybeans, egg yolks, and cauliflower are good sources, as are fish and liver.

Vitamin B₁₂ is a water-soluble red crystalline substance which is stable to heat but vulnerable to light or strong acid or alkaline solutions. Cooking does not destroy it. B_{12} is also known as cyanocobalamin because it contains the trace element cobalt.

For absorption and utilization, B_{12} depends on the presence of several other factors: an intestinal secretion called the *intrinsic factor,* hydrochloric acid, calcium, B_6, iron, and folic acid. Though present in most tissues, vitamin B_{12} is stored primarily in the liver and kidney and is released as needed to the bone marrow and other tissues.

B_{12} is important to the functioning of cells, particularly those of the gastrointestinal tract, nervous system, and bone marrow. It also acts as a coenzyme in DNA synthesis and is more potent than folic acid in stimulating blood cell formation.

Vitamin B_{12} deficiency is rarely caused by a poor diet, except for extreme forms of vegetarianism; rather, deficiency is usually the result of faulty absorption. People who have had their stomachs surgically removed cannot absorb B_{12}. Regarding symptoms, a number of doctors have cited a type of psychosis that shows up with pernicious anemia; it is therefore suggested that doctors routinely measure the serum B_{12} levels of mentally disturbed patients.

A minimum requirement has yet to be established; while your body's needs are low, large doses do not appear to be harmful.

Vegetarians can get their quota of B_{12} from seaweed—about 2 to 3 ounces per day—or capsules. This vitamin is also found in butter, eggs, milk, fish, and liver.

In its pure form, *folic acid* is a bright-yellow crystalline substance which is barely soluble in water. Of the B vitamins, it is most easily destroyed by heat and light.

The chief function of folic acid is the prevention of anemia, for it aids in the growth and reproduction of red blood cells. Folic acid combines with B_{12} in many processes and facilitates the synthesis of compounds necessary for the manufacture of DNA and RNA and for the conversion of amino acids. Folic acid itself is synthesized by certain intestinal bacteria, such as the coliform organism.

Lack of protein impairs the proper utilization of folic acid. Deficiency results in diarrhea, inflammation of the tongue, gastrointestinal disorders, and all the accompanying symptoms of anemia. Anemia is commonly suffered by older people with poor diets and by pregnant women and infants whose intake of folic or ascorbic acid is low.

A minimum daily requirement has not been set, but your diet should not ignore this vitamin. Foods rich in this vitamin are brewer's yeast, spinach and other dark green leafy vegetables, wheat germ, oysters, salmon and chicken.

All living cells contain the B vitamin *choline;* its primary function is to metabolize and transport fat from the liver. Choline is also central to the transmission of nerve impulses. Deficiency leads to muscle weakness, damaged muscle fibers, and excessive scarring. Severe lab-induced choline deficiencies in animals have resulted in kidney degeneration, liver inflammation, and fat deposits in the aorta.

German doctors have successfully treated hepatitis with choline. Researchers in Italy have used this vitamin to relieve hyperthyroid conditions.

Choline requirement has not been established. Your body produces its own supply so long as protein and other B vitamins are present. Dietary sources include soybeans, peas, spinach, brewer's yeast, wheat germ, egg yolk, and liver.

The B vitamin *inositol* first gained public attention in 1950, when an article in *Newsweek* reported that it was thought to lower cholesterol levels. Inositol is a sweet water-soluble substance essential to the production of lecithin. Inositol synthesis takes place within the cell. Combined with choline, this vitamin has been used to reduce the level of fat in the blood of patients recovering from heart attacks.

Deficiency results in poor lecithin production, increased cholesterol, fatty liver and blood sugar, and other disorders. These symptoms are countered by a diet including dried lima beans, cantaloupe, grapefruit, peaches, oranges, peanuts, raisins, wheat germ, brewer's yeast, and cabbage. Meat eaters have a good source in beef brains and hearts.

Little is known about *para-aminobenzoic acid,* one of the most recently discovered B vitamins. It is necessary for the body's production of folic acid. It is antagonistic to sulfa drugs, which supplant para-aminobenzoic when introduced into the body. Thus the unpleasant side effects of sulfa drugs might also be the symptoms of a para-aminobenzoic deficiency. These symptoms include digestive problems, nervousness, and depression. This vitamin has recently been shown to be an effective sun-screening agent.

Sources include other foods high in vitamin B, such as brewer's yeast, wheat germ, whole wheat, eggs, milk, and liver.

Pangamic acid, or B₁₅, was discovered only recently; it aids in the regulation of fat metabolism, increases the assimilation of oxygen in the tissues, and stimulates the glandular and nervous systems. It also increases the body's tolerance of reduced oxygen supplies—common in smoky, smoggy areas—and guards against carbon monoxide poisoning.

There has been considerable controversy over B₁₅, which was banned until recently by the F.D.A. Russian scientists, however, have reported successful treatment of atherosclerosis and other serious conditions with pangamic acid.

Sources include brewer's yeast, whole wheat, wheat germ, green leafy vegetables, eggs, milk, and butter. And, of course, liver.

As with vitamin E, much controversy has raged over the powers of **vitamin C.** Some regard it as a miracle worker; others insist that, other than preventing scurvy, it is just another vitamin. Certainly vitamin C is, in one respect, different from all other vitamins; most animals have in their liver an enzyme that converts glucose into ascorbic acid or vitamin C—but humans, apes, and guinea pigs cannot manufacture vitamin C.

In 1750, Captain James Lind, a Scottish naval doctor, questioned why sailors after a few months at sea contracted scurvy—marked by darkening and easy bruising of the skin, weakness, internal bleeding, swollen joints, bleeding gums, shortness of breath, and, at times, death. Lind discovered that vegetables and fruits remedied these symptoms; in 1795, he persuaded the Admiralty to add limes to the staple diet of every sailor—hence the nickname "limey."

Vitamin C is essential to the proper functioning of the cells and tissues of all animals. Most species manufacture their own supply of vitamin C at a rate relative to their own body weight —for a 150-pound human adult, approximately 2 to 15 grams. The gorilla, like the human, receives his vitamin C only from dietary sources; he eats approximately 4.6 grams (4.6 thousand milligrams) of vitamin C per day, which corresponds to

2 grams per day for a human adult. Thus the levels set by the National Research Council—70 milligrams for adults, 80 milligrams for teenagers, 100 milligrams for pregnant women and old folks—are allowances far below the amount consumed by the ape. These recommended levels also fail to take into account the factors which deplete your vitamin C supply. A single cigarette wastes 25 milligrams of vitamin C; air and water pollution, everyday stress, and alcohol all tax the body's stores of this vitamin. People who smoke or live in polluted areas or lead stressful lives need much more vitamin C than is recommended by the National Research Council.

One of this vitamin's primary roles is in the formation of collagen, the gelatinous substance found in connective tissue, cartilage, and bone. A deficiency of vitamin C hampers the repair processes. Bones become brittle, arteries break and hemorrhage, joints become painful, teeth loosen, and wounds won't heal: all the classic symptoms of scurvy.

Vitamin C is an effective detoxicant. It combats the harmful effects of carbon monoxide, sulfur dioxide, inorganic poisons such as mercury, and various drugs and bacteria. It is this detoxification process that uses up the vitamin C of those who smoke or live in a polluted city.

The brain has the highest concentration of vitamin C. Many experimental subjects claim that their sense of well-being increased when they were given larger doses of vitamin C. Conversely, deficiency can result in extreme confusion and depression.

Vitamin C has also been an effective weapon against atherosclerosis (the buildup of fat deposits in the linings of the arteries). Generally, smokers' vitamin C levels are lower than those of nonsmokers, men's lower than women's, and older persons' lower than young people's; in other words, those who are most prone to coronary thrombosis have lower vitamin C levels. Some doctors have ventured to suggest that atherosclerosis is the direct result of long-term vitamin C deficiency; in support of this view, certain tests demonstrate that ascorbic acid reverses atherosclerosis in rats and guinea pigs.

Vitamin C has been shown to make pregnancy and labor more comfortable. Pregnant women taking large doses have fewer leg cramps, greater skin capacity to resist the pressure of the uterus, a shorter and easier labor, and no tendency to postpartum hemorrhaging.

By far the most celebrated claim for vitamin C is that it can prevent and cure the common cold. The controversy has yet to be resolved. Nobel Prize winner Linus Pauling, the father of this theory, recommends a minimum of 1 to 2 grams of vitamin C per day; a maximum of 2.3 to 9 grams. Pauling recommends that at the first sign of a cold you should take 500 to 1000 milligrams of vitamin C every hour for several hours; if the symptoms persist, increase your dosage to 4 to 10 grams daily until the cold is gone. It should be taken after meals, because large doses on an empty stomach have a laxative effect. Also, avoid taking aspirin, which hinders the effectiveness of vitamin C.

Recent tests have indicated that a high consumption of oxidized vitamin C destroys genetic materials within the cells —so make sure your vitamin C supply is fresh.

Merton P. Lamden, of the University of Vermont, warns that daily doses of 4 to 9 grams of vitamin C increases the excretion of urinary oxalate, a product of vitamin C metabolism. An increased level of urinary oxalate, he says, encourages the development of kidney and bladder damage.

The best sources of vitamin C are the juices of citrus fruits, such as oranges, grapefruit, lemon, and lime. Alfalfa, kale, turnip greens, green peppers, broccoli, almonds, asparagus, bananas, brussels sprouts, cantaloupe, collards, strawberries, tomatoes, and mustard greens also contain vitamin C.

The importance of vitamin C in our diet is obvious. What is still not clear is how much of it we need. This is not a question that is easily answered, because of our biological individuality. No two people have the same requirements for vitamin C to maintain "optimum" health. Therefore, be aware of those conditions which increase your needs: stress, alcohol, fever, surgery, poor diet, anxiety, strenuous exercise. Lack of citrus fruits and dark-green leafy vegetables, consuming aspirin, air pollution, and cigarette smoking all affect your daily vitamin C requirements. Fortunately, up to 1 to 3 grams daily during periods of vitamin C deficiency will not normally be harmful. Keep your supplements small and take after meals. Of course, it is possible to obtain 100 to 200 milligrams daily from a well-balanced diet, which will suffice if you are healthy.

CHAPTER
17

MINERALS

APPROXIMATELY 4 PERCENT OF OUR TOTAL BODY WEIGHT consists of minerals. Minerals are the elements that remain largely as ash when plants and animal tissue are burned. Your body contains up to forty different types of mineral elements; only seventeen, however, seem to be essential to human nutrition.

Calcium and phosphorus constitute three fourths of the total mineral content of your body; potassium, sulfur, sodium, chlorine, and manganese account for most of the rest. These are known as macronutrients. The other minerals are present only in very minimal amounts, representing less than .01 percent of the total body weight, and are referred to as trace elements, or micronutrients. Some of these elements—nickel, cadmium, vanadium, arsenic, and cobalt—are not considered essential, but there is evidence nonetheless of their participation in some important biological reactions. Other elements —gold, silver, aluminum, tin, and lead—do not seem to play any metabolic role.

Under normal circumstances, your body maintains a constant level of these mineral elements by carefully balancing their intake and excretion, a process known as homeostasis. The small intestine absorbs, excludes, and excretes all excesses in the juices; the large intestine reabsorbs what your body might need after the bodily fluids have left the small intestine. Finally, the kidney balances the level of these elements in the blood.

Calcium, for example, is normally absorbed and excreted by both the intestinal juices and the urine. If the blood calcium level is low, your body will absorb more calcium from the intestinal tract, and excrete less in the urine. Conversely, should the blood calcium level get too high, the intestinal barrier will inhibit calcium absorption, and the kidney will excrete the excess.

Such homeostatic control of minerals is vital, because an accumulated excess of any mineral can be toxic. At the same time, deficiencies are unhealthy. The control mechanisms for such minerals as sodium, chlorine, and potassium are well defined. Those for iron, copper, and manganese are known to exist but not understood, while the control mechanisms for chromium, zinc, and cobalt have yet to be located. To this date, there is no known mechanism which regulates fluorine, iodine, molybdenum, or selenium.

Many essential processes depend upon minerals to maintain their integrity and proper functioning:

— The formation of protein requires the presence of calcium and sulfur.
— The nervous function of the digestive tract relies upon the vagus nerve, which cannot function properly without potassium.
— Vitamins often cannot be absorbed through the intestinal barrier without the presence of certain minerals. Vitamin B12, for example, is absorbed only in the presence of cobalt, a trace mineral.

— Minerals must combine with certain vitamins for the removal of internal waste products.
— Insulin contains zinc, and diabetes results from an insulin shortage; thus there is possibly a link between diabetes and zinc deficiency.
— Minerals such as calcium influence muscular contraction and nerve response.
— Minerals regulate the flow of bodily fluids.
— Blood coagulation depends on the presence of minerals.

Minerals cannot be synthesized and must be obtained from food sources. The mineral content of a food is determined by both the mineral content of the soil and the degree of adulteration through refining. Many nutritionists believe that our diet no longer supplies adequate levels of the trace elements. This is due in no small part to farming practices which deplete the soil of its trace minerals; farmers have, for many years, added only nitrogen, phosphorus, and potassium to the soil. But what about the other minerals, the trace elements?

Several studies have shown that current farming practices have, in fact, stripped the soil of many of the trace minerals. A survey conducted by the U.S. Department of Agriculture revealed that, on the average, the old-fashioned and open-pollinated corn contained 82 percent more crude protein, 37 percent more copper, 197 percent more iron, and 113 percent more manganese than the variety which is grown today. And, as might be expected, commercial fertilization depletes the mineral content of soil, whereas organic fertilization enriches it.

Even when food is grown in mineral-rich soil, much of its mineral content is destroyed by overprocessing. Ironically, just as science begins to discover the importance of minerals to our health, the food industry is denuding foods of their mineral content. Most of the high-calorie, fatty processed foods available today are void of minerals; refinement strips whole wheat of 60 percent of its calcium, 71 percent of its phosphorus, 76 percent of its iron, 78 percent of its zinc, 85 percent of its magnesium, and 68 percent of its copper.

Raw vegetables, seeds, grains, and fruits are the richest mineral sources. The American diet frequently requires supplements of iron, calcium, iodine, and zinc.

The body of a normal, healthy individual contains from 3 to 5 grams of **iron**: of that amount about 80 percent is in constant use, primarily in the red blood cells and muscles, while the rest is in storage. Iron is absorbed only with difficulty. The body absorbs only 2 to 10 percent of the iron from a vegetable diet; iron from animal protein is absorbed more readily—10 to 13 percent—and, in turn, seems to improve overall iron absorption. The vegetarian must therefore monitor and supplement his or her intake of iron. The major determinant of iron absorption is the body's immediate needs. When the store of iron is depleted—by, say, an increase in new blood formation, or excessive bleeding—your iron absorption improves. Growing children, pregnant women, and anemics all absorb iron at a higher rate than do other people.

Your system excretes very little iron. With a storage capacity of 1000 milligrams of iron and a daily loss of only 1 milligram, the average adult male has an iron reserve sufficient for nearly a thousand days. While women lose a few milligrams of iron per day during menstruation, their reserves still amount to 200 to 400 milligrams. Despite all this, iron deficiency *is* quite prevalent—the result of chronic blood loss, faulty iron absorption, an increased growth of blood volume, pregnancy, or a low-iron diet over a long period of time. Symptoms of iron deficiency are fatigue, decreased resistance to infection, soreness in the mouth, palpitations after exercise, pallor, and pale blood cells. Iron-deficiency anemia is corrected by large doses of inorganic ferrous iron, together with vitamins C, B_{12}, folic acid and protein. Equally important is a diet which includes foods rich in easily absorbed iron.

The reverse, an overload of iron reserve, leads to hemosiderosis, which may develop in people who regularly use iron utensils when cooking or who, by other means, ingest large dosages of iron over a long period. This condition, and a toxic reaction to it, is rare, because as your iron store increases, your body limits absorption in the intestine.

The recommended daily allowance for iron is 10 milligrams for adults, but 18 milligrams for older women. Infants are born with an iron reserve which lasts about three months, after which the recommended daily allowance is 10 to 15 milligrams during the first year. The RDA for children between the ages of one and three is 15 milligrams, and for those between three and twelve it's 10 milligrams. The RDA for boys aged twelve to eighteen is 18 milligrams.

The average diet contains 6 milligrams of iron per 1000 calories. Since caloric requirement for boys and men is higher, they meet their iron requirement more easily than do most girls and women. Although cereals and breads are very often fortified with iron in an effort to raise the iron content of the average diet, many nutritionists believe a greater supplement is needed.

The sources of iron for the vegetarian are dried apricots, prunes, molasses, kale, mustard greens, lima beans, lettuce, peas, turnip greens, watercress, collards, brussels sprouts, cucumbers, cauliflower, broccoli, and asparagus. And an iron supplement would also be wise.

The body contains only 20 to 23 milligrams of **iodine,** an essential mineral. Though traces of iodine are found in all the bodily tissues, the concentration of iodine in the thyroid gland is about 2500 times greater than that in any other tissue.

Iodine is isolated from organic compounds in the gastrointestinal tract and readily absorbed as inorganic iodide; it is then transported via the bloodstream to the thyroid gland, where it is oxidized into iodine and bound to protein to form thyroxin and two other hormones.The main function of thyroxin is to regulate oxidation in the cells; thus it influences the physical and mental growth of the body, the function of nerve and muscle tissues, circulation activity, and the metabolism of all nutrients.

If the iodine supply is insufficient, the cells of the thyroid gland swell, leading to a condition known as goiter that is marked by an unsightly swelling of the neck. Nine years after the discovery of iodine in 1811, the Swiss physician Coindet determined that it was this mineral which was the curative element in burned sponge, used for centuries to cure goiter. Iodine was finally synthesized in 1927. In the United States, health agencies ensured that Americans got an adequate iodine supply by adding it to table salt, an ingredient of everyone's diet. As a result, goiter is almost unknown in this country.

Both the color and the texture of hair are affected by iodine. Some anemias have been traced to iodine deficiency. And during pregnancy, an iodine shortage can endanger the physical and mental well-being of the fetus.

Because iodine is lost in urine, you should replenish your supply daily. The best source is table and sea salt. Green vegetables grown in iodine-rich soils are good, and seafood is excellent. Drinking water generally contains iodine. The recommended allowance is approximately .1 milligram.

Magnesium accounts for less than 1 percent of your body's total mineral content but is considered essential because of its importance to good health. It is central to the transmission of brain impulses through the nerves and in muscle contraction.

Symptoms of magnesium deficiency include muscle cramps, irregularity, irritability, and convulsions. Magnesium has facilitated the recovery of heart patients and is prescribed in conjunction with vitamin B_6, for the treatment of convulsive nervous disorders such as epilepsy.

Magnesium regulates the metabolism of calcium and vitamin C and, therefore, has control over the neuromuscular system. An excess of calcium in the diet may produce symptoms similar to those of magnesium deficiency, while too much magnesium inhibits bone calcification; the two substances antagonize each other.

The RDA for magnesium is 350 milligrams for males, 300 milligrams for women, 450 milligrams for pregnant women, 60 to 70 milligrams for infants, and 150 to 250 milligrams for children.

Since magnesium is an essential element of chlorophyll, it is a constituent of dark leafy vegetables such as spinach, kale, collards. Nuts, grains, legumes, milk, lima beans, sweet corn, peas, potatoes, bananas, snap beans, sweet potatoes, and brussels sprouts are other good food sources for the vegetarian. Note that flour, rice, corn, and sugar lose from 60 to 99 percent of their magnesium in refining.

Phosphorus, the second most abundant mineral in your body, accounts for 22 percent of its total mineral content. It is found in every cell and in the extracellular fluid. Phosphorus is involved in more bodily functions than any other mineral. Approximately 85 percent is contained by bones and teeth in the form of calcium phosphate, which helps to give them their strength. A phosphorus-containing compound is involved throughout the entire metabolic process by which glucose is converted to energy. Phosphorus is also an essential element of nucleic acids, found in the cytoplasm of all cells, and influences cell division, reproduction, and transmission of hereditary traits.

Your body absorbs phosphorus best when it is ingested in the presence of vitamin D with an equivalent amount of calcium. Phosphorus absorption is hindered by large amounts of antacids.

Phosphorus deficiency is associated with calcium deficiency, rickets, and osteomalacia. Symptoms are weakness and appetite loss.

The RDA of phosphorus is 800 milligrams for adults, 1200 milligrams for pregnant women, 1200 to 1400 milligrams for children, and 240 milligrams for infants. Phosphorus is widely distributed in our foods, so a deficiency is unlikely. Most calcium-rich foods satisfy our phosphorus needs; most foods, excepting green leafy vegetables and milk, contain more phosphorus than calcium, so you should include sufficient green vegetables and milk in your diet to maintain a proper balance.

Brazil nuts, peanuts, oatmeal, dried beans, and peas are rich phosphorus sources. Also good are sweet corn, kale, collards, brussels sprouts, broccoli, asparagus, turnip greens, and cauliflower. Phosphorus is contained in cereals in the form of phytic acid, which is absorbed inefficiently. Fruits are a poor source.

Calcium is the most abundant mineral in your body, accounting for 2 percent of your total body weight and 39 percent of the total mineral content. Approximately 99 percent of this mineral is found in the bones and teeth.

Phosphorus and calcium are usually described together, for they comprise 95 percent of the mineral content of the bones and teeth. A change in one effects a similar change in the other. An excess of either one will result in the poor absorption of both and the excretion of one or the other. The best dietary ratio of calcium to phosphorus is 1½ to 1.

Besides being necessary to bone growth, calcium is essential to the blood-clotting mechanism, nerve transmission, and muscle contraction. A lack of calcium in the system causes irritability, particularly in growing children. Calcium's soothing effect on our nerves becomes obvious when we drink a glass of milk before going to bed. Calcium can also relieve premenstrual tension and cramps.

Calcium should be balanced with vitamin D—milk, fish oil, or sunlight. Vitamin D increases permeability of intestinal membrane to calcium, so the lack of it results in a corresponding calcium deficiency. Protein foods and moderate amounts of fats also facilitate absorption, but excessive and saturated fats have the reverse effect. Sweets impair calcium absorption because they, like calcium, require large amounts of gastric juices in their digestion. Grains should also be separated from calcium foods: the phytic acid they contain can bind with the calcium in the stomach to form calcium phytate, which cannot be absorbed.

Calcium deficiency forces the body to draw on calcium stores in the bones; as much as 40 percent of the bone calcium may be released before an X ray can spot it—usually after the bone has broken or fractured. The most infamous disease of this sort is rickets, in which calcification fails to take place in the crucial early years of bone growth and body structure. The earliest signs among children are a distended belly and swollen joints. The result: softened, deformed bones that are evidenced by bowed legs, pigeon chest, and enlarged wrists and ankles.

Other deficiency diseases are osteomalacia and tetany, which are common among older persons. All people over fifty-five experience some reduction in the amount of bone and the corresponding symptoms: weakness, appetite loss, aches and pains, brittle bones, cramps, stoop shoulders, and a decreased height. The best remedy for these ailments is an increased consumption of calcium, vitamins A and D, and protein, coupled with a program of reasonable exercise.

The daily requirement for calcium has been set at 800 milligrams for adults; calcium, however, is not very soluble, and only about 30 percent is actually absorbed. This allowance, therefore, is perhaps low: some nutritionists suggest 1 to 1.4 grams per day. Calcium needs are certainly much greater for women during pregnancy and lactation and for children during the growing years of twelve to sixteen, when teeth and bones grow rapidly. The recommended daily allowance for pregnant women is 1200 milligrams; for children, 1200 to 1400 milligrams.

Children who drink two to three 8-ounce glasses of milk

a day and follow a well-balanced diet usually maintain an adequate level of calcium. Those children who are either allergic to milk or lack the enzyme amylase—necessary for the proper digestion of calcium—should receive supplements of calcium powder.

Vegetable sources of calcium are collards, kale, turnip greens, mustard greens, watercress, broccoli, rutabaga, snap beans, lima beans, and cabbage. Dairy products such as milk, yogurt, cottage cheese, and hard cheeses are good sources; irradiated milk has vitamin D added, which helps calcium absorption. Calcium supplements are great values, especially calcium phosphate, which should be taken two or three times a day between meals. Remember that vitamins A, B complex, C, and D, iron, and phosphorus are necessary for the absorption and metabolization of calcium.

Minute amounts of **selenium** are distributed all through the cells. The liver and kidneys have the highest concentrations. Because selenium is an effective antioxidant, it has a close association with vitamin E. Selenium has been found to reverse the symptoms of vitamin E deficiency in animals; it can also replace vitamin E in those reactions which require only antioxidant properties. Selenium and vitamin E function together in the body to prevent tissue damage caused by free radicals. By itself, selenium promotes growth and fertility.

Scientists have only recently become aware of selenium's potential. Most research to this point has been conducted on animals, and substances do not necessarily affect humans and animals alike. But the animal research has yielded some amazing results: selenium, along with vitamins A and C, seems to restrict the action of cancer-causing agents, and doctors have found that patients with gastrointestinal cancer have blood selenium levels substantially lower than those of people in good health.

Selenium, because it enhances antibody production, benefits your body's immunity system. It may also be able to stabilize high blood pressure by detoxifying cadmium, a pollutant common in industrial areas and released in cigarette smoke.

Too much selenium, however, can be toxic, probably because of its association with sulfur in certain compounds and because it inhibits the action of certain enzymes.

The recommended daily allowance for selenium has yet to be established, but a daily intake range of 50 to 150 micro-grams will most likely meet your needs. If you smoke or live in a polluted area, you should take special care to include sufficient selenium in your diet.

Unrefined grains and onions are the best sources (unrefined foods have three or four times more selenium than processed foods). Vegetables and fruit contain very little of this mineral.

Very small amounts of **chromium** are found in your body—about 20 parts per billion parts of blood. Yet even in such minute quantities, it is an important nutrient.

Chromium is thought to stimulate the activity of enzymes involved in the metabolism of energy and glucose. Chromium is a major component of the organic substance known as the glucose tolerance factor, which determines the efficiency of sugar and carbohydrate metabolism. It also assists insulin in moving glucose through the membrane into the cell. This means that the poor glucose tolerance of some diabetics may be alleviated by supplementing their diets with chromium. One clinical study reports that the glucose tolerance improved in four out of six diabetics when chromium was administered daily. Other studies indicate that a 250-milligram daily dose of chromium causes significant improvement in hypoglycemics. Chromium is present in high concentrations at birth and during early childhood; its level declines in some tissues as you get older, which could explain the glucose intolerance that comes with middle age.

Chromium deficiency is also thought to be a contributing factor in coronary disease. Chromium is part of the process by which fatty acids and cholesterol are synthesized in the liver; autopsies have revealed that some heart-disease victims have no chromium in their heart vessels.

The RDA for chromium has not been established, but most nutritionists feel that the chromium content of the American diet is too low to maintain adequate tissue concentration; this deficiency is the result of refined foods—especially carbohydrates—and soil levels, since chromium is not used in fertilizers. Thanks to his heavy refined sucrose diet, the average American has only about 1.7 milligrams of chromium in his body, as compared to the 9 milligrams of the average Asian. The American diet furnishes daily about 80 to 100 milligrams of chromium, but only about 5 micrograms are absorbed. To guard against a deficiency, you should eat only unrefined foods, such as whole-wheat bread, and cut all refined carbohydrates down or out of the diet.

Brewer's yeast, corn oil, whole-grain cereals, and dark leafy vegetables are the best sources of this mineral, and fish and meat are good sources. Supplement tablets are less than efficient because the chromium they contain is not easily absorbed by the body.

Only 2 to 3 grams of **zinc** are distributed throughout your cells—primarily in the pancreas, kidney, liver, brain, testes, eyes, hair, and nails. The concentrations in the brain and spermatozoa emphasize the importance of zinc to fertility, sexual maturation, and mental health. Autopsies of some elderly persons have revealed low amounts of zinc in their brain cells.

Zinc functions largely as a constituent of the numerous enzymes involved in digestion and metabolism. An integral part of the RNA molecule, it is thought to maintain the stability of the molecular configuration. Zinc directly influences insulin's effect on carbohydrate metabolism. Its healing properties are well known: zinc ointment has been used for wounds and abrasions for generations, and zinc sulfate lotion is a current acne treatment.

Hepatitis, chronic infection, excessive sweating, anemia, acute rheumatic fever, and alcoholic drinking deplete your body's zinc supply. The symptoms of zinc deficiency are impaired growth, iron-deficiency anemia, leg ulcers and restricted blood flow in the legs, reduced mental alertness and forgetfulness. A deficiency in pregnant women can cause malformations of the fetus and birth control pills may deplete your zinc supply.

Your body absorbs zinc easily, except when it is taken in combination with too much calcium. A 10- to 15-milligram daily dose is sufficient to most people's needs. Pregnant women require 20 milligrams, lactating women about 25 milligrams.

Pumpkin and sunflower seeds, brewer's yeast, bone meal, nuts, wheat germ, beans, eggs, and fish are fine sources of this mineral.

Potassium is the most important element inside the cell, and over 98 percent of your body's supply of this mineral is in the form of intercellular fluid. Potassium counterbalances the action of sodium outside the cell by maintaining the correct concentration and amount of fluids within the tissues; when this balance is lost, you experience tissue swelling, vertigo, heartbeat irregularities, and allergies. Any potassium loss —brought about by diuretic drugs, fasting and dieting, stress, or diarrhea—will weaken muscle contraction, thus affecting the heart muscles and the intestinal peristalsis which evacuates the colon. Excess sodium can also deplete your potassium supply.

Because of its contribution to muscle development, potassium is especially important to your diet during athletic training. Potassium should also become a major part of your diet during heavy stress periods or following surgery.

No RDA has been set for potassium, but you require between 5 and 15 grams, depending on your salt intake and your physical condition. A potassium overdose is possible;

the symptoms are weak heart action, mental confusion, and a numbness in the extremities.

Sources include oranges, sunflower seeds, apricots, nuts, lima beans, spinach, collards, potatoes, brussels sprouts, broccoli, kale, mustard greens, bananas, celery, carrots, beets, and peas.

Though present in all body cells, **sulfur** is concentrated chiefly in the keratin of skin and hair, in nails and connective tissue, and in insulin. Sulfur generally occurs as a constituent of amino acids, vitamins thiamine and biotin, and one or two carbohydrates; once absorbed, these agents are involved with a number of metabolic activities, principally oxidation-reduction reactions. Sulfur compounds are essential for proper blood coagulation and the transference of energy.

No RDA has been established for sulfur, but a well-rounded diet should easily meet your needs; a deficiency is marked by brittle nails and splitting hair. Protein and B vitamin foods contain sulfur; wheat germ, nuts, legumes, egg yolk, milk, cheese, beef, and fish are excellent sources.

Sodium, a prominent element in extracellular fluids, is found throughout your body. Sodium is closely related to potassium: they balance each other much in the same way as do phosphorus and calcium. Excess potassium in your diet can deplete your sodium, and vice versa.

Together with potassium, sodium keeps constant the osmotic pressure on both sides of the cell wall. Sodium's primary function is in the control and makeup of intercellular fluids. The naturally occurring balance between the amount of sodium inside and outside the cell is necessary for the proper transmission of nerve impulses. Correct sodium levels are also important for muscle contraction.

Manufacturers add salt to foods as a flavoring and preservative; sodium therefore saturates the American diet. Too much sodium results in water retention and, over a long time, hypertension. Low-sodium fluid levels generally occur in the hot months when you sweat excessively; vomiting, diarrhea, burns, surgery, and a long salt-restricted diet can also cause sodium deficiencies. Symptoms are nausea, headache, low energy, leg and stomach cramps, and, in severe cases, mental confusion.

No RDA has been set, but sodium is abundant and deficiency rare. Fruits, vegetables, and grains are low in sodium, so the vegetarian should use table salt. The best vegetables are celery, kale, spinach, beets, watercress, carrots, turnip greens, collards, mustard greens and cabbage. The richest sources of sodium are protein foods like egg white, fish, poultry, milk, and meat.

Fluorine is an integral part of the body's tooth and bone structure. Due to its presence, the mineral crystals in your teeth are larger than those in the bones and, consequently, more resistant to erosion by bacteria. At the same time, the high concentration of fluoride on the outside enamel of your teeth—six to ten times that of the fluoride on the inside structure—makes the teeth resistant to decay by reducing the solubility of acids on the surface.

A deficiency results in the breakdown of fluoride in your bones and teeth; bones become brittle and teeth fall out. On the other hand, excessive fluoride can cause mottling of the teeth, a condition in which the enamel loses its glaze and becomes pitted and stained. Too much fluoride can also cause osteosclerosis, depressed growth, and bone fluorosis, which resembles arthritis.

No RDA has been established for fluoride. Although the average diet supplies from .3 to .5 milligram of fluoride, the main source is drinking water: 6 glasses provide 1 to 1.5 milligrams. Spinach, rice, tea, soybeans, onions, and lettuce are good sources. Seafood is excellent.

Chlorine is distributed throughout the body in the form of chloride. The highest concentrations are in the cerebrospinal fluid and in the gastric and pancreatic juices of the intestinal tract. Chlorine is a principal component of your body's extracellular fluids and together with sodium helps to maintain proper water balance and osmotic pressure.

Chlorine is widely used as an antibacterial agent in drinking water. Considerable evidence, however, suggests that chlorination is a dangerous practice which may contribute to our country's increased arteriosclerosis and heart disease. Excessive chloride forms on the walls of the arteries a plaque which eventually clogs them.

Chlorine deficiency results from profuse sweating, vomiting, diarrhea, and sodium or potassium deficiency. Lack of chlorine can effect your digestion, bringing on weakness, apathy, and mental dullness.

No RDA has been set, and the average diet contains sufficient chlorine. Table salt (sodium chloride), drinking water, and kelp are the best sources; rye flour is less obvious but also good.

Copper, necessary for the formation of healthy red blood cells and hemoglobin, is also involved in iron absorption and in the release of iron stores from the liver.

Approximately 30 percent of dietary copper is absorbed by the body. An increased intake of zinc and molybdenum will increase your copper requirement, for these trace minerals are antagonistic. Once absorbed, copper is transported to the liver, where a third is absorbed and the rest excreted, sweated out, lost in the menstrual flow, or deposited in the eyes.

Copper deficiency is rare, but the symptoms are anemia, weight loss, defective keratinization, loss of hair color, reduced reproductive capacity, fetal abnormalities, and sudden death. Also rare is a vast overdose of copper, which is toxic. Symptoms are hepatitis, renal failure, and neurologic disorders.

The RDA for copper has yet to be set, but the American diet supplies about 2.5 to 5 milligrams daily, which is believed to be sufficient. The sources are widely distributed, with legumes, cereals, and mushrooms being outstanding examples.

Manganese is an essential mineral present in all tissues. The body effectively conserves its manganese, reabsorbing what is not excreted in the bile. Too much calcium and phosphorus can interfere with its absorption.

The effects of a deficiency are unknown in humans, but manganese is considered essential nonetheless because of its crucial role in many vital biochemical reactions. Manganese activates numerous enzymes and is necessary for normal bone development. It also participates in the synthesis of fatty acids and cholesterol.

Deficiency is unlikely, assuming a well-balanced diet. Cases of manganese toxicity are confined to miners, who regularly inhale the dust; it accumulates in their liver and central nervous system, causing weakness and mental problems.

The average American diet supplies about 6 to 8 milligrams of manganese, which more than matches your daily needs.

Bran, blueberries, sunflower and pumpkin seeds, nuts, tea, beet tops, and pineapples are the richest of the sources.

Your body contains only minute amounts of **molybdenum.** No RDA has been established; nevertheless molybdenum is considered an essential nutrient. It acts as a cofactor of two important enzymes and is necessary for the mobilization of iron from the liver. It competes with copper for the same metabolic sites, so too much copper can deplete your molybdenum supply.

Some evidence suggests that excessive molybdenum levels can cause a toxic reaction, resulting in diarrhea, anemia, growth lag, and bone abnormalities.

The sources are widely distributed and include legumes,

whole-grain wheat, green leafy vegetables, milk, and organ meats, especially liver.

The only known biological function of **cobalt** is the synthesis of vitamin B_{12} by bacteria in the intestinal tract. Inefficiently absorbed, it can be ingested only as part of vitamin B_{12}. Most cobalt is stored in the liver, the remainder in the pancreas, spleen, and kidneys.

Cobalt deficiency leaves you weak, listless, and anemic. Since cobalt probably influences the rate of iron metabolism, a deficiency may cause an iron buildup in the liver.

The average diet supplies 5 to 8 milligrams of cobalt, which seems to be quite sufficient. Vegetarians, however, find a cobalt supply rather more difficult to come by: since vegetables and grains are very low in B_{12}, the cobalt is not absorbed by the body.

Organ meats and tissues are high in cobalt, which is added (interestingly enough) to American beer. Vegetarians should improve their B_{12} intake if they are to avoid a cobalt deficiency.

Approximately 25 milligrams of **vanadium** are stored in your body fat. Animal studies show that vanadium prevents tooth decay and is essential to growth. A deficiency can cause abnormal bone development and impair reproductive capacities. The most accessible sources are vegetable oils and concentrated fats.

FACTS TO PONDER

— Essential minerals interact with each other and with other nutrients in the body. An excess above the requirement of one mineral may upset the balance and function of other minerals. Too much of one mineral can aggravate mineral imbalance.

— All essential minerals, as well as vitamins A and D, are

toxic in some amount above the requirement: approximately one or two times the daily requirement taken in a concentrated dose.
— Minerals are usually far more toxic when taken on an empty stomach.
— Excess amounts of several essential minerals interact unfavorably with iron and calcium, two essential minerals known to be deficient in the American diet.
— Anemia is a common result of excess intake of several trace elements, including zinc, copper, and manganese.
— Your body has difficulty absorbing iron. Ascorbic acid (vitamin C) increases this absorption. Zinc interferes with it.
— Iron deficiency is recognized as a public health problem in the United States. Women of childbearing age and children are the most common victims.
— Meats are generally high in zinc; fruits and vegetables are low. It is almost impossible to meet the RDA for zinc without eating meat; therefore supplements are advisable for vegetarians.
— According to the Consumers Union, fast-food meals contain more than thirty times the RDA for iodine. No one has established how much iodine is *too* much, but a long-term effect of excessive iodine intake is disruption of thyroid function.
— Iron supplements should be kept out of the reach of children.
— Your body's chromium supply decreases as you get older.
— Heavy beer drinkers may suffer from cobalt toxicity; cobalt is added to beer to form a good foam.
— Selenium is one of the most toxic essential elements.
— Nickel is in your diet but you have no need of it. Oral intake of nickel is apparently nontoxic, but inhalation is highly toxic and can cause cancer.
— Silicon is probably an essential nutrient, but the human intake is unknown. Silicon is so ubiquitous in our environ-

ment that extraordinary conditions were needed to achieve silicon deficiency in lab experiments.

— Vegetarians may become deficient in sulfur if they do not eat eggs!

— One of the areas of neglect in the establishment of a meaningful calcium RDA is the consideration of the interrelationship of calcium with other nutrients and dietary components.

— Your body absorbs only 5 to 15 percent of the iron in your diet. Ascorbic acid helps you absorb it, but large amounts of fiber and cellulose from vegetables, whole grains, and cereals interfere with it.

— Phosphorus is best absorbed when ingested with equal amounts of calcium. Vitamin D also aids in phosphorus (and calcium) absorption.

— The greatest loss of minerals and the one least appreciated is the simple removal of all nutrients by refining processes used to convert raw agricultural products into food.

CONCLUSION

THE WORD *vegetarian* MEANS "TO ENLIVEN," AND THROUGH-out *The New Vegetarian* we have tried to show how you can plan and balance your diet and improve your health through eating, whether you are a meat eater or not.

If you want to eat meat, it is imperative that you be aware that the meat you buy may be chemically treated and there-fore potentially dangerous. By following the guidelines in our chapters on meat, protein, and food co-ops, you can shop for meat intelligently and make your purchase with confidence. If, for economic or hygienic reasons, you decide to reduce or eliminate meat from your diet, the chapters on protein, fat, and carbohydrates will explain how incomplete proteins can be combined to give you the same nutritional value as the complete protein found in meat products.

We have tried to dispel many of the myths surrounding nu-trition—the controversy over cholesterol, for example. We have shown that there is no hard evidence to prove that elim-inating cholesterol-rich foods such as milk, eggs, cheese, yo-ghurt, and meat will prevent heart attacks. We have also shown that ingesting a handful of vitamins is no substitute for eating whole and natural foods. In short, we stress a well-balanced diet, with moderate amounts of wholesome, unprocessed and fresh foods from the four basic food groups.

It is our hope that *The New Vegetarian* will encourage you to experiment with the many rational alternatives in selecting, preparing, and utilizing foods so that you too will be enlivened.

APPENDIX
FOOD CO-OPS:
SURVIVAL TACTICS

FEW PEOPLE HAVE ESCAPED THE BRUTAL SPIRALING COSTS of food. Between July, 1970, and July, 1975, food prices jumped a scandalous 54.2 percent. Prices continue to rise at the rate of 19.5 percent each year. Even if money were no object, the quality of your food is. High-quality produce and meat are a rare commodity these days; indeed, often it is just not available unless you grow your own or buy from a special outlet. Consequently, many Americans are turning toward the small-group solution to these problems: the buying co-operative.

The basic idea of a co-operative is simple: individuals and/or families pool their money and buy large quantities of food directly from wholesalers, manufacturers, farmers, and food-processing plants. The members of the co-op then purchase, package, and distribute their own food, and thus not only avoid middleman markups and packaging costs but also retain greater flexibility as regards the quality of goods. Groups, unlike the individual, can buy from farmers and producers in quantity.

Further, the complaints of a co-op carry far greater weight:

a source that does not mind losing one customer over a bruised eggplant will certainly think twice if it is a question of losing thirty or forty regular customers. A co-op can reduce regular food prices by as much as 40 percent depending on the size of the co-op and the type of food being purchased. The greatest savings are on produce, because supermarkets charge a high percentage markup on produce to cover spoilage losses and refrigeration costs. And while co-op savings are less for poultry, dairy, and baked goods, not only is reduction of 10 percent preferable to the full cost, but the quality is most likely better.

Co-ops vary in size and organization: many co-ops have only a dozen members, while others have memberships numbering in the millions. The Co-operative League of the U.S.A. was formed in 1916; today its members are serviced by special League supermarkets across the country. Other large co-ops grow their own beef—organically and without hormones and other drugs—and operate their own farms for organic produce.

There is a great deal of information that can guide you through the trials of initial organization. Gloria Stern's *How to Start Your Own Food Co-op: A Guide to Wholesale Buying* (Walker and Co., 1974) is a thorough handbook which gives detailed instruction for establishing the co-op's division of labor, ordering and buying food, handling finances and any other problems. It is easier to join an existing co-op than to start a new one: for information on co-ops near you, write to the Food Co-op Project, Loop College, 64 East Lake Street, Chicago, Illinois 61601. William Ronco's *Food Co-ops: An Alternative to Shopping in Supermarkets* (Beacon, 1974) contains a list of nearly a thousand co-ops throughout the country.

Whether you shop as an individual or as part of a co-op, certain tactics will always save you money on food.

— Shop less often. Drawing up a weekly list should allow you to buy everything you need for the week in one trip. Making one trip a week will also save you gasoline and time, which is money.

— Never shop when you are hungry. Surveys have shown that hungry shoppers spend an average of ten dollars more a week on groceries.

— Buy a minimum of convenience foods. Processed foods are usually three times the price of the original ingredients.

— Buy the staples first and keep a mental tally of how much they add up to. You'll be less inclined to spend money on unnecessary items if you know how much you've already spent.

— Buy store brands; generally as good as the name brands, they are also much cheaper. Use unit pricing to compare the costs of similar items.

— Beware of price multiples: items marked three for a dollar are not always the bargains they appear to be.

— Buy seasonally. Do without January tomatoes, which are gray and mealy but cost eighty cents a pound. Plan recipes that use the fruits and vegetables that are in season. You will save money and learn to appreciate the seasonal availability of produce.

— Select foods according to their use. For example, fancy-quality whole walnuts are not needed for a recipe that calls for chopped nutmeats. When the result is the same, why spend more?

NOTES

CHAPTER 1: BECOMING NUTRITIONALLY AWARE

1 / National Livestock and Meat Board, 444 North Michigan Avenue, Chicago, Illinois 60611, Meat and Health Series No. 2, "Meat and the Vegetarian Concept" (1976), p. 19.

2 / National Livestock and Meat Board, *Meat Board Reports,* Vol. 10, No. 1 (January, 1977), p. 9.

3 / Mervyn G. Hardinge, M.D., Ph.D., and Hulda Crooks, "Nonflesh Dietaries," *Journal of the American Dietetic Association,* Vol. 45 (December, 1964), p. 541.

4 / Irvin E. Liener, ed., *Toxic Constituents of Plant Foodstuffs* (New York, Academic Press, 1969), p. 52.

5 / "Nitrates Converted to Nitrites = Trouble," New York *Daily News* (October 31, 1975).

6 / Mervyn G. Hardinge, M.D., and Frederick J. Stare, M.D., *Modern Medicine* (April 15, 1965), p. 99.

7 / *Advanced Nutrition Reader*, N.I.A. Special Research Project on Protein (1975), p. 8.

CHAPTER 4: MEAT

1 / Beatrice Trum Hunter, *Consumer Beware* (New York, Simon and Schuster, 1971), pp. 124–25.

2 / Jon A. McClure, *The Meat Eaters Are Threatened: An Insider's Exposé of Conditions in America's Meat Markets* (New York, Pyramid Books, 1973).

3 / "Frankfurters," *Consumer Reports* (February, 1974), p. 75.

4 / *Ibid.*, p. 76.

5 / Jacqueline Verrett and Jean Carper, *Eating May Be Dangerous to Your Health* (New York, Simon and Schuster, 1974), pp. 136–56.

6 / *Ibid.*, pp. 141–42.

CHAPTER 5: MILK AND DAIRY PRODUCTS

1 / J. R. Campbell and R. T. Marshall, *The Science of Providing Milk for Man* (New York, McGraw-Hill, 1975), p. 137.

2 / F.D.A. news release, February 22, 1956.

3 / *Effects, Uses, Control and Research of Agricultural Pesticides.* A Report by the Surveys and Investigations Staff, U.S.D.A., presented at Hearings Before a Subcommittee on Appropriations, 89th Congress, 1st Session, House of Representatives, Department of Agriculture Appropriations for 1966, Part I, p. 174.

4 / Campbell and Marshall, *op. cit.*, p. 489.

5 / Beatrice Trum Hunter, *Consumer Beware* (New York, Simon and Schuster, 1971), p. 231.

6 / Hans Falk, Paul Kotin, and Adele Miller, "Milk As an Eluant of Polycyclin Aromatic Hydrocarbons Added to Wax," *Nature*, Vol. 183 (April 25, 1950), pp. 1184–85.

7 / "Salmonella, the Ubiquitous Bug," *F.D.A. Papers*, Vol. 1 (February, 1967), p. 14.

8 / "Milk: Why Is the Quality So Low?" *Consumer Reports* (January, 1974), p. 75.

9 / Sidney Margolius, *Health Foods, Facts and Fakes* (New York, Crown Publishers, 1973), p. 119.

10 / *Ibid.*, p. 120.

11 / Campbell and Marshall, *op. cit.*, p. 631.

12 / S. K. Kon, *Milk and Milk Products in Human Nutrition*, F.A.O. Nutrition Studies, No. 27, Food and Agricultural Organization of the United Nations (Rome, 1972), p. 55.

13 / George Stewart, *Introduction to Food Science and Technology* (New York, Academic Press, 1973), p. 171.

14 / *Cheese and Cheese Products, Definitions and Standards Under the Federal Food, Drug and Cosmetic Act*, F.D.A., Part 19, Title 21, Code of Federal Regulations (November, 1959), p. 21.
15 / Peter Millonas, "U.S. Impounding Pesticide Tainted Cheese Imports," *The New York Times* (September 12, 1969).
16 / Campbell and Marshall, *op. cit.*, p. 642.

Chapter 6: The Chicken and the Egg

1 / Helen Charley, *Food Science* (New York, Ronald Press, 1970), p. 399.
2 / Beatrice Trum Hunter, *Consumer Beware* (New York, Simon and Schuster, 1971), p. 137.
3 / Gerald Astor, "The Day the Sky Fell on the Egg People," *Esquire* (May, 1976), p. 143.
4 / Hunter, *op. cit.*, p. 138.
5 / *Ibid.*, p. 139.
6 / Steve Lohr, "Hens Are Willing But People Aren't," *The New York Times* (July 11, 1976), p. 1 of Business and Finance section.
7 / Nancy Lyon, "Cholesterol," *Town & Country* (January, 1977), p. 38.
8 / "What Came First, the Egg or High Cholesterol?" *Los Angeles Times* (October 2, 1975), p. 14.

Chapter 7: Fish

1 / James Trager, *The Food Book* (New York, Avon Books, 1970), p. 42.
2 / *Ibid.*, p. 243.
3 / "The Mercury Contamination of Food," *Caveat Emptor*, Vol. 6, Nos. 6, 7 (June–July 1976), p. 119.
4 / Trager, *op. cit.*, p. 243.
5 / *Ibid.*, p. 223.
6 / Helen Charley, *Food Science* (New York, Ronald Press, 1970), p. 403.
7 / Beatrice Trum Hunter, *Consumer Beware* (New York, Simon and Schuster, 1971), p. 191.
8 / Trager, *op. cit.*, p. 234.
9 / S. M. Roy, "Shellfish Poisoning Always Possible," *U.S. Medicine* (September, 1970), p. 7.

10 / Harold Bengsch, "The Nature of Shellfish and Ecological Factors Contribute to their Role in Food Borne Human Disease," *Journal of Environmental Health*, Vol. 34 (January, 1972), p. 373.

CHAPTER 13: AGRIBUSINESS AND FOOD QUALITY

1 / Daniel Zwerdling, "Boom Times for Agribusiness," *Skeptic*, No. 10 (1975), pp. 23–24. Reprinted from *The Progressive* (1974.)

2 / *Ibid.*, p. 24.

3 / Ron Ridenour, "Interview with Carol Foreman," *Skeptic*, No. 10, 1975.

4 / Zwerdling, *op. cit.*, p. 26.

5 / Interview with Dr. Elmer George, director of the New York State Food Laboratory, April 11, 1977.

6 / "Organic Foods," a Scientific Status Summary by the Institute of Food Technologists, *Journal of Food Technology* (January, 1974).

7 / *Ibid.*

8 / Jack Lucas, *Our Polluted Food: A Survey of the Risks* (New York, John Wiley & Sons, 1975), p. 78.

9 / Reay Tannahill, *Food in History* (New York, Stein and Day, 1973), p. 383.

10 / Thomas K. Derry and Trevor I. Williams, *A Short History of Technology from the Earliest Times to A.D. 1900* (New York, Oxford University Press, 1961), p. 686.

11 / Tannahill, *op. cit.*, p. 384.

12 / Beatrice Trum Hunter, *Consumer Beware* (New York, Simon and Schuster, 1971), p. 259.

CHAPTER 15: CARBOHYDRATES

1 / A. Jeanes and J. Hodge, *Physiological Effects of Food Carbohydrates*, A.C.S. Symposium Series No. 15 (Washington, D.C.: American Chemical Society, 1975), p. 316.

2 / Esther Monroe, *Sprouts to Grow and Eat* (Brattleboro, Vermont, Stephen Greene Press, 1974), p. 2.

3 / James Trager, *The Food Book* (New York, Avon Books, 1970), p. 27.

4 / E. Baker and D. S. Lepkovsky, "Bread and the War Food Problem," Riverside College of California (June, 1943).

5 / Beatrice Trum Hunter, *Consumer Beware* (New York, Simon and Schuster, 1971), p. 271.

6 / I. M. Sherman and P. J. Richards, "Commercial Breads as Sources of Vitamin E for Rats Determined by the Hemolysis Test," *British Journal of Nutrition*, Vol. 14 (1960), p. 85.

7 / Trager, *op. cit.*, p. 307.

8 / Blanche Droz, "Fiber, the Missing Ingredient," *Town & Country* (April, 1976), p. 101.

9 / A. Jeans and J. Hodge, *loc. cit.*

10 / *Ibid.*, p. 54.

11 / Richard Passwater, *Supernutrition* (New York, Dial Press, 1975), p. 16.

BIBLIOGRAPHY

Alfin-Slater, R. B., "Polyunsaturated Fatty Acid Tocopherol Interrelationships." *American Journal of Clinical Nutrition*, Vol. 23, No. 8 (August, 1970), p. 1100.

————, Wells, P., and Aftergood, L., "Dietary Fat Composition and Tocopherol Requirement: IV. Safety of Polyunsaturated Fats." *Journal of the American Oil Chemist Society*, Vol. 50 (1973), pp. 479–84.

Altschul, A. M., Proteins: Their Chemistry and Politics. New York: Basic Books, Inc., 1965.

Anderson, B. A., Kinsella, J. E., and Watt, B. K., "Beef Products: Comprehensive Evaluation of Fatty Acids in Foods." *Journal of the American Dietetic Association*, Vol. 67 (July, 1975), pp. 35–40.

Bailey, Herbert, The Vitamin Pioneers. New York: Pyramid Books, 1968.

Biezenski, J. J., "Fetal Lipid Metabolism." *Obstetrics and Gynecology Annual*, Vol. 3 (1974), pp. 203–33.

————, "Maternal Lipid Metabolism." *Obstetrics and Gynecology Annual*, Vol. 3 (1974), pp. 203–33.

Billimoria, J. D., Pozner, H., Metselaar, B., Best, F. W., and James, D. C. O., "Effect of Cigarette Smoking on Lipids, Lipoproteins, Blood Coagulation, Fibrinolysis, and Cellular Components of Human Blood." *Atherosclerosis*, Vol. 21 (1975), pp. 61–76.

Brown, Edward Espe, *Tassajara Cooking*. Berkeley: Shambhala Publications, Inc., 1973.

Campbell, J. R., and Marshall, R. T., *The Science of Providing Milk for Man*. New York: McGraw-Hill, Inc., 1975.

Carcione, Joe, and Lucas, Bob, *The Greengrocer: The Consumer's Guide to Fruits and Vegetables*. San Francisco: Chronicle Books, 1972.

Chen, Philip S., *Mineral Balance in Eating for Health*. Emmaus, Pennsylvania: Rodale Press, 1969.

Courtner, Gay, *The Beansprout Book*. New York: Simon and Schuster, Inc., 1973.

Davis, J. G., *Dictionary of Dairying*, supplement to 2nd ed. London: Leonard Hill Publishers, 1965.

Donde, U. M., and Virkar, K., "The Effect of Combination of Low Dose Progestogen Oral Contraceptives on Serum Lipids." *Fertility and Sterility*, Vol. 26, No. 1 (January, 1975), pp. 62–66.

————, "The Effect of Contraceptive Steroids on Serum Lipids." *American Journal of Obsterics and Gynecology*, Vol. 123 (December 1, 1975), pp. 736–41.

Ellis, J. M., and Presley, James, *Vitamin B₆: The Doctor's Report*. New York: Harper & Row, Publishers, Inc., 1973.

Feeley, R. M., Criner, P. E., and Slover, H. T., "Major Fatty Acids and Proximate Composition of Dairy Products." *Journal of the American Dietetic Association*, Vol. 66 (February, 1975), pp. 140–46.

Ford, Marjorie Winn, Hillyard, Susan, and Koock, Mary Fauld, *Deaf Smith Country Cookbook*. New York: Collier Books, 1973.

Fristrom, G. A., Stewart, B. C., Weihrauch, J. L., and Posati, L. P., "Comprehensive Evaluation of Fatty Acids in Foods." *Journal of the American Dietetic Association*, Vol. 67 (October, 1975), pp. 351–55.

Gangl, A., and Ockner, R. K., "Intestinal Metabolism of Lipids and Lipoproteins." *Gastroenterology*, Vol. 68 (1975), pp. 167–86.

Goldbeck, Nikki and David, *The Supermarket Handbook: Access to Whole Foods*. New York: Signet, 1976.

Goodhart, Robert S., and Shils, Maurice E., *Modern Nutrition in Health and Disease.* Philadelphia: Lea & Febiger, 1973.

Guthrie, Helen A., *Introducing Nutrition.* St. Louis: The C. V. Mosby Company, 1967.

Harris, Robert S., and von Loesecke, Harry, *Nutritional Evaluation of Food Processing.* New York: John Wiley & Sons, Inc., 1960.

Hunter, Beatrice Trum, *Consumer Beware.* New York: Simon and Schuster, Inc., 1971.

————, *The Mirage of Safety.* New York: Charles Scribner's Sons, 1975.

Kirschner, H. E., *Nature's Healing Grasses.* Yucaipa, California: H. C. White Publications, 1960.

Kloss, Jethro, *Back to Eden.* Santa Barbara, California: Lifeline Books, 1972.

Krause, Marie V., and Hunscher, Martha A., *Food, Nutrition, and Diet Therapy*, 5th ed. Philadelphia: W. B. Saunders Company, 1972.

Lappé, Frances Moore, *Diet for a Small Planet.* New York: Ballantine Books, Inc., 1971; rev. 1975.

Latour, John P., *The ABC's of Vitamins, Minerals, and Natural Foods.* New York: Arco Publishing Company, Inc., 1972.

Lindair, Victor H., *You Are What You Eat.* New York: Lancer Books, 1972.

"Lipid Metabolism and Its Control" (symposium). *Proceedings of the Nutrition Society*, Vol. 34 (1935), pp. 203–87.

Lopez, S. A., Vial, R., Balart, L., and Arroyave, G., "Effect of Exercise and Physical Fitness on Serum Lipids and Lipoproteins." *Atherosclerosis*, Vol. 20 (1974), pp. 1–7.

Margolius, Sidney, *Health Food Facts and Fakes.* New York: Crown Publishers, 1973.

Marine, G., and Van Allen, J., *Food Pollution: The Violation of Our Inner Ecology.* New York: Holt, Rinehart and Winston, Inc., 1972.

McClure, Jon A., *The Meat Eaters Are Threatened: An Insider's Exposé of Conditions in America's Meat Markets.* New York: Pyramid Books, 1973.

Null, Gary and Steve, *Protein for Vegetarians.* New York: Pyramid Books, 1975.

Nutrition Reviews, *Present Knowledge in Nutrition*, 4th ed. New

York and Washington: The Nutrition Foundation, Inc., 1976.

Ohsawa, Georges, *Zen Macrobiotics*. Los Angeles: Ohsawa Foundation, 1965.

Ohsawa, Lima, and Stiskin, Nahum, *The Art of Just Cooking*. Kenagawa-ken, Japan: Autumn Press, 1974.

Pauling, Linus, *Vitamin C and the Common Cold*. San Francisco: W. H. Freeman & Company, Publishers, 1970.

Pfeiffer, Carl C., ed., *Neurobiology of the Trace Elements Zinc and Copper*, supplement I. New York: Academic Press, International Review of Neurobiology, 1972.

Posati, L. P., Kinsella, J. E., and Watt, B. K., "Dairy Products: Comprehensive Evaluation of Fatty Acids." *Journal of the American Dietetic Association*, Vol. 66 (May, 1975), pp. 482–87.

————, "Eggs and Egg Products: Comprehensive Evaluation of Fatty Acids in Foods." *Journal of the American Dietetic Association*, Vol. 67 (August, 1975), pp. 11–15.

Pratt, D. E., "Lipid Analysis of a Frozen Egg Substitute." *Journal of the American Dietetic Association*, Vol. 66 (1975), pp. 31–33.

Schroeder, Henry A., *The Trace Elements and Man*. Old Greenwich, Connecticut: The Devin-Adair Co., Inc., 1973.

Shelton, Herbert M., *Food Combining Made Easy*. San Antonio, Texas: Dr. Shelton's Health School, 1951.

Shurtleff, William, and Aoyagi, Akiko, *The Book of Miso*. Kenagawa-ken, Japan: Autumn Press, 1976.

————, *The Book of Tofu*. Kenagawa-ken, Japan: Autumn Press, 1975.

Shute, Wilfrid E., *The Vitamin E Book*. New Canaan, Connecticut: Keats Publishing, Inc., 1975.

Strauss, J. S., Pochi, P. E., and Downing, D. T., "Skin Lipids and Acne," *Journal of Dermatology*, 1975, pp. 27–31.

Talking Food Flyers. Charlestown, Massachusetts: Talking Food Company, 1973.

Trager, James, *The Food Book*. New York: Avon Books, 1970.

U.S. Department of Agriculture, Agricultural Research Service, Agricultural Handbook No. 8, *Composition of Foods: Raw, Processed, and Prepared*, 1973.

Verritt, J., and *Carper, J., Eating May Be Hazardous to Your Health.* New York: Simon and Schuster, Inc., 1974.

Vranic, M., "Turnover of Free Fatty Acids and Triglyceride," an overview. *Federation Proceedings,* Vol. 34, No. 13 (December, 1975), pp. 2233–37.

Wade, Carlson, Magic Minerals: Key to Better Health. New York: Arco Books, 1967.

————, *Yeast Flakes Cookbook.* New York: Pyramid Books, 1973.

Walker N. W., Raw Vegetable Juices. New York: Pyramid Books, 1976.

Webster, James, Vitamin C, the Protective Vitamin. New York: Award Books, 1971.

Wellford, Harrison, Sowing the Wind: The Report on the Politics of Food Safety. Ralph Nader's Study Group Reports. New York: Grossman Publishers, Inc., 1972.

INDEX